# B-17
## COMBAT MISSIONS

# B-17

# COMBAT MISSIONS

## FIGHTERS, FLAK, AND FORTS: FIRST-HAND ACCOUNTS
## OF MIGHTY 8TH OPERATIONS OVER GERMANY

## MARTIN BOWMAN
### FOREWORD BY MAJOR GENERAL LEWIS LYLE

METRO BOOKS
NEW YORK

*Editorial Director:* **Will Steeds**
*Project Editor:* **Laura Ward**
*Designer:* **Philip Clucas** MCSD
*Photographer:* **Neil Sutherland**
*Production:* **Robert Paulley**
*Color reproduction:* **Modern Age Repro House Ltd**, Hong Kong

Elephant Book Company and the author particularly wish to thank the
following for their help in preparing this book: Ron Batley, Chairman and
Curator, 100th Bomb Group Memorial Museum, Thorpe Abbotts, Norfolk,
England; Natalie Finnigan, Imperial War Museum, Duxford, England; Larry
Goldstein; Dr Walter E Brown, President & CEO, Mighty Eighth Air Force
Museum, Savannah, GA; Major General Lewis Lyle; Michael P Faley, 100th
Bomb Group historian.

This 2008 edition published by Metro Books,
by arrangement with Elephant Book Company Limited,
14, Dryden Court, Renfrew Road, London, SE11 4NH, United Kingdom.

Metro Books
122 Fifth Avenue
New York, NY 10011

ISBN-13: 978-0-7607-8935-3
ISBN-10: 0-7607-8935-5

Printed and bound in China

10  9  8  7  6  5  4  3  2

Jacket and front cover illustration: *Clash Over Haseleunne* by Robert Bailey
(website: www.baileyprints.com)

# Contents

# Foreword

The ten crewmembers of a B-17 Flying Fortress were each confined to a rather small space in which to perform the responsibilities of their position in the airplane. As the pilot of a crew, I flew in the left-hand seat of the cockpit, with my copilot next to me on the right. Six of the crew, all gunners, were situated in the back of the plane, where I could not easily see them. It also was not feasible to get up out of the seat when we were under fire by enemy fighters.

As a command pilot, the crews were close to you and you had a routine. Each crewman had his own responsibilities, which I trusted him to meet. After the Mission Briefing, the first thing we did was to inspect the airplane. I never did the inspection. I wanted to give the crew jobs that were important. Each crewmember was to have his position and his gear in proper order for combat. I gave them that full responsibility. My copilot along with the entire crew performed the final pre-flight inspection of the aircraft. The important job of readying the airplane itself was the responsibility of the ground crew chief. I always arrived at the hardstand just minutes before engine start-up for the mission. The crew would be there and ready. I would ask the crew chief if the airplane was ready. With his affirmative, he got my salute, and I went up through the hatch into the cockpit.

From the outset, my crew understood that they were not to talk or even eat until we hit the ground after the mission was completed. Many crews liked to talk while they were in the air, some even singing songs and shooting the breeze about their escapades of the previous night. If you were talking, your mind was not on the business at hand. The navigator and the bombardier up front always had their own jobs, keeping them pretty busy. In the radio compartment, the radio operator stayed occupied with radio monitoring and transmissions. It was a routine they all got used to and nobody complained. After takeoff, I depended on each crewmember to keep me informed of everything that they saw from their crew position. It was vital for me to have a complete picture of what was going on around the aircraft. I wanted to be kept abreast of what they saw back there. They used the proper words. If they saw an enemy airplane coming in, they had to let everyone know: a direct callout of fighters in just five seconds.

In that regard, I became known on the airbase as a strict disciplinarian with the various crews I flew with. I made sure they knew that I was the only person operating the aircraft and was the only crewmember that could do something with the airplane to avoid trouble in the air and to get them back home. With their input, that was something I got pretty good at as the number of missions mounted.

The crews developed a bond as their tour of combat together progressed. This bond persisted after the War and continues up to the present day. They experienced combat under frightening circumstances, and each airman depended on every other crewmember on their airplane for their survival. These men speak a language today that even their closest family members do not understand. These crews—flying together as one—were the reason for the success of the Eighth Air Force in World War II.

Major General Lewis Elton Lyle, USAF (Ret.)
Commander, 303rd and 379th Bombardment Groups, 8th Air Force

*Major General Lew Lyle participated in the Cold War as the head of the Strategic Air Command's Committee on Planning under the direction of General Curtis LeMay. His Committee was responsible for the development and implementation of America's nuclear deterrent programs against Russia. He is Founder and a Trustee of the Mighty Eighth Air Force Museum in Pooler, Georgia. Lew and his wife, Betty, reside in Hot Springs, Arkansas.*

# Introduction

"The more Fortresses we have, the shorter the war is going to be," predicted Colonel (later General) Curtis E. LeMay in England in 1943. He was referring to the B-17 Flying Fortress, America's most famous bomber of World War II. Developed from a number of prewar prototypes, a few Fortresses were operated by RAF Bomber Command in 1941 before the US entered the War but the "Boeing Boys in blue" (as the RAF crews were called) were not an unqualified success. During 1942 and early 1943, small numbers of Army Air Corps' B-17s saw action in the Pacific against the Japanese. Later, Fortresses also equipped several Bomb Groups in the Mediterranean. Perhaps the Fortress's greatest contribution, though, was in the "Big League," as part of Eighth Bomber Command in eastern England from 1942 until the end of the War in 1945. Fortresses (and Liberators) spearheaded the bomber offensive by day while RAF Bomber Command completed the 24-hour "round the clock" bombing campaign mainly at night.

Heavy losses, especially on the Schweinfurt raids of late 1943 and "Big Week" in February 1944, were constant reminders that on long-range missions especially, the bomber was vulnerable to flak and fighters. The stark reality was that had it not been for the Mustang and other Allied escort fighters, the story of the Fortress would have had a far different outcome. Many combat crewmen recognized the limitations but largely they never faltered, flying combat tours in awful conditions, hoping that they would survive and return to the ZOI in one piece. Often their fortitude carried them through, even though the odds were stacked against them. During 1942–45, B-17s in the ETO flew over 290,000 sorties in Europe, losing over 4,600 of their number in combat. Facts such as these masked the hyperbole. The generals referred to the B-17 as "the best combat airplane ever built" and claimed that "without the B-17, we might have lost the War," but the reality was quite different. In the words of the Air Corps song, "If you'd live to be a gray-haired wonder, keep your nose out of the blue." "Nothing," it was said, "can stop the US Air Corps." Certainly the *Luftwaffe* tried—and failed.

This, then, is the story of the men who flew the Fortress: their feelings, fears, and foibles, and what they thought about their aircraft, their equipment, and their life expectancy. Often their stories are far removed from the tales of stirring deeds that filled the newspapers and magazines of the period. This book tells of laughter, friendship, death, fear, exhilaration, stupidity, superstitions, discipline, respect, and outrage. Also, of course, it tells of the sheer horrors faced mission after mission by these "gladiators of the air."

Martin Bowman
Norwich, England, March 2007

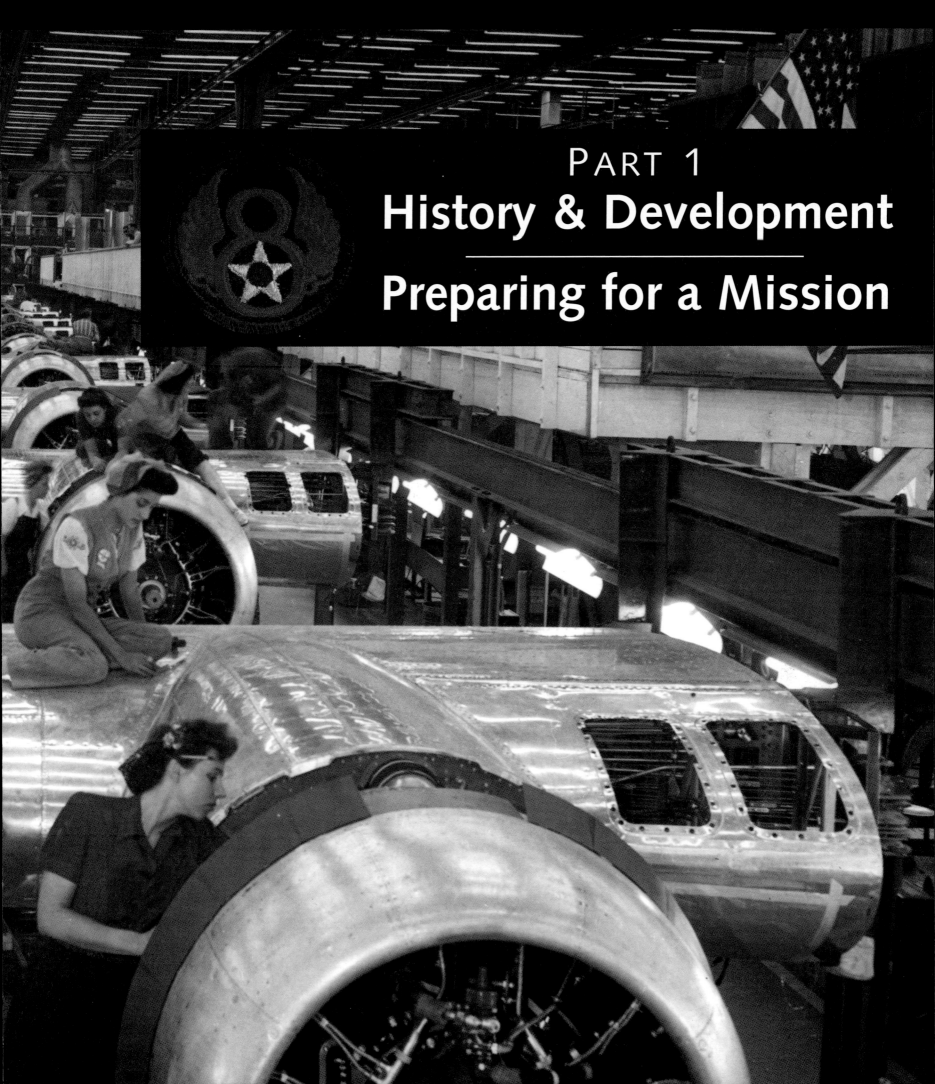

PART 1
# History & Development
## Preparing for a Mission

# History and Development

**"They took the Flying Fortress up to 40,000 feet,
'Cause they've only got a teeny weeny bomb."**

**R**AF Bomber Command, having flirted briefly with the Fortress in 1941, were unimpressed with the "Queen of the skies" and the popular ditty could have been its epitaph. The Royal Air Force made every conceivable effort to help the 8th Bomber Command get into the war as quickly as possible, but many remained skeptical about its ability to bomb in broad daylight. Drawing on their own bitter experience of the disastrous daylight bombing campaign of 1939–40, few believed that General Ira C. Eaker's 8th Bomber Command in England could succeed where the *Luftwaffe*, during the Battle of Britain, and the RAF, had failed. Major Paul W. Tibbets, Group Flying Executive Officer of the 97th Bomb Group and charged with formulating tactics at Polebrook, recalls, "The seven weeks of training between our arrival in England and our first raid paid off handsomely. I shudder to think of the results had it not been for the intensive practice afforded during this period . . . I remember some of the discussions held with RAF officials who tried to dissuade us from daylight bombing. These centered on their belief that we would be 'shot out of the air' by fighters and flak. Consequently, most of us were apprehensive since it appeared we were up against 'supermen' and that our fate was in their hands."

Eventually the British, notably Prime Minister Winston Churchill, came to accept the American method of bombing, with the USAAF bombing by day and the RAF Bomber Command by night in a round-the-clock bomber offensive. And it was the Fort that helped form the mainstay of the 8th Air Force bombing missions in the ETO (European Theater of Operations).

American faith in daylight precision bombing was unshakable. In 1941 American exponents of air power had concluded that it could destroy German industry because, in theory, 90 per cent of the bombs dropped on a clear day would explode within 1,250ft (380m) of the MPI (Mean Point of Impact). This belief had originated in the 1930s when it was thought that unescorted long-range bombers could get through to a target if they were armed sufficiently and organized into massed formations. Some believed that air power alone could directly influence the course of a war by having strategic air forces fly long-range missions and destroy an enemy's industrial infrastructure. This belief developed into an unofficial doctrine of air power and Major General Henry H. "Hap" Arnold and his

Below: *The XB-15 in the Boeing Seattle factory in 1937. The 35-ton plane had a 149ft (45m) span and was powered by four Allison V-1710 inline engines.*

staff formulated a policy (AWPD/l) of relentless air attacks against Germany, strategic defense in the Pacific Theater, and air operations in the defense of the Western Hemisphere. First priority was given to attacking Germany's electric power grid; its rail, road, and canal systems were deemed to be the next most important targets, followed by its oil and petroleum industry. It was argued that strategic bombing of these targets, together with the neutralization of the *Luftwaffe* and of naval facilities, might even render a land campaign unnecessary.

In 1938 the Army Air Corps (AAC) had recognized that it would have monumental problems in developing a

planes nor the trained manpower to fight a war successfully on all fronts at this stage of the conflict. At the time of Pearl Harbor, a heavy bomber squadron comprised eight aircraft. Combat squadrons were normally organized into groups, each bomber group usually consisting of four squadrons with a total compliment of 35 aircraft. The Air Corps had planned in April 1939 for 24 groups, but by October 1941 the target had increased to 84. Two months later the Air Corps had, on paper, 70 groups but only three of these were fully equipped with B-17 Flying Fortresses, of which there were fewer than 200 examples in service. Arnold also wished to

tremendously expanded Air Corps. In January 1939 President Franklin D. Roosevelt asked Congress to strengthen America's air power, declaring that it was "utterly inadequate." The AAC clamored for more four-engined bombers, but by June that year the AAC had barely 13 operational B-17s. Major General Arnold, the AAC chief of staff, realized that the US had to plan for the possibility that it would become involved in the European War. In June 1941 President Roosevelt had approved the plan for the formation of a new, autonomous army division: the Army Air Forces (AAF), although the Air Corps and Air Force Combat Command were to remain in being until March 9, 1942. Even when the Japanese bombing of Pearl Harbor on Sunday December 7, 1941, plunged the US fully into the war, America would still direct its greater strength against Nazi Germany, which declared war on the US the next day. And it would be B-17s based in the United Kingdom that would form the main offensive weapon. The US, however, had neither the

*Above: So great was the Model 299's wingspan that when it was rolled out at Boeing Field on July 17, 1935, it had to be maneuvered sideways out of the hangar on wheeled dollies.*

*Above top: Paul Tibbets, who flew on the first B-17 mission from England in August 1942.*
*Below: General Ira C. Eaker, who saw the AAC as a precision daylight bombing instrument.*

increase the number of pilots trained from 500 a year to 4,500 every two years. When the US entered the war, the 384,535 men in the AAF was a far cry from the two million men needed, but training facilities were already in place and expansion was rapid. Forty-one primary flying training centers were in operation and the US was turning out 37,000 pilots annually.

The Boeing B-17 Flying Fortress and the Consolidated B-24 Liberator four-engined bombers were to be the prime weapons in the US offensive in Europe and the method, as mentioned before, would be daylight precision bombing. The early fame of the Boeing Airplane Company had been earned as a result of its position as the leading American supplier of single-seat fighter aircraft between 1924 and 1936. In the early 1930s production switched to the more

lucrative transport business, and in 1934 Boeing Aircraft moved into bomber construction, too. On April 14, 1934, the US Army's General Staff issued a request for design proposals for "Project A," an aircraft capable of carrying a one-ton bomb 5,000 miles (8,000km). Boeing proposed the Model 294 or the XBLR-1 (Experimental Bomber, Long-Range), as it was initially known. On June 28, 1934, Boeing won a contract for design data, wind tunnel tests, and a mockup: the 35-ton XB-15 was the result. The plane had a 149-foot (45-m) span and was powered by four Allison V-1710 inline engines. On July 18, 1934, the US Army Air Corps issued a specification for the next production bomber to replace the Martin B-10. This new "multi-engined" bomber had to be capable of carrying a 2,000lb bombload at a speed of 200–250mph (320–400kmph) over a distance of 1,020–2,000 miles (1,600–3,200km). Manufacturers would have to find the funds themselves, but at stake was a contract for 220 bombers. Boeing decided to proceed with a four-engined bomber called the Model 299, which was already in the design stage (for "multi-engined" applied to four as well as two engines). Rushed to completion in just one year, the Model 299 was flown for the first time on July 28, 1935, at Boeing Field, Seattle, by the company test pilot, Leslie Tower.

Richard L. Williams, a *Seattle Times* reporter, wrote, "Declared to be the largest land plane ever built in America, this 15-ton Flying Fortress, built by Boeing Aircraft Company under Army specifications, today was ready to test its wings . . . "

While the role of later versions was to be offensive, the Model 299 was conceived for a purely defensive mission: to protect the US coastline from foreign surface fleets. It was this designation—and not the later formidable defensive machine-gun armament—which suggested the famous name of "Flying Fortress."

On August 20, only a month after the rollout, the Model 299 was flown from Seattle to Wright Field at Dayton, Ohio, to begin service trials in competition with the twin-engined Martin 146 and the Douglas DB-1. The Model 299 completed the 2,100-mile (3,380-km) trip much of the way on autopilot, in a record-breaking nine hours non-stop with an unbelievable average speed of 233mph (375kmph). Competitive testing was almost complete and the Air Corps about to confer the title XB-17 on the aircraft when, on October 30, 1935, the Model 299 crashed and burst into flames. The subsequent investigation revealed that it had been caused by the tail controls not having been unlocked prior to takeoff. Before the crash the Air

Corps had been considering an order for 65 B-17 bombers. In January 1937, however, production contracts were awarded to Douglas for 133 twin-engined B-18 bombers, while Boeing received only a service test order of 13 flight articles and a static test model under the designation YB-17. This was changed to Y1B-17 shortly before the first one was ready for test flying on December 2, 1936.

The YB-17 was flown for the first time on December 2, 1936, and despite a landing mishap when the bomber turned over, the first Y1B-17s were cleared for service. Between January and August 1937, 12 Y1B-17s were

Below: The Norden bombsight had been developed by Carl L. Norden to meet the need for a gyro-stabilized base for the US Navy's bombsight.

Right: Bombs Away! The USAAF expected that 40 per cent of its bombs would be dropped within 500 yards of the MPI. But precision bombing called for daylight attacks, and the ideal conditions prevailing on US test ranges were not often to be found in Europe.
Far right: Magnifying glasses used to evaluate strike photos such as this one, made on the raid on Magdeburg, Germany, on August 5, 1944.

Opposite page, far left: Six YB-17s of the 2nd Bomb Group over New York City in February, 1938, during their goodwill trip to Buenos Aires, Argentina.

Opposite page, above right: Testing was almost complete and the Air Corps about to confer the title XB-17 to the Model 299 when, on October 30, 1935, the aircraft crashed and was destroyed in the fire.

delivered to the 2nd Bombardment Group at Langley Field, Virginia. Lieutenant-Colonel Robert Olds' group pioneered the early use of the B-17, and it gained a well-earned reputation for rugged construction and safe operation with no serious mishaps during three years of strenuous flying.

In June 1937 GHQ Air Force Commander General Frank Andrews had recommended to the War Department that all future bombers should be four-engined; twin-engined bombers meant the Army would be tied to a support role for the ground troops in any future battle. Andrews, like General Billy Mitchell before him (who had been court martialed for voicing his beliefs back in 1925), was convinced of the need for a genuine strategic bomber capable of destroying America's enemies before they reached the battlefields. But funds for bombers were still a low priority. In May 1938 the War Department declared that experimentation and development would be confined to aircraft "designed for the close-in support of ground troops." In February 1938 six B-17s led by Colonel Olds made a successful goodwill trip to South America, reminding any would-be aggressor that the Air Corps could now fly bombers over long distances. In May the AAC upped the ante by sending three B-17s on a "navigational exercise," to intercept the Italian liner Rex 725 miles (1,170km) off the coast of America. Olds and his

navigator, Lieutenant (later General) Curtis E. LeMay completed the task and dropped a message on the deck of the liner. This brilliant feat of navigation proved that an invasion force at sea could be intercepted before it could harm coastal defenses. The US Navy retaliated by trying to limit the Army Air Corps' area of operation to under 100 miles (160km) from the American shore!

In the 1930s inter-service rivalry was rife, with the Navy and Army fighting over the limited funds available to the military. In 1921 the Norden bombsight had been developed by consulting engineer Carl L. Norden, a Dutch-born expert on gyroscopes, in response to a request by the US Navy, which needed a gyro-stabilized base for its existing bombsight to enable it to be used at high altitude. Norden's device appeared in prototype form in 1923, but was only good for targets that remained stationary. The improved gyro-optical sight followed in 1924; this model incorporated a timing device to indicate the precise moment for bomb release. In 1931 the celebrated Mk.15 Norden gyroscopically stabilized bombsight appeared, and the Air Corps ordered it. In 1935 tests carried out by two Martin B-10 groups using the Mk.15 produced impressive results. By 1940 it was "claimed" that AAC bombardiers in B-17B high-altitude bombers at ranges at Muroc Dry Lake in California's Mojave Desert could put a practice bomb in a pickle barrel

*Left: It was claimed that a practice bomb could be put in a pickle barrel from 20,000 feet, but this was a wild exaggeration.*

from 20,000 feet (6,100m). The Norden was estimated to be six to eight times more accurate than the bombsight used by the RAF.

The B-17B had resulted from the Y1B-17 and 17A, and the B-17C, which flew for the first time on July 21, 1940, was a more combat-worthy model, incorporating recommendations made by Britain and France as a result of their experience with bombers in air combat. Two limited-vision gun cupolas, fitted to the sides of the fuselage on earlier models, were replaced with streamlined Plexiglas tear-drop-shaped windows, while the top gun blister was replaced with a sliding Plexiglas hatch. The under gunner's blister was replaced with a large "bath tub" containing a single .50 caliber machine gun.

A .30 caliber gun could be fired from any of the six ball sockets in the nose. Armor plate and self-sealing fuel tanks were fitted and the bomb load remained the same at 4,996lb (2,266kg). A further batch of 42 B-17Cs required so many modifications as a result of the RAF's experience that they were redesignated B-17Ds in September 1941. Outwardly, the "D" differed from the "C" in the addition of engine cowl flaps and twin-gun installations in the belly and upper positions. Internally, more armor plate was added, a new self-sealing fuel tank system installed, and changes were also made to the bomb release, oxygen, and electrical systems. In May 1941 21 B-17Ds were flown to Hawaii and the remainder were sent to the 7th and 19th Bomb Groups.

Results of the European combat experience and lessons learned in the Pacific were incorporated into the extensively improved B-17E, which was ordered on August 30, 1941. Armament was increased, although the greatest threat was still perceived—incorrectly as it proved—to be from the rear. Army Air Corps strategists did not believe that a Messerschmitt 109 pilot would ever try head-on attacks with such a fast-closing speed between fighter and bomber. Boeing received orders for 812 B-17Es and about 100 examples had been delivered to the Air Corps by the time of the Japanese attack on Pearl Harbor on December 7, 1941. A handful of bomb groups fought the Japanese in the Philippines and Java and the B-17 continued to operate in the Pacific Theater until 1943.

The first B-17Es of the 97th Bomb Group landed in Britain in July 1942 and this unit flew the first American Fortress mission on August 17. After 512 B-17Es had been built, the remaining 300 aircraft on the contract were converted to B-17F production standard. The B.V.D. pool was created when Boeing agreed to let Lockheed-Vega at Burbank, California, and Douglas Aircraft at Long Beach build the B-17F under license. Outwardly, the "F" differed from the B-17E in having a frameless Plexiglas nose, which gave the bombardier better all-round visibility but no fewer than 400 changes and modifications were made, most of them being carried out on the production line itself. New Wright R-1820-97 Cyclones with wider Hamilton Standard "paddle" propeller blades meant that the standard 1200-hp could be raised to 1380-hp ("war emergency" power) to give a top speed of 325mph (523kmph). The leading edge of the engine cowlings had to be re-shaped and shortened so that the blades could clear the cowling when feathered. The installation of "Tokyo Tanks" in the wings and an 820-gallon tank in the bomb bay increased the tankage to 3,630 gallons. Maximum bombload was 9,600lb (4,350kg), but the normal combat load was nearer 4,000lb (1,814kg). At the beginning of 1943, 8th Bomber Command in England had four B-17F groups totaling 200 aircraft. Altogether, B-17F production totaled 3,400. Boeing built 2,300 and starting in July 1942 in new factories built specially for the purpose, Douglas and Lockheed-Vega delivered 600 and 500 respectively.

The B-17G, which featured a chin turret, staggered waist gun windows, and a modified tail-gun position flew for the first time on May 21, 1943, and the model began equipping bomb groups in England in September. Altogether, 8,680 B-17Gs were built. Boeing built 4,035 B-17Gs and Douglas and Lockheed built 2,395 and 2,250 respectively. At the peak of B-17 production in June 1944 the Boeing Seattle factory was rolling out 16 Fortresses every 24 hours. The last B-17G rolled off the Lockheed-Vega production line on July 29, 1945, bringing to an end a total production run of 12,677 B-17 Fortresses.

*Above: The B-17G, which featured a chin turret, flew for the first time in May 1943.*

There was no doubt that the aircraft and American bombing equipment were among the best in the world, and yet the much-publicized "pickle-barrel" bombing accuracy was a myth. The US Army Air Corps started out bombing in daylight using gyroscopically stabilized bombsights to carry out precision bombing of specific German targets by day. The USAAF expected that 40 per cent of its bombs would be dropped within 500 yards

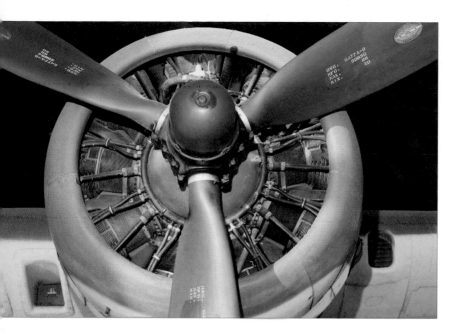

*Left, far left, and below: Wright R-1820-97 Cyclones. The wider Hamilton Standard "paddle" propeller blades meant that horse power could be raised to 1380-hp, giving a top speed of 325mph. The leading edge of the engine cowlings had to be re-shaped and shortened.*

pathfinder techniques to light the objectives while at the same time introducing a range of blind bombing/navigational devices, which were adopted and in some cases, refined, for use by the USAAC. About 80 per cent of 8th Air Force missions in the last quarter of 1944 used some type of radar bombing devices, either for navigation or targeting.

Two years earlier General Ira C. Eaker had summed up the American approach by saying, "We must never allow the record of this war to convict us of throwing the strategic bomber at the man in the street." Events before final victory were to prove otherwise; and as far as the US air war was concerned, it was the man in the street from every city, town, and homestead in America who was trained for bombing missions that was the instrument.

of the MPI. However, precision bombing called for attacks in daylight and the ideal conditions prevailing on the ranges in California and Texas were not often to be found in Europe, as 8th Bomber Command soon found to its chagrin. During most of 1943 only 24 per cent of bombs dropped by the 8th Air Force fell within 1,000 feet (304m) of the MPI. Elmer Bendiner, a Fortress navigator, recalled that after a raid on Hüls, " . . . our superiors were pleased with us because we had dropped 422 tons of bombs and, according to the reconnaissance photos, only 333.4 tons had been wasted on homes, streets, public parks, zoos, department stores, and air-raid shelters. This passed for precision . . . One of the axioms suggested by the British declared that only a fool would go over a target twice in the same mission. That advice was actually useless to us; it was meant for the upper echelons who had already formulated their own rules, which would require crews to go around and around as often as need be to put the bombs into the pickle barrel, for that was why we were there. I admired the British for not feeling quite so compulsive about the matter."

RAF Bomber Command had resorted to area bombing at night using

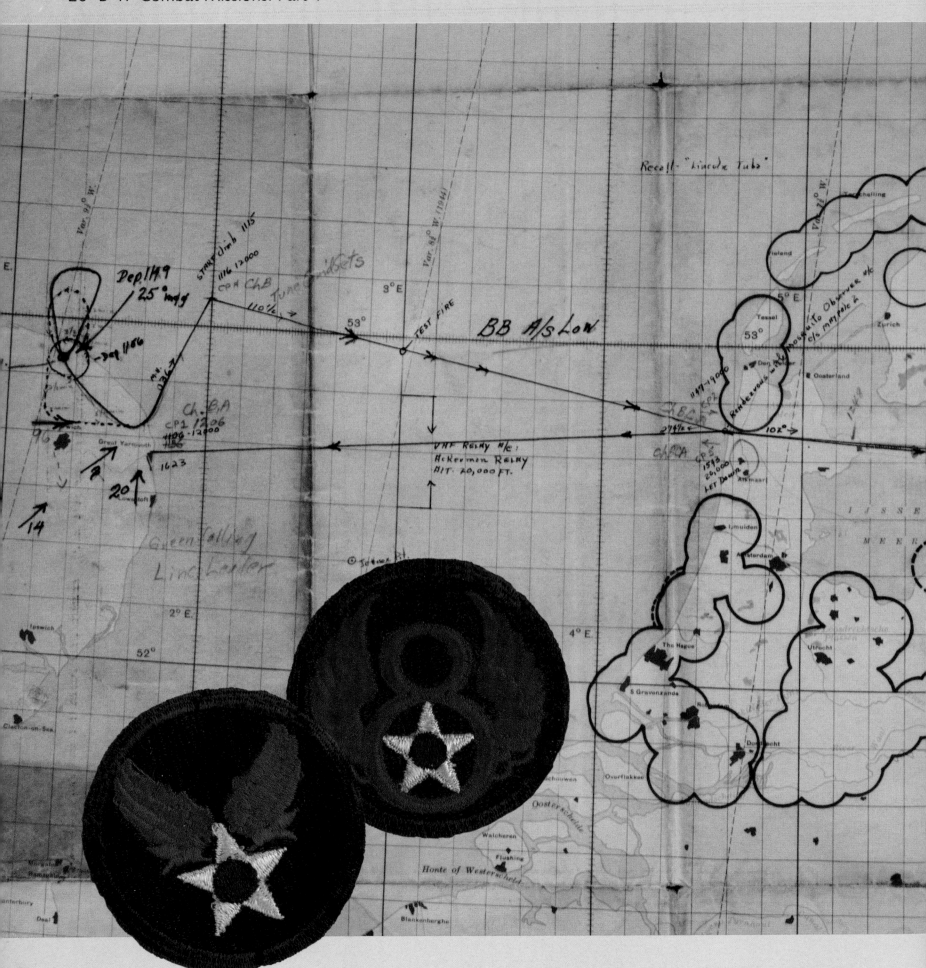

# Preparing for a Mission

*"They came out of the wheat fields, the factories in the cities. They were the guys just off the street. Some of them only had a few weeks' training, a few months at most. As soon as the commander said 'I think I can make it,' they sent him out."*—Major General Lewis Lyle

During 1942–45, B-17s in the ETO flew over 290,000 sorties in Europe, losing 4,688 of their number in combat. At the outset B-17 groups could be counted on the fingers of one hand. The force was just several hundred strong and only big enough to equip one, and then two bombardment wings, and raids were usually shallow penetration missions to targets in France and the Low Countries. But as the War progressed the 8th became so big and so powerful that it was referred to as the "Mighty Eighth," and it was not uncommon for raids involving a thousand to two thousand aircraft to be flown on any given day. By the late summer of 1944 Fortresses equipped all the groups in the 1st and 3rd Bomb (later Air) Divisions which were controlled by 8th Bomber Command. Each Air Division was subdivided into Combat Bombardment Wings with usually three to four bomb groups in each. Throughout the war all the heavy bomb groups were concentrated in the English counties of Huntingdonshire, Bedfordshire, and Cambridgeshire, and parts of Norfolk and Suffolk. Every new group that arrived in East Anglia to join the vast armada was better trained than those that had gone before, and every replacement crew that was sent to any one of four bomb squadrons that characterized every group knew what was expected of them. What most young fliers were unprepared for was the stark reality of it all.

From July 1942 to December 5, 1942, the AAF used the Foreign Service Concentration Command to deal with the special problems of overseas movement, but in December this function was restored to the four Continental Air Forces. This action was accompanied by instructions

Above: *Crew briefings were part of the pre-mission ritual. Occasionally, however, as in the early dawn of June 6, 1944, the news was welcomed and joyfully received—for it was "D-Day!"*

that all units destined for overseas duty should be carefully checked in accordance with a new inspection system, called Preparation for Overseas Movement, which was under the supervision of the Air Inspector. By 1943 preparations needed to move an air unit overseas took more than four months. It normally took almost 120 days and 17 separate actions by HQ officers to move the unit to its port of embarkation. All crews had to be declared operational by the Preparation for Overseas Movement (POM) Inspectors before they could leave the ZOI (Zone of Interior, or the US).

Few had any inkling as to which theater of war they would be sent. Air echelons of every new group would fly to their assigned departure point, and the pilots would then be handed a sealed envelope containing

*Opposite page: A section of a mission briefing map to Berlin shows the assembly patterns, the route in and out across Holland, and the all-important known flak areas (marked in red). "Big B" was a feared target throughout the War. Inset are the Air Forces' badge (left) and the 8th Air Force's famous "Winged 8" badge.*

Destination Orders, which were only to be opened one hour after departure from the Continental US. Then, and only then, would they know for sure where they were headed. The hazardous Northern Ferry Route usually meant Britain and the ETO. The same was usually true of the long Southern Ferry Route, via South America and North Africa, but the ultimate destination could just as easily have been the Pacific. Meanwhile, the ground echelons had already sailed and were en route. Those destined for Great Britain normally made landfall in Scotland and flew on to East Anglia.

For most men the transition from balmy training bases in the US to a combat zone was earth-shattering. In the movie *Twelve O'Clock High,* the CO tells the new arrivals that they aren't going home: "You're all going to die. In fact, consider yourselves already dead!" Though the movie—about a B-17 group, and written by Bernie Lay Jr.,—is fictional, it was based on first-hand experience, and it struck at the heart of problems associated with combat exhaustion and stress. A major cause was the fact that combat crews realized they could—at least theoretically—be wiped out in 20 missions if the average loss of five per cent per mission (then a conservative estimate) was not reduced. As a result, morale was at a very low ebb during the winter of 1942–43. When, finally, something was done, a combat tour in the ETO was initially 25 missions but in 1944 this was increased to 30 missions and eventually it was raised to 35. There were no "easy" missions either—even a "milk run" could turn "sour." One crewmember who beat the odds to survive 51 missions logged just over 410 combat hours, an average of roughly eight hours a mission. Between January and June 1944, of the 2,051 crew who started a tour of 25 missions, 1,195 of them could expect to be killed in action.

New crews were sent to the Combat Crew Replacement Center before being assigned to bomb groups as replacements. If they had not already heard about conditions in a combat theater then their introduction to life on base could be harsh, and gave them much to ponder. One pilot's diary entry after his arrival one cold November day was brief and uninspired: "Arrived at base at 1800. It isn't so hot. No barracks. No blanket. No heat. Slept in a cold room and about froze." Howard E. Hernan, gunner, 303rd Bomb Group, recalls the conditions: "The combat crews were kept separate from the rest of the base personnel and we lived primarily in the NE corner of the Molesworth base in small Nissen huts with 12 men to a hut, making two crews. Most generally, right next door lived eight officers who formed the rest of the two crews. We had a little coke stove, but toilet facilities were a little lacking. We had a couple of flush toilets but no facilities to take a shower, so we rigged up a couple of barrels with a charcoal stove underneath to get a little warm water. A dirty body at high altitude was so much harder to keep warm and it always surprised me that better washing facilities for the combat crews were never provided."

Technical Sergeant Walt Hagemeier Jr., radio operator, 306th Bomb Group, remembers the rain: "We landed and it was just pouring with rain. It had been light rain just shortly before and we got on the ground and got over to our dispersal area, and I mean it just opened up about three faucets; it just came down in buckets. I didn't know what to think of it. The buildings were so unusual; most of 'em were Quonset huts. We were there two days before we got our pass to go into town. Of course, we were briefed on the money situation, and so on. We were briefed on what to expect, and went into town the first time, and thought it was great. I thoroughly enjoyed myself all the time, really. We had an attitude, 'Here today, Gone tomorrow and the devil may care'."

Combat losses tended to be hushed up so as not to undermine the men's morale, so unless a neophyte crewman knew someone personally who had gone down, reality hit home hard. Wilbur Richardson, a gunner, arrived at Rougham to join the 94th Bomb Group on April 11 with three other crews: "Later in the Mess Hall we learned that four crews failed to return from Poznan, Poland. Such news to hear on arrival. For the month of April, 25 crews were lost. What would our fate be?" Larry Goldstein, a radio operator in the 388th Bomb Group, recalls, "When we asked, 'Why the empty beds?' we were told that they were left by men who had gone down recently. This was rather discouraging." John A. Holden, a navigator in the 452nd Bomb Group adds, "When we arrived at our Quonset hut at Deopham Green, so many officers had been killed there was no room to hang our clothes. One door was blocked

Above: *Arrival in England was something of a culture shock for US servicemen, and a variety of booklets and guides were produced to acquaint them with the English people and their customs, and about life in the ETO.*

with piles of uniforms. Our crew borrowed a wheelchair from supply and moved most of the clothing and footlockers out. It took us two days to empty the barracks." William C. Stewart, a 19-year-old gunner who "never really expected to make his 20th birthday" arrived at Podington to join the 92nd Bomb Group and was quite unprepared for what he saw. "The truck drove to the helmeted MPs at the main gate that opened in the link fence that protected the area. It was fairly flat countryside and we

Left: *The Nissen huts were notoriously difficult to keep warm.*
Below: *Nissen huts accommodated 12 enlisted men (EM) or eight officers, or two crews to a hut. Each hut had a coke stove, a couple of flush toilets, but no shower facilities.*

drove down the one main road of the base, past clustered areas on the left and right of wood and tarpaper barracks. Every so often there would be a painted sign that could be read from the road. One was, 'This Group flies the tightest formation in the ETO.' Another read, 'This Group takes no evasive action on the bomb run.' I moved my gear into a barracks and threw it onto one of the lower bunks, which was conveniently near one of the two warm 'pot-bellied' stoves. One of the men said, 'You can take that bunk if you want but it belonged to our engineer, who got it through the head on a mission a couple of days ago.' With no further words I selected another bunk, farther away from the heat of the stove."

A mission would be set in motion at around 1700 hours at the daily Operations Conference at the headquarters of the 8th Bomber Command at High Wycombe, in a room buried beneath 30 feet (9m) of reinforced concrete. The Commanding General would ask for a report on weather conditions in the target areas: this would determine whether the raid would be a deep-penetration mission into Germany or beyond, or a shallow-penetration mission to France or the Low Countries. Late in the afternoon, the bases in East Anglia would be alerted by the warning order and bomb trailers would begin transporting the bombs from the dumps to the bombers waiting at dispersals. The Field Order, a yard-long message containing details of targets and aiming points, fighter support, aircraft required, routes out and back, bombing altitudes, zero hour, and radio procedure, was teletyped to the Air Divisional headquarters for operational staffs to study. If the weather held, at around 2330 hours the Combat Wings and their bomb groups would receive the Combat Order from the Air Divisions. Following the teletyped orders, S-2, the Intelligence chief, the group commander, and the group navigator would gather in the Intelligence Room. There, the Duty Officer would have pinned a large piece of transparent talc over the wall map with the routes to their target and back marked with a red grease pencil. Then it only remained for the takeoff and briefing times to be set. Takeoff at

0700 hours meant that briefing had to be at 0400, with breakfast at 0330. There were separate navigators' briefings, pilots' briefings, and gunners' briefings.

In the meantime, everyone from the CO, the flak officer and S-2 to the cooks and the ground crews would get everything ready for the "off." The squadron commanders and the lead navigators and bombardiers arrived first. Crews slept in their beds piled high with blankets, uniforms, and anything else they could lay their hands on to keep out the freezing east wind, dreading the knock at the door which told them the mission was on. At around 0300 hours CQs (Charge of Quarters) would start their wake-up calls at the brick-and-tin barrack huts scattered around most every base. It was a rude shock to be wakened on a cold English morning. Those that could sleep were still dreaming about the night before, when they might have been drinking at the local pub, or playing Blackjack until late. Once the crew had answered their names, this

harbinger of doom shouted, "Breakfast at 0330; Briefing at 0400; Start Engines at 0600; Taxi out at 0630 and takeoff at 0700." This was no dream. They could hear the sounds of Wright Cyclones being run up and pre-flighted on the hard stands around the perimeter of the airfield. Crews donned flying coveralls, heated suits, and boots, and headed to the mess halls where the cooks were putting on a mission breakfast.

The sky would still be dark as they walked to the mess halls. It took about ten minutes, depending on the weather. Inside was a hubbub of conversation while the base kitchens served breakfasts of dehydrated eggs, which came in square boxes, bread with apple butter, orange marmalade, and black coffee. Sometimes they ate oatmeal and powdered milk; not because they liked it, but because it was warm and filling. (It could be a man's last meal for some time, and he might have to walk home.) Howard Herman in the 92nd Bomb Group at Podington recalled: "What a life. Up at 0400 and the only sleep we got was in the afternoons and also, we were only getting two meals a day." Larry

know what their target was; rumor and speculation would be swept away by the pull of the curtain from the mission map. Richard Bing, a radio operator in the 388th Bomb Group at Knettishall, recalled, "At

*Left: The yard-long Field Order is studied by operational staff.*
*Below left: It was only at the briefing that crews would find out for sure what their target was to be.*
*Below right: Combat crews, tired and pensive, listen intently to the briefing. Most dreaded hearing the words, "Berlin" or "Merseburg," and would pray instead for a "milk run" to France.*

Goldstein remembers, "We tumbled out of a warm bed, dressed warmly, shaved in cold water and boarded a GI truck in darkness to the mess halls for a breakfast we were not sure we could eat because of our nervous stomachs. Each man was wondering, 'Will we make it back today?'" Wilbur Richardson was one who soon learned to shave well, "because high-altitude flying necessitates an oxygen mask and facial hairs can cause a good deal of irritation. Also, it could get awfully cold. The temperature varied from -10° (-23°C) to -70° (-56°C). Because of this there was little or no food or water. Our 'blue bunny' heated suits did not always work efficiently."

Fresh eggs confirmed that a combat mission was in the offing and the first problem was whether you could get them down. Howard E. Hernan, on the subject of breakfast, pointed out: "Combat crews were entitled to bacon and fried eggs on the morning of a mission, but there were not enough to go around. Sometimes we had powdered eggs and if they had been prepared right you couldn't tell the difference."

If waking up was hard and breakfast unpalatable, then the briefing was where nerves really tightened. Then, and only then, would crews really

6am, tired crewmembers assembled at squadron briefing. A white sheet covered the wall at the far end of the room. Behind its cleanness was a map of Europe and our dirty work for the day. Hopefully, we prayed, it was a short run to France."

George Rubin was a waist gunner in the 486th Bomb Group and his mission ritual rarely ever changed, right up to the day he was shot down: "I'd get up feeling groggy and put on my long johns over my regular underwear, woolen socks, shirt and pants, and then my flying suit over all of this. Tie up the laces of my GI shoes and put on my green lined flight jacket. It is cold and windy as I step out into the night, carrying my towel and toilet kit and walk slowly over to the latrine and the water closet. Other crewmembers are already there. There is very little conversation. Make do with a fast wash up and maybe a shave. Not too close or your face will be irritated by the oxygen mask. Then back to the Quonset to get a scarf and a knit cap to wear.

"It's cold and clear as I walk the quarter mile or so to the mess hall wondering where the bombing mission is going today? I enter a long, well-lit and warm building filled with airmen getting their breakfast or eating it. It's hard to feel hungry. Partly it's due to the hour and also the nervous gut feeling about the mission. There is very little conversation at the table. Just drink your coffee and pick at the food. Then it's back out into the dark and the cold night. A gray light has started to fill the sky in the east. It's another long walk to the flight lockers.

"Open your locker and take off flight jacket and flying suit and put on electrically heated suit, another pair of socks, and electrically heated flying boots. Put the flight suit on over all of this and then the flight jacket goes back on. Electrically heated gloves are placed in the jacket pocket and the flying helmet is put on or carried. Don't forget oxygen mask and Polaroid flying goggles. GI shoes are slung over a shoulder and I put on a pair of warm gloves and a scarf. Leave your wallet and other identification in the locker. I hope that if I don't return these items will find their way home to my parents. Next door I sign out for my parachute and escape packet consisting of a compass, map, German money and phrasebook, and a .45 caliber pistol.

"Then it's a short walk to the briefing room; a long Quonset with rows of chairs and a covered map at one end. I have a sick feeling when I look at the strings going deep into Germany. This will be a long mission. There are very few questions.

"We are dismissed from the briefing and leave now for the hardstand and our plane. Some walk, others bike, or ride over in a jeep. The sky is now light as dawn approaches. I arrive at *Oh! Miss Agnes*. The ground crew is at work loading the bombs. Today it will be 12 500lb demolition bombs. I check with the ground crew about the A-4 bomb shackles and inspect all the .50 caliber machine guns. All are in place and so is the ammo. I walk around the plane, then swing on board through the waist-door hatch and deposit my parachute near the left waist gun. This is a safe place. Then I begin my pre-flight check. Oxygen-pressure full on the dial. The dial next to it shows the little lips moving up and down—oxygen is coming out. Check the emergency bottles and the large oxygen tank on top of the ball turret. They are full. Connect intercom; check that I can hear and that the throat mike is transmitting my voice. Check that the guns and the ammo clips are in place. Outside again the other crewmembers and me help the ground crew pull the props through the usual nine times to clear out the cylinders. Take a last look around the field and re-enter through waist hatch. Watch as the rest of the crew comes aboard. Each has done a pre-flight of their equipment and the entire plane. I sit in the waist. It is a time of tense quiet. The spell is broken by the whine of the No.3 engine starting up. 'Clear. Contact!' The prop rotates slowly then the engine catches. Smoke comes out of the exhaust and the engine is running. This is followed by 4, then 1 and 2. All four are running smoothly. The pilot releases the brakes and we move off the hardstand and line up behind other planes in the squadron. We wait for the green flare from the control tower to signal that the mission is 'on' or the red flare that means the mission is 'scrubbed.'"

Most were not sorry if the mission was "scrubbed." It meant another day to live.

**Above:** *Crew wearing B-4 life preservers and carrying their chest parachute packs and flak helmets, leave their briefing room and walk out to their B-17, mid-1944.*
**Below:** *B-17s in group formation setting out from their base in East Anglia in the early morning to rendezvous with the other groups in the bomb wing.*

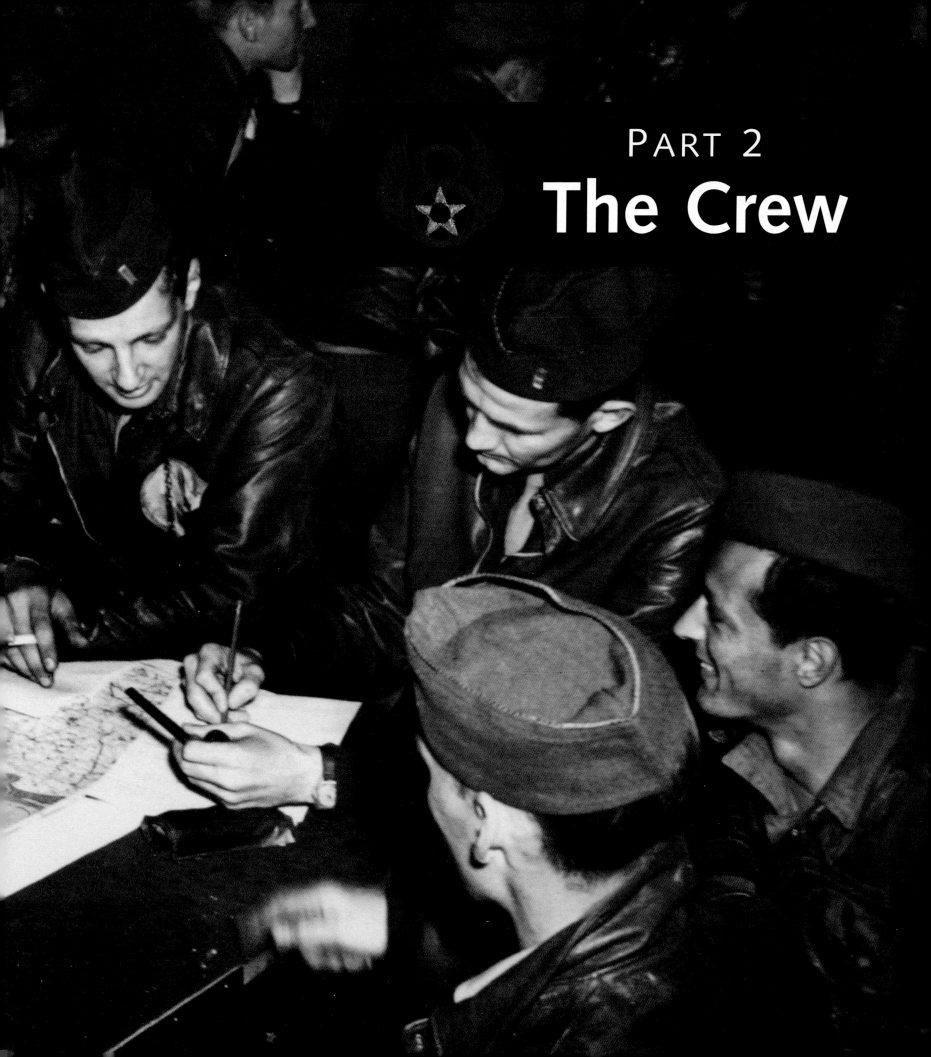

PART 2
# The Crew

# The Pilot and Copilot

*"The B-24 was not faster than the B-17. We simply flew it 10mph faster to make it more stable and to prevent it from stalling out. The Davis wing provided far less lift than the B-17 wing. After all of the trouble we had getting the B-24s off the ground with three times as long a run, it was a real pleasure to be flying an airplane that seemed to want to fly."*—Ellis B. Woodward, a lead crew pilot in the 493rd Bomb Group

Originally, bombardment training took 90 days. All personnel assigned to the AAC for aviation cadet training were given a five-week basic military course which included exhaustive physical, psychological, and mental tests to determine their fitness for the flying program, and to ascertain the specialty for which they were best suited. After basic training, each man was ready to begin training in his specialty. The flying training program took up to 36 weeks to complete, with 12 (later reduced to 10) weeks each for primary, basic, and advanced pilot training. Most had never even driven a car before, let alone flown an aircraft, but they were expected to fly solo after six hours' tuition. Those who achieved this, progressed to advanced and transition flying training, at the end of which, based on performance and choice, they would be earmarked for heavy or medium bombardment, transports, troop carriers or twin-engined fighters.

Flying as a pilot with a ten-man crew seemed to some to be a glamorous thing to be a part of, but only a select few were offered this chance. If they were honest, the B-17—or "Big Ass Bird"—was *the* plane every US bomber pilot wanted to fly, especially when the alternatives could be the B-24 Liberator or the B-26 Marauder. The latter

*Left: B-17G cockpit showing the typical black instrument panel and flying control yokes. Pilots were particularly vulnerable to the head-on attacks of the Luftwaffe fighter pilots.*

was known universally as the "widow maker," and the Liberator as "the crate that the B-17 came in."

Many of those who failed (or "washed out") in pilot training were retrained as bombardiers or navigators. But those who graduated successfully from advanced training were awarded the silver pilot's wings of the AAF, and appointed as flight officers or commissioned as 2nd lieutenants. Before they began to train in units, pilots learned to fly the type of aircraft they would handle in combat. Those men earmarked for B-17 assignment took a ten-week transition course before reporting to unit training groups, where they were welded into fighting teams.

Once in the ETO (European Theater of Operations) heavy bomber missions varied considerably in duration and intensity depending on the complexity, destination, and numbers involved. Assembly and formation procedures could consume an hour or more so that even so-called "milk runs"—easy missions—to northern France took up four and a half hours of flying time. A round trip to Berlin could take nine to ten hours, sometimes more. A mission to the Ruhr could last seven hours, Brunswick eight, and Dresden nine. Often the chances of being killed or badly wounded depended on the position flown in the formation and the level of exposure to flak and fighters. When Bernie Lay, Jr. flew with the 100th Bomb Group to Regensburg he had looked at the crew sheet, where the line-up of the lead, low, and high squadrons of the group was plotted for each mission. On the chance suggestion of one of the squadron commanders, the operations officer erased his name and shifted him to the high squadron as copilot in the crew of Lieutenant Murphy. Neither of them knew it but that operations officer saved Lay's life right there "with a piece of rubber on the end of a pencil." Even so Lay knew that "it was a cinch" that his group would be the "softest touch for the enemy fighters, being last man through the gauntlet. Furthermore, the *Piccadilly Lily* was leading the last three ships of the high squadron—the tip of the tail end of the whole shebang. We didn't relish it much. Who wants a Purple Heart?"

During fighter attacks the pilot and copilot, without a gun to fire, could only sit and watch. The pilot and copilot positions on the B-17 were the most vulnerable of all because the best chance of knocking a bomber out of formation was to kill the pilots in the cockpit. The *Luftwaffe* therefore employed the head-on approach, attacking 10 degrees above the horizontal, otherwise known as "12 o'clock high." When this was found to be effective the *Luftwaffe* refined the tactic further, employing larger attacking formations, and simultaneous

attacks by fighters (rather than attacks in trail, one after another). On January 13, 1943, when the leading 305th Bomb Group were hit by upward of 25 FW 190s attacking in line astern, making their attacks from head-on at the same altitude as the Fortresses, they downed one B-17 and damaged another ten. In the lead ship, Major Taylor was killed by a cannon shot in the chest and his copilot was wounded. A pilot's armor-plated seat was useless in these situations, and pilots soon took to wearing steel helmets and, later, flak vests and flak helmets as well. But until escort fighters became available in late 1943 the only remedy was to put more and more guns at the front of the Fortress to deter frontal attacks.

*Page right, clockwise from top left: Officer's OD wool garrison or "Crusher" cap, with folded crown crest; look-down view on the front section of the B-17G; close-up of the Boeing boss fitted to the control wheel; control wheel from one of the 2,995 examples built by the Douglas company under license; pilot's operational equipment with throttles, propeller controls, and control switches.*

## How Not to Fly the B-17

There were many pitfalls to flying a B-17. Due to the proximity of the switches in the cockpit it was not uncommon on approach to landing to select "undercarriage up" instead of "flaps down." (Eventually the "U/C Switch" was relocated to the base of the windshield.) This booklet, published during the war years by Headquarters, AAF Office of Flying Safety, was one of many publications produced by the organization to improve flight safety.

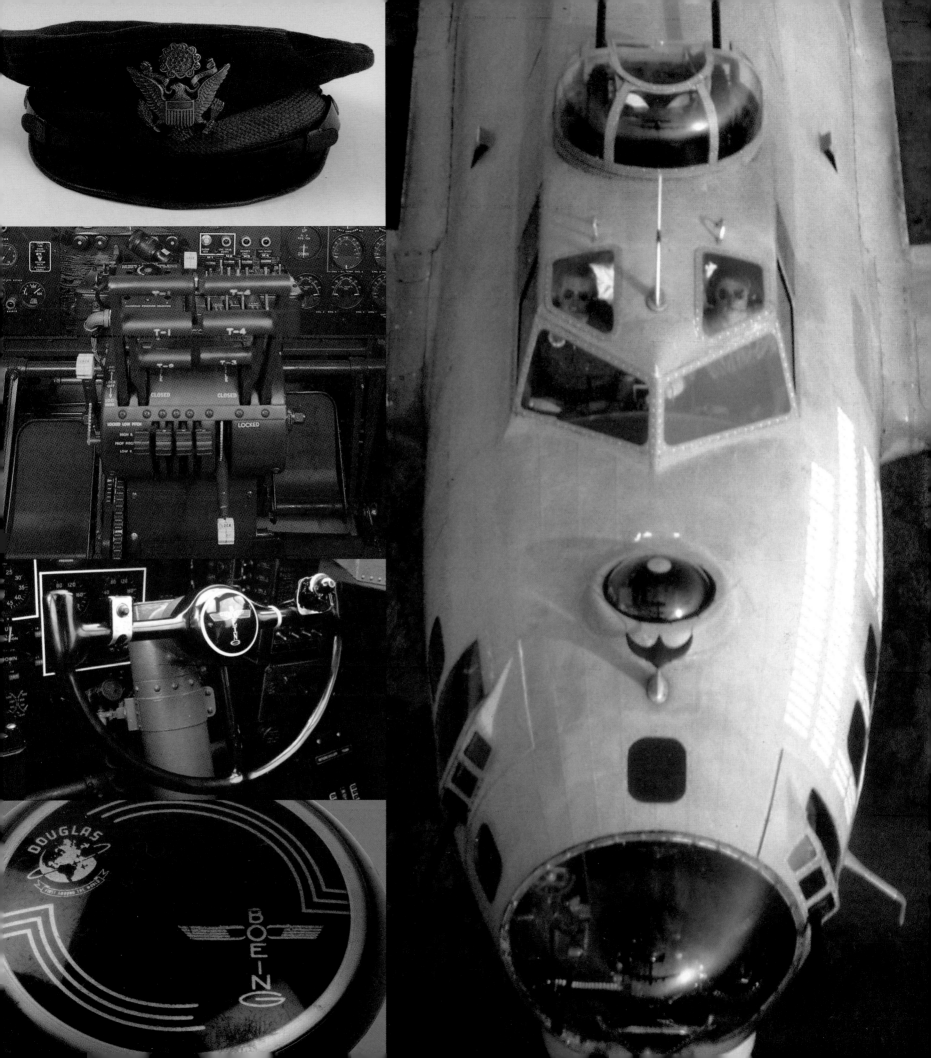

# In the "Big League"

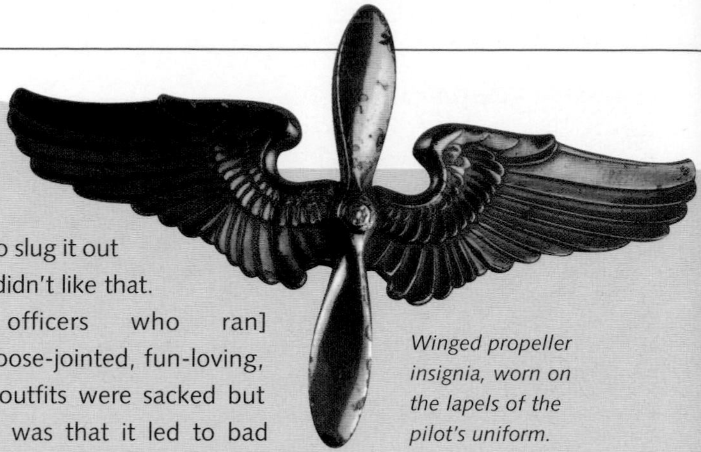

Formation flying in combat boxes for mutual protection and concentrated bombing was 8th Bomber Command's *raison d'être*. In 1942–43 a group was made up of about 20 planes. That was "Bush League" deep in the heart of the Ruhr. Moving up to the "Big League," a 15-mile "aerial parade" might have been unwieldy, but, as the enemy found, it was dangerous to fool with. Robert Morgan, pilot of the *Memphis Belle*, talked about the importance of maintaining formation on missions:

"I would like to make one suggestion to improve the training of bomber pilots. Cut down on transition training—landings and takeoffs—and emphasize high-altitude flying and formation flying. I could have used a lot more of that . . . Keep your formation. I can't emphasize that too strongly. At first the idea seemed to be to get the bombs out and then go hell-bent for home. But we learned how important it was that the formation be maintained. There were a few cases when we turned a formation nearly around to pick up a man who was straggling. The Germans always tried to break up the formation and then jump the stragglers . . . If we concentrated our firepower by keeping formation the only thing they [the Germans] could do was to slug it out with us. They didn't like that.

"[Senior officers who ran] lackadaisical, loose-jointed, fun-loving, badly trained outfits were sacked but the real crime was that it led to bad formation flying. This in turn resulted in high losses and a dangerous drop in morale. Morale is always good when results are good. As groups like the Bloody Hundredth discovered to its cost, German fighter pilots sought out the weaker groups, singled out the easy pickings and picked off cripples and stragglers almost at will. Once a Fortress became a straggler, the *Luftwaffe* would, as one crewman put it, "gang up on the limping Fort like the buzzards gang up in the sky over the desert when a horse goes down in the hot sand."

[For Morgan, teamwork was also vital for survival:] "If you want to know in just one word how we were able to go through hell over Europe 25 times and get back home without a casualty . . . I'll give it to you. The word is TEAMWORK. Until you have been over there, you can't know how essential that is. We had 10 men working together, each ready and able to help out anybody else who might need him. If it weren't for the gunners using the interphone to keep me posted on what they can see, it would be almost impossible for me to fly the airplane in combat. I can't get up and look around. Those fellows are my eyes."

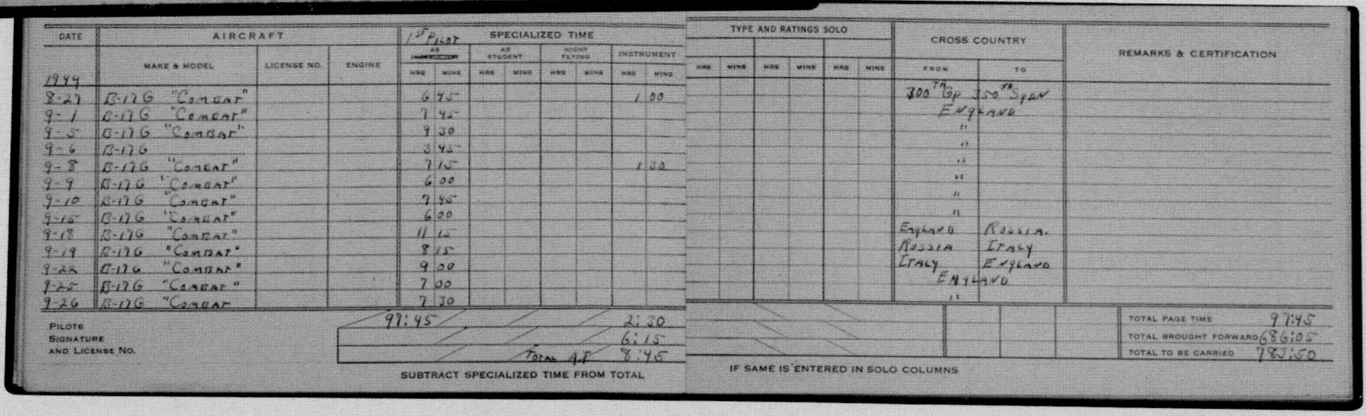

**As for the copilot's role, James A. Verinis—Morgan's deputy in the *Memphis Belle*—had this to say:**

"To begin with, let me say to the fellows who go over as copilots that they probably won't be copilots long. The chances are that if they are good they

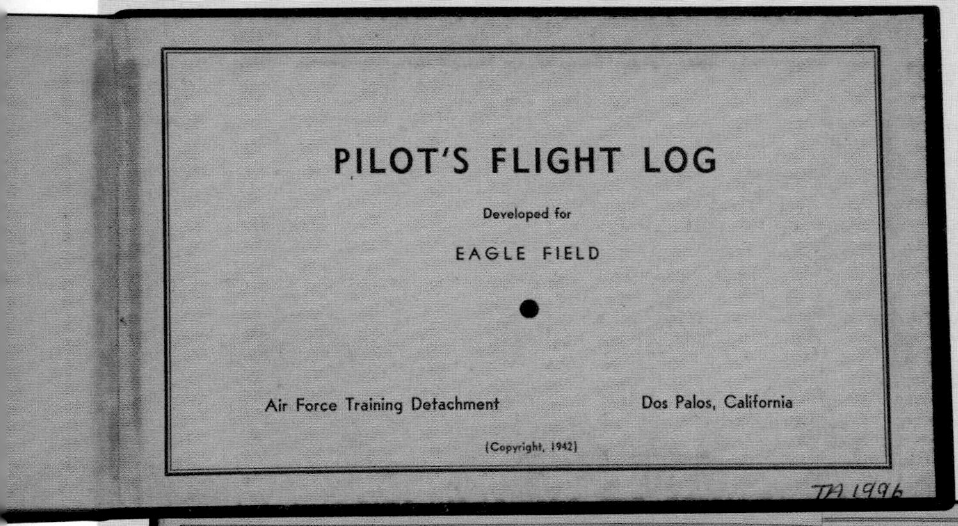

*Winged propeller insignia, worn on the lapels of the pilot's uniform.*

PILOT'S FLIGHT LOG

Developed for

EAGLE FIELD

Air Force Training Detachment          Dos Palos, California

(Copyright, 1942)

*Above right: Take-Off, the handbook of the Corps of Aviation Cadets of the Air Corps Replacement Training Center (Air Crew), issued to cadets in training in the ZOI (US).*

*Left and above left: Pilot's Flight Log developed for Eagle Field at Dos Palos, California, by the Air Force Training Detachment in 1943.*

Take Off

THE OFFICIAL HANDBOOK

of the

Corps of Aviation Cadets

of the

Air Corps Replacement Training
Center (Air Crew)

of

The Southeast Air Corps Training
Center

Above: *B-17G Fortresses in the 487th Bomb Group in formation in 1944. Formation flying in combat boxes for mutual protection and concentrated bombing was 8th Bomber Command's favored mode of operation. German fighter pilots sought out the weaker groups, singled out the easy pickings, and picked off stragglers with ease.*

will get their own ships. So don't get the idea that you are going to fight the war as a copilot. You should be prepared to take over your own ship and crew any minute you are called upon to do so. But while you are copilot, you have very definite responsibilities. As copilot, you should do everything you possibly can do to relieve the pilot. The pilot has tremendous responsibilities and I consider it the copilot's job to relieve him of all the worries that he can. There is no question about the need for a copilot in the B-17. The strength of one man is not sufficient to kick it around in combat. Usually, the copilot will do at least half the flying, but the pilot takes over in actual combat. But even in combat, when the pilot is flying the ship, the copilot should keep his hands on the wheel and his feet on the rudders. In that way he is ready, when needed, to apply pressure in the direction the pilot indicates . . . Now that the boys know they have only 25 raids to go before they get a let-up, morale is good. As long as they have a goal, as long as they know there is a stopping place, they're OK. If they felt they had to go on indefinitely, the spirit wouldn't be so good. Don't misunderstand me. It's no picnic over there. If anything, the missions are getting tougher. These daylight raids on the Ruhr Valley must be hell. I've never been over the Ruhr myself. But

the boys know that their equipment is good. They know that our bombers surpass anything that anybody else has."

**Second Lieutenant Robert "Bob" McCallum, pilot of *Queen Jeannie* (306th Bomb Group)—he was killed in action on October 14, 1943— thought it was "no fun being a copilot":**

"When an easy one [mission] comes along they take a new first pilot and let him go in your place, to sort of let him see what a raid is like before he has to go on his own as a first pilot. And a lot of times, you get ranked out of a raid by a general or a colonel, so you never finish up with the pilot you started with . . . A pilot and a copilot pal around together a lot. They're usually closer than anybody else in the crew. They split up the flying time, about every fifteen minutes, switching generally every time the big hand on the clock hits 12, 3, 6 and 9. The big difference between the two jobs is the pilot has to decide what to do when you get in trouble."

# The B-17 vs the B-24

**There was intense rivalry between B-17 and B-24 crews, as Ellis B. Woodward, a lead crew pilot in the 493rd Bomb Group, remarked:**

"During all the time we were flying B-24s, we couldn't have been happier with our lot. B-24 pilots and B-17 pilots were always having friendly arguments about which was the best airplane and almost all of the time, the pilots stood up for the airplane they were flying at the time. In our own case, we staunchly defended the B-24 over the B-17. In the early part of the war these were the only American four-engine

Left: *Throttle controls allowed individual or multi-engine adjustment with one hand. Glycol boilers fed by heat from the engine exhaust collectors warmed the flight decks.*

bombers flying in combat, so it was only natural that they would be compared to each other. The pilot of a B-24 was able to cup his hand over the top of the four throttles at one time; he had to hold the throttles upside down on the B-17, because of the way they were designed. There was one more thing that was inconvenient. When the pilot stopped the airplane at the end of the takeoff runway in order to run the engines up to full power to check them out before taking off, he had to ask the copilot to apply the parking brakes for him. The only control for the parking brakes was to the right of the copilot's seat and it was out of reach of the pilot. Weird! It's beginning to sound like we just really didn't care for the B-17 but that simply isn't the case. We loved it with a passion.

"If we had received the same amount of damage to a B-24—large holes in the wing, elevators, and flaps—we felt almost certain that we would not have been able to remain aloft for the four hours that it took us to return to England on our 15th mission, on 12 September, 1944, when we went to Magdeburg.

"In our group, there were two brothers, both of whom were pilots and they liked to fly on the same missions. In addition, their preference was to fly in the same element, one flying in the No.2 position, and the other flying in the No.3 position. Being near to each other and being able to see each other apparently provided them with comfort and solace. However, there was always the possibility that this closeness in formation could turn from comfort into horror and this day it did. The brother flying in the No.3 position suffered a direct hit in the gas tanks while over the target and the gas tanks burst into flames. The flames above the wing appeared to be about 50ft [15m] high, and they stretched from wing tip to wing tip, which measured just over 103ft [31m]. The plane continued on course for a few seconds and then banked into a slow turn to the left. Within a few seconds, the plane went into a steep bank and within another few seconds, the plane exploded. It reminded me of a firecracker. When you throw a firecracker and it explodes, all you can see is a little black powder accompanied by tiny pieces of paper floating to the ground. When this B-17 exploded, it fit the description exactly. There were no distinguishing features in the aftermath. You couldn't see wings, or tails, or engines, or wheels, or parachutes, or people—nothing. It was sickening to watch.

"After witnessing the explosion, we dropped our bombs, cleared the flak area over the target, breathed a sigh of relief, turned left and headed for home. But our relief was to be short-lived. Over the intercom came the dreaded word, 'fighters.' We were leading a flight of 12 B-17s. Within 60 seconds, we could feel some of the hits from 20mm cannon shells ripping through the airplane. And within 90 seconds of the warning, we looked around and found that there was no one left in our squadron except our deputy lead—our right wingman—and us. All of the other B-17s had disappeared, each with nine crewmen aboard. What a catastrophe!

"The reason that we were selected to be a Lead Crew was due to the fact that my total flying experience was substantially more than most of the other pilots in the group. When we landed in England, my total flying

Above: *A B-17 lead pilot wearing his "50 mission crush." The front spring stiffening (or grommet) was removed so that the headset could be worn over the cap in flight.*

time, as a pilot, was more than 1,000 hours, while many of our other pilots had only 350 to 400 hours. Lead Crews flew on average about three or four missions per month, while Wing Crews flew about six or seven missions during the same period. Wing Crews were called upon to fly 35 missions to complete a tour of duty, while Lead Crews completed a tour of duty by flying 30. But the Lead Crews had to adhere to a more rigorous schedule than the Wing Crews. They had to fly every day. They had to take their aircraft up to 15,000ft [4,600m] and check out all equipment: engines, electrical equipment, the instruments, the radios, the machine guns, the bombsight, and the oxygen system. The reason for having to climb to 15,000ft was for the sole purpose of testing the oxygen system. World War II aircraft were not equipped with pressurized cabins. All crewmembers were required to wear oxygen masks when flying at altitudes above 10,000ft [3,000m]. If their supply of oxygen were inadequate, it could produce a state of hypoxia [lack of oxygen to the blood and brain]. While in this state, a crewmember often felt euphoric and this resulted in a few tragic consequences."

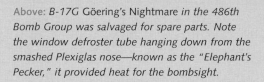

Above: *B-17G* Göering's Nightmare *in the 486th Bomb Group was salvaged for spare parts. Note the window defroster tube hanging down from the smashed Plexiglas nose—known as the "Elephant's Pecker," it provided heat for the bombsight.*

Top right: *B-17F* Old Bill *in the 305th Bomb Group after a raid on May 15, 1943. Twenty-mm cannon fire from fighters over Heligoland had riddled the Fortress, shooting out the Plexiglas nose, and killing navigator 2nd Lt Douglas van Able.*

Above: *Crews inspect* Betty Lou's Buggy, *safely back at Bassingbourn on April 19, 1944 after sustaining heavy damage from enemy fighters over the FW 190 plant. Fighters holed the left wing fuel tank, and knocked out the left aileron and the elevators.*

# To Hell—and Merseburg

Oil targets were among the most feared by pilots and crew alike. Merseburg soon became the main topic of conversation among the old-timers. When Ken Blakeborough, a replacement pilot, arrived at Glatton on Christmas Eve in 1944 he was quick to notice it. Blakeborough threw his baggage on an empty bunk and was told by one of the old-timers in the "Fireball Outfit" that the bed he had chosen had belonged to Gordon Gallagher, who had gone down at Merseburg on November 2. Charles E. Harris, pilot of *Sack Artist* in the Bloody Hundredth, describes what it was like to hit Merseburg three times:

"In each case, the missions were rough, primarily from the heavy concentration of 88mms. The word Merseburg always brings back the memories of flak and more flak! To our crew and I dare say most of the 100th, Merseburg was one of the worst targets, if not THE worst. Our crew had a real rough beginning; badly mauled on two missions and in the

Above: *Newly arrived natural metal finish (NMF) B-17Gs stockpiled on runways and taxiways in England in the run up to D-Day, June 1944.*

Red Cross flak shack after only six missions. But soon after that we were designated a lead crew. On July 29 Major Joe Zeller was the command pilot. (When a command pilot was in the right hand seat, the normal crew copilot was 'promoted' to tail gunner). Until we hit the bomb run, it was pretty much like other missions. But as we started down the run I looked straight ahead and the sky was a continuous flak burst. Being the lead plane, there were no other planes to look at; the preceding Group was far ahead. I think that this was the only mission where I honestly thought to myself: 'We'll never make it through' and I said a quick prayer. Major Zeller was on the radio, in contact with the other groups and his apparent coolness helped settle me back into the routine of

Above left: B-17F Airplane Pilot's Flight Operating Instructions. *The instruction manual was produced by Air Service Command at Patterson Field, Fairfield, Ohio, in December 1942.*

Above right: Section II *graphically showed some of the instrument and handling pitfalls. Pilots had to be aware of the changes between B-17s; the "F" model, for instance, differed from the B-17E in having no fewer than 400 modifications made.*

flying. The pilot of the lead plane was essentially on instruments. Maintaining exact altitude and speed was vital, also the heading provided by the navigator. Once the bombardier took control, the heading became his responsibility. After that one good look forward, I went back to the business of flying on instruments. For the pilot that was a blessing in a way, as it kept his eyes on the instruments and not on what was going on around, but the command pilot, with no actual flying responsibility, got to see everything (poor guy). During the bomb run there were several 'bangs' that indicated flak bursts all too near. My navigator said that the target was smoked out and was leaning over the bombardier, trying to point out where to hit, when he looked thru the nose and saw all of those fighters headed right at us with tracers making it look like the 4th of July. At 'bombs away' I made a fast, descending turn to get out of the flak. At that time, getting away was primary and I left the instruments so that I could see where we were going so as to avoid conflict with any other groups in the area. Because of the evasive action, the group formation always loosened up a bit due to the maneuver. We didn't come home with any holes in the plane, though we did lose some planes out of the group."

*Below: The pilot had to maintain formation and the copilot had to be prepared to take over ship and crew at a minute's notice. It was his job to relieve the pilot of as many of his worries as possible.*

# Converting to "Grenade Carriers"

Above: *Brigadier General James H. Doolittle (right), commanding general of the 8th Air Force November 1943–July 1945, General Carl A. "Toohey" Spaatz (center), and a congressman.*

**In the summer of 1944 General "Jimmy" Doolittle carried out the first stage of his plan to convert all five Liberator groups of the 3rd Bomb Division to the B-17. The 493rd Bomb Group's conversion to Fortresses took place over one weekend with a quick flick through the "handbook," a couple of briefings and then straight into the "practical," as 1st Lieutenant Richard R. Lewis recalls.**
"Captain Earl Johnson took me on a guided tour of the 'new' aircraft. He pointed out what to look for on the pre-flight and he also showed me the 'art' of climbing into the aircraft through the nose hatch—difficult even for an acrobat, let alone an airman in full flight clothing! The B-17 really was a dream to fly—you didn't have to fight it like the B-24."

**Dream to fly or not, for Lieutenant Francis S. Milligan there was a downside to being transferred to B-17s:** "Changing over to Flying Fortresses was practically a guarantee from the 8th Air Force that from now on we would be visiting the Reichland—definitely the 'Big League'. . . Bremen, Merseburg, Magdeburg, Münster, Ludwigshaven, and other German cities became our targets. Hitting the Hitler gang's backyard was a bit different than bombing V-1 launching sites in France. They really loved to shoot at us over the Fatherland. I think they must have given the schoolkids recess at Merseburg, and each one had a flak gun. Flak and rocket trails were heavy over practically every one of the German targets. It was almost impossible to visualize how black the sky became when Jerry started to throw his stuff up at us. Flak always scared me . . . "

# "Mercilessburg:" Storm of Steel

**The big Leuna plant at Merseburg was one of four main oil plants in the Leipzig area in central Germany: it was estimated that it was protected by some 2,200 88mm and 105mm guns. Gordon Weir commented that "Mercilessburg [as the crews called it] was the most fearsome target in Europe . . . being surrounded by more guns—and more heavy guns— than Berlin." For both George P. Fory, and for Fred Huston (a bombardier in the 96th Bomb Group), it was the flak that made "Mercilessburg" memorable—for all the wrong reasons. Fred Huston remembers:**

"My memory of some of the missions we flew are vivid in the extreme; others were just names and [all you remembered was] how many hours it took to get there and back, but the Merseburg-Lutzkendorf-Leuna missions stand out, with a certain amount of terror included. Our first trip there I thought very little about it. It was just another place where the red string ended and the intelligence officer assured us [the mission] was vital to the prosecution of the war. Of course, they said that about every target so we took it with a grain of salt. Some of them didn't seem all that important to a bunch of 20-year-olds who were more concerned with the next pass to London than we were with saving the world. I am sure that I went to Merseburg something like four or five times. I can also recall a sinking feeling in the pit of my stomach every time the string headed that way. When the string reached Merseburg I had my usual cold chills. Merseburg was the first time I saw colored flak. I remember it as red, although there are those who remember it as pale blue. I still think it was red. We were told by someone, probably someone who didn't know either, that it was to call in the fighters. Since we already had more fighters than Custer had Sioux, I thought that it was gilding the lily somewhat to call in something that we already had in abundance. But to me, one fighter was plenty for the day."

For George P. Fory, too, the Merseburg flak was unforgettable—though he recalls it as being "brownish-black:" "Flak-wise, Merseburg was worse than Berlin. There the flak was in curtains and of a barrage type where an area was filled with it, but Merseburg flak was mostly tracking type and always the flak would come up in four bursts at a time, generally 50–75 yards [46–69m] apart and usually staggered in elevation. If you saw three bursts, you wondered if you were in the fourth. The worst part of being in

*Below left: B-17s flying through heavy flak—"thick enough to walk on," as the saying went—in February 1944.*
*Below right: B-17G* Blue Streak *in the 834th Bomb Squadron, 486th Bomb Group, which was shot down over Merseburg on November 2, 1944. All nine members of 2nd Lieutenant David M. Paris's crew were killed.*

the lead was waiting for the flak to start. On one occasion we were in the lead and had passed the 'three minutes to go' point and no flak. About the time I asked the bombardier, 'Where's the flak?' a great big black, brown burst, seemingly big as the airplane, went off directly ahead of us on our level, and immediately we were in it. For an instant I was in a pure 'puckering' state, as were the other crew who

*M4E-2 standardized for mass production as the M4A-2 flyers' flak helmet in 1944.*

**Above:** *Mission map showing the area around Berlin in 1945, with the route to and from the target planned to avoid the worst of the known flak areas, which are outlined in red.*

saw it. Merseburg flak was brownish-black. Berlin flak was black. Munich flak was mixed brownish and pinkish centers. That was the way it looked to me anyway . . . The best words I know of to describe Merseburg flak was that it was 'intense' and 'accurate.'"

# Pre-mission nerves

On the day of a mission, the first pangs would come during the early hours of the morning. The only thought in the minds of pilots and crew was to get back in one piece—and to count the number of missions that were needed to complete the tour. Griswold Smith, a pilot in the 100th Bomb Group at Thorpe Abbotts, recalls:

"At briefing the lights were turned off and they pulled the curtain back from the map on which our route to the target was always marked with a red ribbon. This was always a dramatic moment because no one ever knew where the mission was going until then. On this day it looked as if the ribbon was never going to stop. When the curtain was half way drawn you could hear 'Berlin' whispered all over the room. My heart quickened a little. Finally, it turned out to be Eger, Czechoslovakia, to everyone's relief. Nothing happened on the raid except for the terrific nervous strain caused by the shout, 'Bandits in the area!' on one occasion. We really flew close formation and sweated it out. This was our Air Medal mission—we'd really had our fill of combat by now."

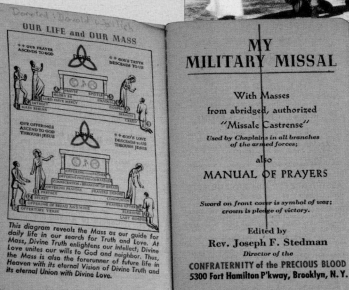

Above: A crew receive benediction before a mission. Overall, the mix of religions and regional backgrounds probably brought the men closer together.
Left and far left: The rigors of combat flying, cold, danger, and equipment failure did not leave time to think about religion, except for each to pray in his way.

waddle over to his barrack and fall in bed until the alert sergeant woke him the next morning for briefing, and the ritual would begin all over again. Second Lieutenant Dick Johnson, a B-17 pilot in the 303rd Bomb Group, talked about how the men coped with the stress:

"We usually lived a day-to-day existence, knowing that the next mission could be our last. Many men reacted differently to the stress of almost daily combat. One day when one of our pilots was shot down my thoughts were not about 'Poor Lieutenant X' but 'My God, I'm glad I wasn't over there.' When I returned from the mission I went into the barracks before I went to debriefing where I met another pilot. 'Hey,' I said, 'Lieutenant X got shot down today.' 'No shit,' he said, 'I wonder if his pants will fit me.' I was shocked but said nothing more. I couldn't imagine anybody being so callous about a friend or acquaintance being shot down and possibly killed. I figured that his attitude might have just been his defense strategy."

After missions like this the mental and physical strain was such that many were too tired to keep up their mission logs or diaries. Missions could come every day with no rest in between. Griswold Smith would return from a mission and the pilots' truck would be waiting to carry him to the mission critique. From there he would stagger over to the Mess Hall and gorge himself. After that he would

Some pilots, like Lowell S. Watts, pilot of *Blitzin' Betsy* in the 388th Bomb Group at Knettishall, "had arrived at that mental state where one more extra-long, extra-tough raid, meant almost nothing to us. It was just another raid. As for myself at least, I'd grown calloused. The tougher the raid now, the better I liked it." Captain John "Tex" McCrary listed some of the ways to die:

"There are so damn many ways to get killed in a Fortress . . . Your oxygen mask can freeze up and you're a stiff in ten minutes. Any one of your four engines or several gas tanks can stop an explosive slug and that spells curtains. Or maybe a couple of your engines go out and you lag behind the formation and then the fighters cut you to pieces. And all this happens about five miles above the earth—and that's the thing that doubles the strain on your nerves—the environment in which your guts have to digest danger is unnatural."

**Right:** *In April 1944 General Eisenhower "christened" General "Ike," a 91st Bomb Group B-17G, at Bassingbourn with Mississippi River water. The name was Major James McPartlin's idea (here he gets a "dunking" in celebration of finishing his missions). Ike completed 75 missions, returning to the US in 1945.*

**Below:** *Charles L. Brown, a pilot in the 379th Bomb Group at Kimbolton, celebrates completing his tour on April 11, 1944, with a swig of "mountaineer tea."*

**When Lieutenant Ralph R. Miller, pilot of *Lady Liberty*, waited to fly his 13th mission he reflected that a few more and he and his crew would reach a point, "from where they could see that Promised Land of 25 missions completed, then *finis* and they would all be past and only memories."** The 13th mission, though, turned out to be unlucky for them, jut as it was to be for another crew, as Leonard W. Herman, of the 95th Bomb Group, remembered:

"There was one crew that had just about completed their tour. However, the pilot had an abnormal number of aborts. Consequently, there was much conversation and insinuations that these aborts were more of pilot doing rather than mechanical failures. In order to prove that this was not the case, the pilot volunteered to fly an additional five missions. He was shot down on his 26th mission."

**When Bill Rose, a pilot in the 92nd Bomb Group, had first started flying, his Squadron CO had told him that "if you can survive seven missions, there's a good chance you'll survive 25." To help himself get through, Rose adopted a tough attitude: kill or be killed:**

"I flew as copilot on my first mission with an experienced pilot to Gdynia, Poland, the longest round trip bombing mission by the 8th Air Force. We had no fighter attacks going in, but on the way back they were waiting over Denmark. This was my first taste of combat. I watched a German fighter come in, met by a wall of tracer bullets. He shot down a Fortress and escaped, seemingly unscathed. My attitude changed. It was kill or be killed. I felt like a Roman Gladiator whose only hope of surviving was to be more cunning, more careful, and more deadly than his opponent. We needed that seriousness for the battle that lay ahead."

# The Navigator

"The only time I've ever seen real, naked terror was in a navigator's eyes—on the ground. He had been grounded but the terror was still echoing in his eyes."

—Captain John R. "Tex" McCrary, *First of the Many*

"*Y*ou can always tell a navigator by his pencils, maps and such. You can always tell a pilot but you can't tell him much,*" went the popular wartime ditty. Harry Crosby, one of the finest navigators in the 8th Air Force says: "We didn't want any Hairbreadth Harry types. We wanted beady-eyed guys just absolutely holding the course, sweating and working hard to keep the subtle settings right in." After pre-flight school, navigator trainees spent many hours learning codes, mathematics, maps and charts, aircraft and naval recognition, principles of flight, aero-physics, and altitude equipment training. They also had to be able to handle machine guns and fire them, so they were sent to flexible gunnery school for a six-week course. Captain Charles B. Leighton, navigator on the *Memphis Belle*, said, "I should have had more gunnery training. The first moving target I fired at was a Focke-Wulf." Navigator school was a 20-week course. Trainees spent 104 hours airborne in Beechcraft AT-7s learning dead reckoning using compass, wind drift, and airspeed to calculate positions and practiced navigating by radio bearings and night navigation techniques. Another 782 hours was spent in ground school learning pilotage navigation (observation of the ground and its features and comparing them to a map), instruments, dead reckoning, radio, celestial navigation, meteorology, and codes and recognition. Trainees were awarded navigator's silver

*Left: B-17G with the navigator's "office" (left). The navigator was under the worst strain of all, having to think all the time, but with nothing to do with his hands but push a pencil. Sometimes he got to use one of the side nose guns, which helped relieve the tension.*

wings, appointed flight officers or commissioned as 2nd lieutenants and sent on to unit training.

William W. Varnedoe Jr recalls ". . . After Pearl Harbor I knew I was destined to fight." By VJ Day, more than 50,000 students had graduated from the specialized navigation schools. Varnedoe went to the Nashville classification center where he was given "all sorts of tests, written, psychological, and psychomotor . . . The latter was a sort of penny arcade of machines to test reaction times and coordination. We were asked to rate ourselves on a scale of 10 = best to 1 = poor as pilots, navigators, and bombardiers. I thought, 'I want to be a pilot, but I'll take any of them, so I'll show I'm good at all three, but show preference.' I rated myself P-10, N-9, and B-8. The tests gave me: P-7, N-10, and B-7. I was assigned Navigator. Others who gave themselves, P-10, N-1, B-1, and got test scores of P-7, N-10, B-7, were assigned to pilot school. Oh, well." Varnedoe was commissioned a 2nd lieutenant and at Avon Park, Florida, he met the rest of the B-17 —the men who would be his "crewmates, war companions, buddies and friends for life."

Abe L. Dolim, a young Hawaiian from Honolulu who had stood and watched helplessly as the Japanese bombed his island and who, after washing-out in flight school in March 1943, became a navigator, recalls, "Air navigation was considered an art and not a science—perhaps it still is. We were taught that the most important asset of a good navigator was the ability to make a sound judgment based on the best information available. As one classmate put it, 'Navigation is a deadly game of educated guessing.' Most navigators did 'follow the pilot' navigation, that is, plotting where the aircraft has been rather than where it is going. For this type of navigation we were over-trained—but where lead navigation was concerned, we required additional training in the new instrumentation and techniques. For my part, I hated to put away my sextant, as celestial navigation was my favorite method. Our instruments were very reliable. The radio compass was subject to the weather or terrain. The 'G Box' (nothing more than a simple television receiver) was affected by enemy interference, which forced the operator to wade through the high 'Grass' and 'Ghosts' to find the true 'Master' and 'Slave' signals or 'Blips.' The trick was to obtain the 'Line of Position' reading within the three seconds allotted to the operator by Jerry. In England, I liked the British maps we were issued. In many respects they were superior to ours. Patches of wood were exactly plotted in their particular geometric forms and the colors were sharper. The names of towns, rivers, etc., were in the language of the country or location. My knowledge of the German language was to be of some use after all."

At the general briefing the target would be announced, and all the other aspects of the mission—ordnance, takeoff time, expected flak, and assembly, would all be covered. Then it was synchronize watches and the crewmen would be dismissed to their special briefings. Navigators would pick up their charts and logs, plot the route to and from the target and alternate target, the estimated time of arrival at assembly points, turning points, initial points, targets, the predicted winds, and weather along the way. All done, they packed up and double-checked that they had everything in their briefcase—charts and flight plan, EGB computer (manually operated and nothing like modern electronics), protractor and dividers, weather card, code data sheets, and several sharpened pencils. Then it was off to the lockers to change into flight clothing.

*Page right, clockwise from top left: The all-important forward entry and escape hatch door in the floor of the B-17 nose; B-17G Mary Alice, showing the two windows above the navigator's station; one of the 50-caliber cheek guns; a photograph of the navigator's station of the B-17, made by Boeing; a window on the war aboard Nine-O-Nine. Frontal activity, high and low pressure areas, and altitude in the ETO plagued every navigator on a mission of any distance—in a fast-moving aircraft, he was always kept busy.*

## Navigators' Information File

This navigator's table shows a mix of memorabilia and instruments that might be taken aboard the B-17. Snatched moments could be spent reading *Yank* magazine, *Stars & Stripes*, or special Armed Service Editions of popular novels.

*The publication (left) was one of several produced by the USAAF to assist the navigator in his tasks. On a combat mission the navigator's table (above) would be covered with maps, charts, and instruments for making computations, and other paraphernalia.*

# Navigators at work

**In July 1943 Captain Charles B. Leighton talked about the navigator's job while on missions in the ETO:**

"We usually have three hours between the briefing and the takeoff. During that time the navigator is busy as hell. He must make sure that he fully understands weather conditions, including any anticipated changes. He must check on any flak areas on or anywhere near the route so that he can avoid them. He must be thoroughly familiar with the formation

*Above: At their special briefings navigators would pick up their charts and logs, plot the route to and from the target and alternate target, the estimated time of arrival at assembly points, turning points, initial points, targets, the predicted winds, and weather along the way.*

that is going on the mission. After briefing, he consults with the pilot to go over the route. It is especially important for the navigator to talk to the radio operator and to make sure that all the radio equipment is ready. The navigator should brief the pilot on how to get back in the event something happens to the navigator. I have tried drawing the route on a small map for the pilot but every precaution should be taken not to let a map get out and it must be destroyed if the ship goes down.

"There are two conditions that might cause a navigator trouble: first, poor weather when he can't see the ground. Second, a fight that takes him out to sea, causing him to lose all his landmarks. So it's good to train yourself to write down your compass heading and to continue your navigation work even through a stiff fight.

"I like being a navigator. I would like to get up and walk around a little sometimes, but I have to work like the devil all the time. But there is

nothing like the satisfaction a navigator gets when he hits his ETA right on the head. When you are the lead navigator, the whole formation depends upon you. The responsibility is frightening sometimes. You should be just as alert if you are the navigator of any of the other ships in the formation. You might lose your lead ship or you might get separated from the formation.

"You get scared sometimes, but usually any feeling of fright or tenseness leaves you when you start mixing it up. The worst scare I ever had was over St. Nazaire. We were at 10,000ft [3,048m]. I could see the bursts following us, one after another. It was only a minute or so, but it seemed like 15 years. When we heard 'bombs away,' we ducked. It wasn't a second too soon. From experiences like that, I learned that it is important to keep your eyes off the flak. It helps a lot. I also got scared the time I ran out of ammunition. It doesn't bother me if I can shoot back. But looking down those barrels and not having anything to shoot is no fun."

**Second Lieutenant William W. Varnedoe Jr., who became 2nd Lieutenant George H. Crow Jr.'s navigator in the 385th Bomb Group, recalls that:**

"No two B-17s that I flew were ever exactly alike. The position of the flux gate compass, the radio compass, the *G Box* [used for navigation], the oxygen outlet, the heated suit receptacle, the intercom control box, the place to plug in the headset and throat mike, varied all over the nose compartment. Each time they had to be hunted down. They were usually so scattered about that when I was attached to the intercom, oxygen, and heated suit, I felt like a fly in a spider web. When moving about I had to be careful not to unplug something. I always stood up for all flights. The B-17 came equipped with a chair for the navigator, complete with a seat belt. But this chair was unattached to the fuselage! We generally gave this chair to the crew chief, leaving no place for navigators to sit down. In return, the crew chiefs would scrounge up all sorts of scrap armor plate. The pilots usually put some in the seat of their chairs. One must protect the vitals! I stacked odd pieces about the nose. Some Forts had so much that I'm sure was not on the weight calculations that I wondered how they behaved in the air. We also had one-man inflatable dinghies. These came in a small package

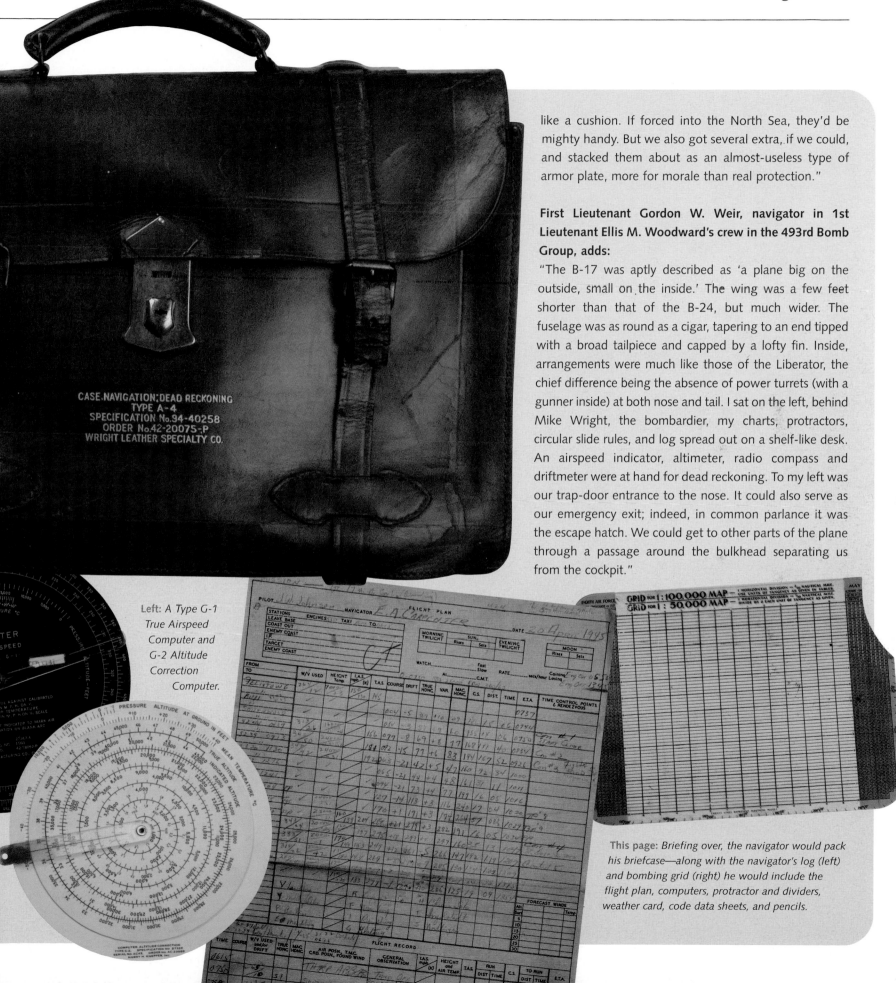

like a cushion. If forced into the North Sea, they'd be mighty handy. But we also got several extra, if we could, and stacked them about as an almost-useless type of armor plate, more for morale than real protection."

**First Lieutenant Gordon W. Weir, navigator in 1st Lieutenant Ellis M. Woodward's crew in the 493rd Bomb Group, adds:**

"The B-17 was aptly described as 'a plane big on the outside, small on the inside.' The wing was a few feet shorter than that of the B-24, but much wider. The fuselage was as round as a cigar, tapering to an end tipped with a broad tailpiece and capped by a lofty fin. Inside, arrangements were much like those of the Liberator, the chief difference being the absence of power turrets (with a gunner inside) at both nose and tail. I sat on the left, behind Mike Wright, the bombardier, my charts, protractors, circular slide rules, and log spread out on a shelf-like desk. An airspeed indicator, altimeter, radio compass and driftmeter were at hand for dead reckoning. To my left was our trap-door entrance to the nose. It could also serve as our emergency exit; indeed, in common parlance it was the escape hatch. We could get to other parts of the plane through a passage around the bulkhead separating us from the cockpit."

*Left: A Type G-1 True Airspeed Computer and G-2 Altitude Correction Computer.*

*This page: Briefing over, the navigator would pack his briefcase—along with the navigator's log (left) and bombing grid (right) he would include the flight plan, computers, protractor and dividers, weather card, code data sheets, and pencils.*

# Filling up—and more

**Navigating and manning guns in the close confines of the B-17's nose was uncomfortable in the extreme, as Abe Dolim confirms:**
"The flak suits we wore were made of laminated metal and weighed about 20lb [9kg]. They were cumbersome and caused one's shoulders to ache but a buddy of mine stopped three pieces of flak with his. We also

*Above and right: 1st Lt Abel "Abe" L. Dolim (on the far left in the photo with his crew), who flew two tours and 51 missions as a navigator in the 94th Bomb Group. By March 1945, he had lost 15lb (6–8kg) and had become impossible to fly or live with.*

wore flak helmets that were really infantrymen's helmets with the sides cut out to accommodate our large earphones. My ears would ring from the engine noise. Condensation from moist breath forms a lump of ice on one's neck, so we wore a muffler to catch the moisture and to keep cold air out. We used silk inner gloves to keep

our hands from sticking to the extremely cold metal parts of the aircraft. Either the extreme cold at -40°F [-40°C] or the tension caused me to pass water frequently. I discovered that no one used the relief tube in the bomb bay for two good reasons. First, the trip with an oxygen bottle was too much and second, if one used it but did not notify the ball-turret gunner to rotate at 6 o'clock, his windscreen was very neatly frosted. We used empty bomb fuze containers, with which the armorer-gunners very generously supplied us. The filled cans froze quickly, and then they were stacked alongside a bulkhead until they were thrown out during the bomb run. During the winter of 1944–45 I heard a conversation between a radioman and his engineer sweating out the returning bombers. The engineer wondered when the navigator would be returning to duty. He's been in the hospital for a week now. And he's put in for the Purple Heart. The engineer turned to his radioman and smiling, said, 'I wonder what he'll tell his kids someday—he sure as hell won't tell them he left a lot of foreskin on a super-cold fuze can over Germany at 26,000 feet [7,925m]. Boy did he ever bleed like a stuck pig.'

"Gas expansion was always a problem among crews at high altitude where air is thin and stagnant in a bomber. Odors of all sorts permeated the combined oxygen supply systems and many were the complaints from crewmembers that had to put up with someone else's gas. On June 5, 1944, we flew four hours on a mission to northern France but had to

PURE-DRIED WHOLE EGGS U.S.A.

abort over the Pas de Calais at 29,500ft [9,000m] because of severe stomach cramps among several crewmembers. Combat crews were not supposed to be fed foods that produced gas but in England they grew a lot of Brussels sprouts, kale, and cabbage. These were the fresh vegetables served, along with occasional cabbage caterpillars. Only crews scheduled for the day's combat mission were fed fresh eggs for breakfast. The rest got powdered eggs as usual. They might also have fried canned salted bacon or a bologna-type sausage, sliced

to clean and adjust their weapons after every mission. Armament technicians checked the barrels for wear. We fired in short bursts of three or four rounds at a time to keep from overheating the barrels. It is hard to believe that even at -40°F [-40°C] a barrel could be damaged, but once the spiral lands of the gun bores were burned up, all that was left was just another piece of scrap iron. Our combined .50s created a tremendous earsplitting, reverberating racket and the entire bomber would seem to vibrate. The stench of exploded cartridges would fill our navigator-bombardier compartment and the floor would be covered with empty .50 caliber casings, so moving about I felt like I had roller skates on my fur-lined boots. Very unlike the Hollywood version of air combat, I did not hear enemy aircraft engine noise or cannon fire, even when the enemy pressed their attack to within yards of our bomber."

*Left: When there were no fresh eggs for breakfast, powdered eggs were whipped into a sticky emulsion, then apparently fried in axle grease left over from the motor pool; the result was a well-vulcanized lump of goo, occasionally flavored with dehydrated bacon bits.*

and fried, which we called 'horsecock.' Then of course there was always that old friend and true army breakfast substitute, creamed chipped beef on toast, affectionately known as 'shit on a shingle.' We were issued one box each of high-carbohydrate ration candy, all we had to eat during the missions, some of which were nine to ten hours in duration. However, the Group always had corned beef sandwiches and coffee or cocoa for us during interrogation. Our GI coffee turned spoons green and it is believed by some that the spoon would dissolve if left in the brew too long.

"We always checked our .50 caliber cartridge belts for 'short rounds' before takeoff. As soon as we attained altitude we charged our .50s to keep one round in the chamber in case of icing. Gunners were required

*Above: Combat crew were issued with one box each of high-carbohydrate ration candy—all they had to eat during missions, some of which were nine to ten hours in duration. However, the Group always had corned-beef sandwiches, and coffee or cocoa ready for them during interrogation.*

# Good—and bad—omens

Navigators are renowned for their sharp, succinct, and accurate reporting, and Norman K. Andrew, in Jack Stanley's B-17 crew in the 487th Bomb Group, was no exception. When Andrew prepared to fly his first mission he was also philosophical, as his diary shows:

"1st mission today, 34 to go . . . They woke us at 1.50am. Briefing time 3:00am. So we knew it was pretty sure to be a long one. Had pineapple juice, fresh egg, hotcakes, sausage, cold cereal, coffee. Target, Schmitt ball bearing works, Nurnberg. Took off 0715— left England 0856. Over enemy coast 0921. Ran into overcast and cloudy weather. Turned back approx. 50 miles [80km] southeast of Aachen. Picked a target of opportunity—dropped on lead ship and leveled the town of St. Vith in Belgium. Encountered flak at Liège—moderate. Landed 1220. Logged five and a quarter hours.'

Left: At debriefing, intelligence officers asked crewmembers set questions about what they had seen, what damage they had suffered, and what other aircraft they knew to have been hit.

had to be up! The atmosphere at briefing was invariably somber but when the briefing officer announced, 'This is it—this is D-Day!' it was different; a lusty cheer shattered the quiet of a moment before. Whoops, whispers and yells echoed from the gray walls. It was an unprecedented and ecstatic vocal demonstration by the fliers who had doggedly been carrying the war to Germany for many months with considerable losses of men and planes. It was the day they had awaited to share with the ground forces and together they would assault the Nazi war machine, hopefully gaining a foothold on the mainland with the ultimate goal of driving the *Wehrmacht* back to the Fatherland and crushing it.

" . . . 'How was it Lieutenant?' [asked the crew chief in charge of keeping the Fortress flying, when Betz returned from the mission] 'What I saw through the breaks in clouds was an unforgettable sight,'" Betz replied. [There was no time to say anything more. A truck pulled up to take the crew to interrogation after which they had to get ready for the afternoon flight,

Above and right: One by one the Fortresses line up for takeoff, then, 30 seconds apart, climb away into the overcast—or, if they were lucky, the "beautiful CAVU," for more than an hour of forming up before the pilot flew the route to the target.

Combat crewmen like Franklin L. Betz, a navigator in the 379th Bomb Group at Kimbolton, could wax lyrical, especially when it was a special occasion. They did not come more special than "D-Day"—June 6, 1944:

"To be awakened about 0400 for a mission was pretty much routine but to be hauled out of the sack at about 0130 to report to briefing—well, something unusual just

and had us running out of fuel about the time we would reach the Channel. Hollywood not withstanding, a single B-17 is mismatched against a flurry of fighters usually. Six Me 109s hit us from the rear. They plastered us good, knocking out the controls and who knows what else. We baled out and got out OK, were buzzed, but not fired upon in our 'chutes by the remaining 109s. We were captured immediately."

**Jones, though, was the only one to escape when his plane went down:** "We picked up heavy flak near Koblenz but no planes were lost or delayed. However, this was just a harbinger of things to come. In no time at all we observed our fighter cover above us being drawn off to defend us against

*Above and right: Northamptonshire farm workers wave to a Fortress coming home after a long mission. A safe return meant another day to live—and another day to fly a new mission.*

his 30th mission. B-17s continued to peel off from the formation and land as the sun shone brightly through the cloud covering that was breaking up. Betz thought it a "good omen."]

**It was a beautiful clear day when Clifford D. Jones, a navigator in the 96th Bomb Group, and Richard Wynn, a navigator in the 100th Bomb Group, set off for a raid on oil targets. But that was as far as the good omens went because both were forced to bale out of their doomed Forts. Wynn, who was on his 14th mission, aboard *Rosie's Riveters*, made famous by Robert Rosenthal, a legendary figure in the Bloody Hundredth, recalls:**

"We were hit in the No.3 engine and lost oil pressure before the prop could be feathered. Cockpit procedure was complicated by the fact that a faulty flare from the lead ship deposited a heavy film of 'guck' over the pilot's half of the windshield, putting the copilot in control of the ship. His visibility was also limited to some extent. With a windmilling prop and all of the drag it created, we were unable to keep up with the formation and became a single straggler on the way home with heavy fuel consumption on a very deep penetration. I did a fuel consumption problem after a while

German fighters. Almost simultaneously, our crew was reporting attacks by enemy fighters from almost all points of the clock. With the exception of the tail gunner who wore a flat, back type parachute at all times, the remaining crewmembers had detachable chest type 'chutes. Attaching a chest 'chute on a buckle harness under a flak vest was extremely awkward. However, considering the pressing attacks, in a brief lull, I decided to loosen my flak vest and put my 'chute on. With all the bombers going down around us, I felt it was just a matter of time and if worse came to worse, I could, at least, make an immediate attempt to escape. A very short time thereafter there was a sudden jolt and shuddering of our aircraft. It seemed to stop in mid-air and then fell off into an uncontrolled fall. Through a miracle I escaped through the B-17's nose hatch and the tail gunner was blown out the rear. None of the other crewmembers would have had their 'chutes on when our plane went down out of control."

*Left: AN5740 master navigational watch, minus its special metal carrying case, made by Hamilton Watch Company.*

# Black Thursday

**Captain David Williams, group navigator, flew on the first Schweinfurt raid on August 17, 1943, in the lead ship, *Oklahoma Okie* and the second, on October 14, 1943, in the *Bad Egg*:**

"I vividly recall the operations order when it came over the teletype in Group Operations at Bassingbourn during the wee hours of the morning of October 14, as I had to do the navigational mission planning while the rest of the combat crews were still asleep. Thus we had already overcome the initial shock which we were to see on the faces of the crews somewhat later when the curtains were dramatically pulled back to reveal the scheduled second deep penetration to Schweinfurt. Mission 115 was my 23rd combat mission and the second time that I would have the dubious honor of being in the very first B-17 over the target. On August 17 [on the first Schweinfurt raid] we were one of only two aircraft which were able to make it back without an intermediate landing. At that we had part of our left wing shot

off from a 20mm frontal attack which resulted in our left wingman being completely shot out of the air. We also had an unexploded 20mm in our left main wing tank. A bullet of unknown caliber came through the top of the nose, passed through my right-hand British glove, through my left pant leg and British flying boot without so much as breaking the skin, then out through the floor. It paid to be skinny at the time!

"It was an eerie feeling once more to be the vanguard, striking out across the Channel toward a target, which had dealt us so many devastating losses just a few months before. All the more so this time since four of our group had already aborted and we were setting course with just seven aircraft comprising the 91st effort. I kept thinking of the ten we had lost in August and somehow could not seem to reconcile the math, which was going through my mind. The navigational chore ahead left little time for such speculation.

"Our crew was extremely fortunate on this trip for I do not recall any casualties and very little, if any, battle damage to the aircraft. Nonetheless, we had a grandstand view of the entire frightening battle, which once more was characterized by vicious frontal fighter attacks. They appeared to concentrate their efforts on the low groups rather than the lead group of aircraft. We expended many thousands of rounds of .50 caliber ammo'

*Left: The disintegrating remnants of a Bf 110 going down on the return from the mission to Schweinfurt on August 17, 1943. The enemy fighter was hit by fire from two P-47 Thunderbolts.*

*Above: The Nazi flag that fluttered over the Kugelfischer ball-bearing plant at Schweinfurt was presented to the 305th Bomb Group after the US 42nd Armored Division captured it in April 1945.*

against the attacking fighters on their way to the less fortunate Fortresses of our wing. Fortunately, the overcast disappeared at the southern German border and the weather was absolutely clear for the remainder of the route to the target and withdrawal until just east of Paris. This provided us with an opportunity for precise navigation and excellent bombing but also provided a field day for the German fighters and anti-aircraft gunners.

"It was a long day, eight hours of logged air combat, four per cent of a complete tour and one-fifth of an Air Medal [after five missions a crewman was awarded the AM]. It was also good for some combat grog, but not quite yet for the lead crewmembers. Our day was not finished. We had to re-plot the mission track and write a report on the day's effort. All in all it was a very tiring day for those who had to plan it, brief it, fly it, and report it. At least there was the satisfaction of having flown the mission as briefed. We lost one aircraft and we made it back."

Above: Fairchild A-10 sextant with an averaging device used in celestial navigation—the sole method of over-water navigation by which a navigator could start from a new point of departure when all other methods failed.

Below: E-6B computer, the best instrument for dead reckoning (DR) computations, wind drifts, conversion for true airspeed and altitude, and for changing statute miles to nautical miles.

Above: Colonel "Mo" Preston, CO 379th Bomb Group, listens to Major "Rip" Rohr on his return from Schweinfurt. Preston noted that Rohr "looked harassed, shaken, and more agitated that I had ever seen him."

# Bad dreams recalled

**Very early in his combat career Abe Dolim had turned off to the rally point and looked toward 5 o'clock to see a sky full of flak with two B-17s in trouble—one on fire and in a shallow dive, and the other exploding after a short vertical dive:**

"I watched several parachutes descend to German soil, then looked for my 'chute pack—it was not within easy reach. I made a note to stack it between my position and the emergency hatch against the bulkhead next to my navigation table. Our chest pack situation was a mess. Some high-ranking congenital idiot in the Air Materiel Command procurement business had decided that we must have two types of chest packs. One had rings on the harness and snapped on the 'chute, and the other type was just the opposite—an embarrassing situation at bale-out time if one was not careful."

and No.4. Wing fell in flames—the ship fell in flames, tight spin to the right. No parachutes observed. I knew they couldn't get out—it was spinning too tight. I'd rather get a direct hit. Three minutes later another one got a direct hit. All I could see was shiny bits of aluminum—just a ball of fire. No one had a chance. On my seventh mission, our first as a lead crew, we had about 8/10ths [visibility] most of the way, 10/10ths the rest. We had no flak, no fighters. Some of the wings coming in behind us went too close to Münster. Osnabrück tried a few bursts, about a mile off our right wing. One of our boys flipped over on his back and tore the wing off of his left wing man. Both went down—must have been prop wash. One ship in the group behind us blew up. What a day! On my eighth mission for some reason I had a feeling of confidence all the way through. We ran into some light inaccurate flak between Koblenz and Mainz as we crossed the Rhine. I was working like mad on my guns. Joe put the left hand gun on the right side and vice versa. I had to change the switches at 25,000ft [7,620m]

*Above and right: 2nd Lt Norbert A. Zwicke, seen holding his machine gun, was the navigator aboard B-17* Nora*. His ground crew issued him with the "special citation" shown to the right.*

**Over France one day, Norman K. Andrew saw a 12-ship formation flying on their left about eight miles away:**

"They plowed right over a flak battery at Falaise. I was looking right at them when one of the ships got a direct hit in the right wing. The wing broke off between No.3

364th Bomb Squadron (H)
305th Bomb Group (H)
Station #105, USAAF, ETOUSA

Special Citation #1
Lt. Norbert A. Zwicke

1.   Under the provisions of T. O. 7-11-XYZ, as amended Jan 1 1943, and rescinded Aug 19 1943, 2nd Lt. Norbert A. Zwicke is hereby awarded the Order of the Big Wheel.

2.   For:
Exceptionally meritorious conduct in battle and under fire ( he was inevitably the first under the navigator's table when fighters attacked).
Unequalled navigation under all circumstances (he could tell his po at a glance—whether he was sitting down or standing up or just lying about).
Completing 25 operational missions over enemy territory (at a loss t Air Force of 19,736 rounds of Cal. 50 ammunition --- to warm his guns --- and 17 rounds accidently fired at one attacking FW 190).
A sense of humor which has proved invaluable in combating the strain of the ETO (otherwise known as "ETO-Happy")

3.   The conduct of Lt. Zwicke has at all times reflected a high degree of credit on the armed forces in general and the Air Forces in particular. (his log of bunk-time is undoubtedly the most extensive in the ETO).

by order of the Crew Chief,
John V. (for victory) Purvis
Master Sergeant
Army Air Forces

Signed:  the ground crew of "NORA"

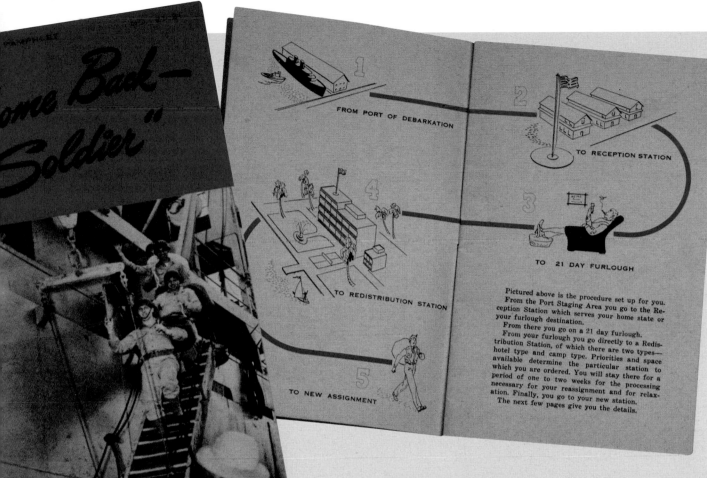

FROM PORT OF DEBARKATION

TO RECEPTION STATION

TO 21 DAY FURLOUGH

TO REDISTRIBUTION STATION

TO NEW ASSIGNMENT

Pictured above is the procedure set up for you. From the Port Staging Area you go to the Reception Station which serves your home state or your furlough destination.

From there you go on a 21 day furlough.

From your furlough you go directly to a Redistribution Station, of which there are two types—hotel type and camp type. Priorities and space available determine the particular station to which you are ordered. You will stay there for a period of one to two weeks for the processing necessary for your reassignment and for relaxation. Finally, you go to your new station. The next few pages give you the details.

*Left and far left: "Welcome Back– Soldier" booklet for returning servicemen. Most young aircrew had grown up during the War. More squadron friends were dead than alive; only a handful had completed a combat tour. They knew of no other life than this accelerated existence, and coming to terms with the changes could be traumatic.*

"When my friends and relatives asked me about the air war I soon realized I could not communicate. How could I possibly expect them to understand what it felt like when you were freezing your ass off at -40°F [-40°C], 25,000ft [7,620m] above Germany in dread of flak and the deadly *Luftwaffe*? I soon learned to use the RAF tack, 'Piece of cake, old boy'. Oh yeah! End of conversation."

and was sweating when I finished—too busy to even watch the flak. The formation was really lousy—all over the sky. Supposed to come in on a mag. heading of 116—came in on 176. Target about 8/10ths covered. Bombed from 27,400ft [8,350m]. On the turn from the target we were carried by an 80-knot wind over the flak area at Gorringen. Flak at target moderate—fairly accurate. At the RP I was watching one B-17 that was circling below us and losing altitude. Obviously hit. The right wing came off at No.4 and the plane caught fire and disintegrated in not over 10 seconds. One 'chute observed. Time of mission 7:45; 4:30 on oxygen. Maximum cold -47°F [-44°C]. Easy trip home."

**In July 1944 a tour was officially 35 missions. Abe Dolim had flown 27 but he had "had his fill" and he did not think he would survive eight more. By signing up for another tour airmen did not have to fly the rest of the first tour and they could go on home leave. Dolim decided to sign up for a further tour, take the leave, and hope that the War would be over before he had to return to fly a second tour. Back home, though, he could not help feeling estranged:**

**After completing his tour, Jule Berndt, once back in the US, "safe and sound from combat," "sat down and tried to evaluate his emotions" about everything he had experienced:**

"It almost seems like a bad dream to me now. I just can't visualize having gone through a complete tour of missions in Europe, of having been in England, over Germany. The memories of those anxious moments over targets, of seeing the face of our wounded ball-turret gunner, of the time over Duisburg and Merseburg when there just didn't seem to be a plausible excuse for emerging unscathed from the clouds of flak that we entered—all these now seem like parts of one of those bad nightmares that are hard to reconstruct after you wake up. The long hours of thinking before falling asleep on the night before a mission, and the anxious moments spent contemplating the thought of dying so young—worrying about such things not just for yourself but also for your parents, who you knew were praying for your safety back home. All this has become just a part of the past, and I am here now, today, whole, alive, and writing about it. It is almost too good to be true."

# The Radio Operator

"A 20mm shell entered the radio compartment, killing Norman Smith, the radio operator, who bled to death with his legs severed above the knees . . . "—Lieutenant Colonel Bernie Lay, Jr., *I Saw Regensburg Destroyed*

**T**he radio room was a rough place to ride. "Radio" manned the open hatch gun and, once the target had been passed, looked in the bomb bay to check that all the bombs had cleared the racks. When in trouble he tuned into the distress frequency on the liaison set and, nearing the coast, sent the "darky-darky" signal—the military equivalent of "May-Day."

Before a mission, once all the crews, officers, and non-commissioned officers had been briefed together, each would be given a separate briefing at which time they received a canvas packet containing coded data called a "flimsy." "Flimsies"—daily identification codes—were printed on rice paper so that they could be swallowed before baling out, to prevent them being captured by the enemy. Pilots, navigators, bombardiers, and radio operators would also each receive an Information Signals sheet, so that before climbing into a B-17 they would know call signs, code words and VHF channels, fighter call signs, and answering call signs. A radio operator would know from his flimsy that, for instance, "London Bridge is Falling Down," was that day's VHF recall phrase—the signal meaning the mission was being aborted—but if he was to be incapacitated on the mission then the pilot's flimsy would contain the information he needed.

Once airborne, each Fortress would, at the appointed altitude, orbit around an assembly beacon (a ground installation that emitted a signal). Each pilot would know the position he had been allocated in the formation from

*Left: The radio operator's position showing the SCR-287—a liaison radio consisting of a BC-375 receiver (below, on the table), BC-348 transmitter, and two tuning units.*

the briefing. Takeoff was in the same order and, once airborne, it remained only to locate the squadron leader or assembly ship—he would be firing a combination of flares in colors such as red and green. When the pilot saw his color, he joined up, tacking onto the leader in his proper slot while continuing to orbit. When all the aircraft were in the combat box, it headed out toward the North Sea or English Channel, depending on where the mission was going. "During all of this time" recalls Ben Smith, "there was complete radio silence, as the German interceptor stations were monitoring constantly. I doubt if we ever fooled them. I don't remember their ever being asleep when I visited Germany."

In 1942 the fledgling B-17 Groups about to spread their wings in Europe had been formed in the turbulent weeks following Pearl Harbor, and their training had been deficient in many respects. Some air gunners had received little or no training in aerial gunnery, and some radio operators could not send or receive Morse. Deficiencies were remedied gradually while the "new" groups got to grips with the enemy. As more and more aircraft took to the skies during 1943 and into 1944, and a weird chatter unfamiliar to many filled the airwaves, the radio operator's workload increased dramatically. At the end of the basic training period radio operator mechanic gunner trainees received 20 weeks of combat crew radio operation and repair training. All enlisted men in an aircrew were aerial gunners and received training as such, but with the introduction of the Sperry top turret atop and behind the cockpit, the radio compartment gun position was gradually phased out. In January 1944 the radio-room gun was given an improved field of fire by a frameless hatch with a K-5 mount that allowed 90° movement of the gun in zenith. However, the gun was installed only in early production batches of the B-17G, and it was eliminated altogether in later production batches.

As for equipment, B-17s had three main aircraft communications sets. The Command Radio (SCR-274-N) provided for short-range voice communication with nearby aircraft or ground stations. It was used for contact with airfield control towers within a maximum 30 miles (48km). The Liaison Radio (SCR-287-A) provided for long-range, two-way voice and Morse code communication between aircraft and a ground station, though in the 8th Air Force it was normally used purely for coded signals by W/T (wireless telegraphy). The set was used to send mission progress signals or distress calls when at long range. The VHF Command Radio (SCR-522-A), finally, was the principal operational set for verbal communication with bombers and fighters. It had a range of about 150 miles (241km) for an aircraft at 20,000ft (6,000m). If an aircraft got into distress the radioman became a crucial cog in the rescue. He would send out distress signals and position

fixes if over the sea. The radioman was also responsible for the Radio Compass (SCR-269-G), which was used in direction finding with "Buncher" and "Splasher" systems for assembly and in undercast conditions. In the spring of 1943 the 8th Air Force began making use of the dozen or so RAF Splasher medium-frequency radio beacons, and crews were given a list of call-signs and frequencies for the Splashers selected for the day's mission. At first Splashers were used as rendezvous points for bomb groups, and proved invaluable for assembling combat wings. The B-17 radio operator was provided with a schedule of times and frequencies, tuning the radio compass accordingly. Bunchers were British low-powered radio beacons specifically for assembling US heavy bombers in all weather conditions. The SCR-269-G, tuned and controlled by the radio operator, presented visual display indicators on the pilots' instrument panel and over the navigator's table, or aural reception in modulated code.

*Page right, clockwise from top left: A US Army portable frequency meter, used to calibrate the radios; though standard on a B-17 it was often not carried—they were dead weight; with the introduction of the Sperry top turret the radio compartment gun position (center) was phased out. It was used only in early production batches of the B-17G; Signal Corps Radio Receiver BC-1033-B (right); right side bulkhead, with the bomb bay behind (bottom), with the SCR-274-N Command Radio, which the pilots used for short-range voice communication with nearby aircraft or ground stations.*

## Combat Crew

A training pamphlet produced by the USAAF training commands, which were issued to combat crews before they embarked on the Northern or Southern Ferry routes to their theater of operations. If they were unlucky they could be sent to the backwater of Kiska in the Aleutians.

### THE RADIO OPERATOR

"I think any radio man who has heard lead buzzing by his ear will back me up on this one." The tech sergeant talking was pounding a key over Kiska a month ago.

"A day will come in combat when the job of getting home is up to the radio operator. Maybe you'll be heading into a British airport in radio silence—and have to flash a blinker signal or else the guns below will start popping ack-ack. Maybe you'll be floating in the South Pacific on a life raft—and your ability to handle the emergency equipment will decide how long you'll play tag with the sharks."

"Maybe you'll get in a jam like me—somewhere north of Kiska. We were on the run home—and the fog rolled up like it was made of jello—frozen jello. The only hope we had was the radio compass and it turns out the navigator had never been introduced to the gadget. These were the early days of the war. Officially, I knew nothing about it—but one night when I was too busted to get in the poker game, I got out the tech orders on the compass and ran over them—just to kill a couple of hours.

"I didn't know much—but what I knew got us back—through a fog so thick that we were not sure we had hit the home field till we started bouncing. The navigator knew his compass the next trip. People learn quick in combat—if they live.

"The idea is to learn before you get in combat. Most of you, here from radio school, will make the discovery that there is a lot of differ-

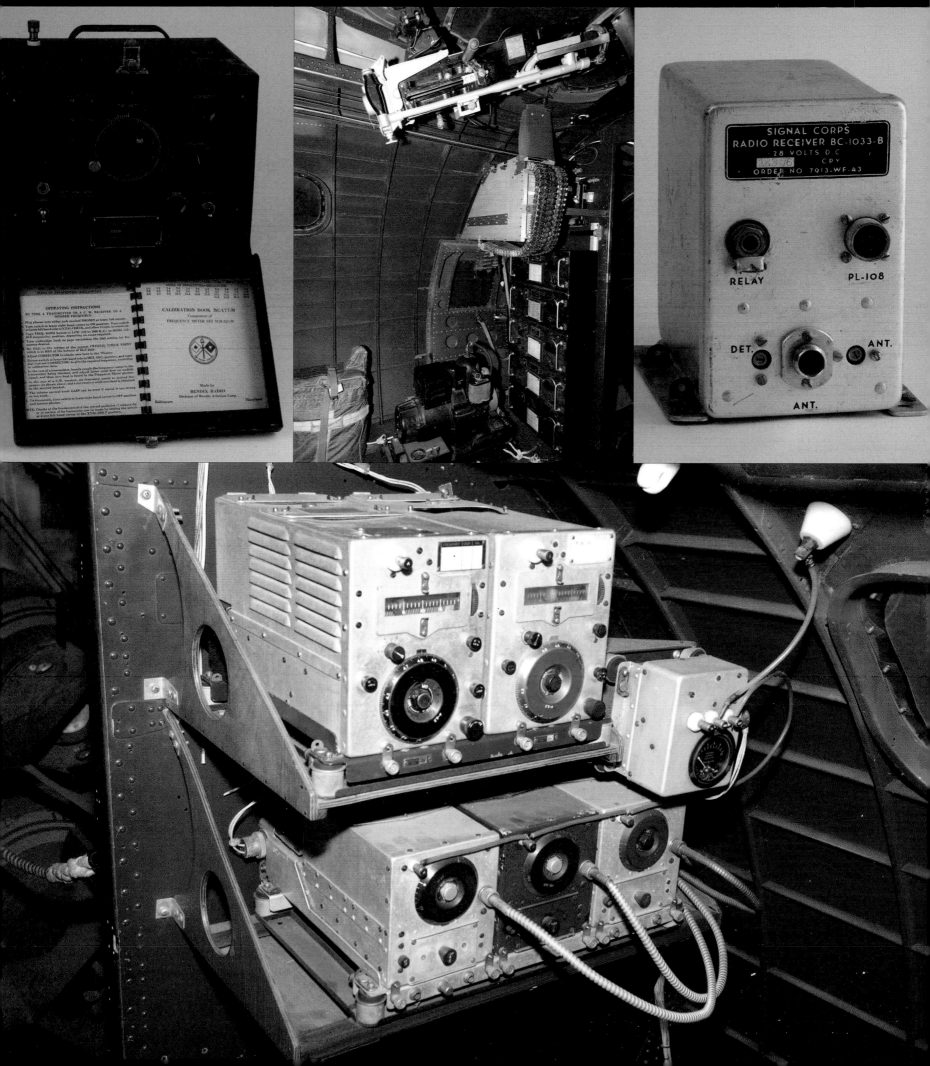

# Radio op in training

Above: *Technical Sergeant Larry "Goldie" Goldstein at Knettishall in 1943 wearing his HS-33 radio headphones over his A-3 flight cap.*

**Twenty-year-old Larry Goldstein from Brooklyn started his military service on October 16, 1942. Little did he know that he would volunteer in the near future for flying duty:**

"I was classified by the Air Corps as a potential radio operator and was sent to Chicago to attend a school. The Army had taken over several of the large hotels as barracks and schools. Chicago in the winter was a cold place to be, especially when we arrived from Miami in November in our summer uniforms. From November, when I arrived, to March, when I left Chicago, I suffered through a very cold winter with a great deal of snow, ice, and very cold winds. My GI friends and I found out why this city was called 'windy city.' Three months later I graduated as a radio operator and within a week I was sent to Boca Raton, Florida, to a special radar school and promoted to corporal. After arriving there several of my buddies and I decided that this was not the army job we wanted, thinking that we might be sent to some island in the Pacific. Each Friday we had to take a written test and if you failed you were immediately shipped out to another base. I found myself in Salt Lake City at a replacement depot. It was here that I volunteered for flying status. Along with my GI friends I was impressed with the glamor of flying, and all that went with it—the silver wings of a gunner, the promotions, and the flight pay. This all occurred almost by accident, because this was strictly offered only to those who qualified by military training; I was considered to be so qualified. I was hustled off to aerial gunnery school even before I had a chance to rethink my decision. I was not aware at that time that the Army Air Corps was in the process of building the largest combat air force in the world, and had plans to take the aerial war to the enemy over his territory.

"Wendover Aerial Gunnery School, Utah, was way up in the hills. It was so remote that the GI comment was, a man going AWOL for five days would only be charged for three because he could be seen walking on the salt flats for the first two days. If ever a place could be classified as a sample of hell this was the place.

*A radio headset as worn on low-altitude flights on training missions in the US.*

June and July, with temperatures ranging near 100°F [38°C], was unbearable. It was so hot that I had to cool off with a shower whenever possible, usually several times a day and this was not easy because we had to rely on water trucked in from the air base on a 24-hour basis. Wendover was the only gunnery school without flying training. The need for radio operators and engineers was so great that they pushed several classes through without ever firing a shot from an airplane. Our training was all ground-work, including firing machine guns at moving targets mounted on jeeps. Those silver aerial gunners' wings, promotions, and the thought of flight pay kept us going. I graduated and was awarded my wings along with a promotion to sergeant. This was a proud moment because I knew that I was about to participate in the making of history. Perhaps my GI pals and me were unrealistic as to what was ahead of us."

[Once assigned to a plane, Goldstein found that his pilot, Belford J. Keirsted] "was a strong, quiet man from Uniontown, Pennsylvania, a tough coal town. 'B.J.' had a dark, brooding look about him. He and his

Above: *Trainee radio operators with their instructor (top). The headsets were not normally worn on combat missions in the ETO, as the flight helmet had the earphones attached.*

sister Dorothy had toured the country before the war as the ballroom dance team of 'Jan and Janis' (Belford and Dorothy apparently lacked pizzazz). At our first meeting 'B.J.' had asked us to work hard, become proficient at our jobs and possibly some day one of us might be responsible for the rest of the crew's survival.

He, along with copilot Clifford 'Ace' Conklin, prodded the crew to achieve perfection and at the same time were also working hard to sharpen their skills. Conklin was a Jock from New Paltz, New York. He had been a business student. When Conklin was assigned to Keirsted's crew he was crestfallen. He thought, 'I don't want to be with this crew—we've got a ballroom dancer for a pilot!' but Keirsted proved he had more on the ball than a set of twinkletoes. Quiet, reserved, he exuded a calm authority that was universally respected and admired. More than that, the men liked Keirsted. 'He was just a nice guy, period,' Conklin would say. 'He never had a bad thing to say.'

"Our crew gelled immediately and we worked well together. I had a great deal of faith in the abilities of 'B.J.' and 'Ace' as pilots and I felt safe with them at the controls. They seemed to be aware of potential trouble that was always around us and were always prepared to handle an emergency if it happened. This was a comforting thought because there always was the element of danger present."

*Not as warm as the AN-H-16, later versions of the A-11 helmet were made of sheepskin and lined with deerskin.*

*Wiring looms and plugs for connection to the radio output.*

*A "throat mike," as used for inter-crew communication.*

**Above:** *A-11 intermediate helmet made of leather, lined with chamois, and with black rubber mounts for ANB-H-1 receivers, and oxygen mask. The AN-H-16 winter helmet differed from the A-11 in having fur inside.*

**Right:** *Larry Goldstein at Wendover Aerial Gunnery School in July 1943.*

# Surviving the tour

**If a crew survived eight to ten missions they were considered lucky. Larry Goldstein remembers what it was like making the full tour in "B.J.'s" plane:**

"Our 25 missions were not simple—each one was worse than the last. 'B.J.' Keirsted kept repeating that 'we will make it.' When we met our first ground crew chief when our own plane was assigned to us, 'B.J.' asked him how many crews he had. He said, 'You are my third, the other two went down.'

*Left: Ambulances at the ready and crews staring skyward for ominous red flares denoting wounded aboard, all waiting as the returning Fortresses prepare to break off and land.*

'B.J.'s answer to him was, 'We will make it, you can mark it down.' We were not as sure as he was, but his self-confidence rubbed off on us. The 388th command demanded precision-tight formation flying which brought more guns to bear and increased our overall protection. Enemy fighters seldom hit good formation flying outfits. Our pilots prided themselves on good formation flying but, on our 12th mission, soon after flying into a cloud bank, there were B-17s all over the sky. 'B.J' decided to abort, as there was no formation to join. We were over enemy territory and just the danger of mid-air collision was enough to make that decision.

*Above: A smoking Fortress, probably a victim of flak, falls out of formation as others, streaming contrails, head for the safety of home—and leaving any straggler an easy prey, ripe to be picked off by enemy fighters.*

"On our 22nd mission, to Posnan, fighters hit us and as we had no support all the way we had a battle on our hands. We were airborne for 11 hours and the fact that we landed at Knettishall in almost total darkness was in itself a miracle. We were exhausted and could hardly get to the mess hall for the evening meal.

"We completed our 23rd and 24th [missions] and then finally, on March 4 we flew our 25th. 'Big-B' [Berlin, Germany] was the target. The extra-early briefing was attended by all three chaplains: Jewish, Catholic, and Protestant—which increased the sense that this was an important occasion. We hoped the mission would be scrubbed, and we constantly watched the control tower for a red flare. It never came. Takeoff and assembly were normal but we were a little bit more on edge. Just before we reached the target there was a recall of the formation for the second straight day. As a crew we made a decision by vote over the intercom to drop our bomb load on some target. Kent 'Cap' Keith, our cowboy from Montana, picked out a railroad marshaling yard on the German-French border. We dropped out of formation to make our bomb run despite 'Ace' Conklin's warning that the formation was getting farther and farther away.

"After 'bombs away' we climbed back toward the formation, which was now many miles ahead. Our bomb-bay doors were closing and, according to Keith, they were closing as they should. My job was to check those doors visually. I did. They were open. Several more attempts to close them were futile, so 'B.J.' gave the order for Jack Kings to leave his top turret and hand-crank them closed. Suddenly, there was a loud explosion. A Me 109 must have seen a straggling Fort and fired several 20mm shells at us. Little did we know that we were severely damaged.

"We finally broke out over France. Phil 'Bloodhound' Brejensky was unable to plot a course, and I was asked to get a heading. I contacted the RAF distress channel for help. God bless them because they answered immediately in the clear with a course for England, but the Germans immediately jammed it. Technical Sergeant Wallace Gross, who was one mission behind his crew and had volunteered to fly the ball position, was not eager to be there [in the ball turret] for the whole flight, and was sitting on the radio-room floor. He was a crackerjack radioman, and immediately set up another frequency. Again I transmitted, and again the receiver message was jammed. We began to panic but Wallace put in a third unit and we received a heading, which I gave to the navigator. When we broke out of the clouds over the Channel and saw the white cliffs of Dover it was the most beautiful sight that I could ever hope to see. At this moment I did not realize the importance of my radio work. I had been too scared, but my training had paid off.

"The rest of the flight should have been routine—but it wasn't. We were probably the last aircraft to land. Everybody had seen us get hit and they figured that we were lost. As we came over Knettishall our landing approach was normal until touchdown: [we found we had] no brakes. We went off the end of the runway and did a slow ground loop coming to a halt. The fire trucks all rushed to our aid but they were not needed. The medics wanted to know if the radio operator was hurt. When someone on our plane said I was OK one of the firemen pointed to a tremendous hole in the right side of the radio room. It was then that I realized that we had flown like that for three hours. I was probably too scared to realize how dangerous it had been. Nevertheless, it was 25 [missions completed] and home. I guess someone up there was looking out for the 'Worry Wart' crew. We walked away from the plane and said our own individual prayers of thanks. A few days later 'B.J' ordered us all to accompany him to the base chapel, and there we really became one crew that was thankful for our completing our missions without a major injury."

84-1

Hqs. ONE HUNDREDTH BOMB Gp. No. 00783

**CRASH PASS**

The Bearer CAPTAIN U. A. CARLETON TAC 99

IS ALLOWED TO PROCEED TO AIRCRAFT ACCIDENT

By Order of The Station Commander (S.9:99) Major Adjutant

*Above: A Crash Pass issued to Captain Bill Carleton, a squadron engineering officer in the 100th Bomb Group.*

*Top left: Extensive damage to the radio room area of a B-17G after a 88mm flak shell entered the left-hand side of the aircraft and caused an exit blast on the right side. In the process the floor was torn away and the radioman was blown out of the aircraft to his death. The pilot and copilot finally got the crippled Fortress down without brakes.*

*Left: B-17G Lucky Patch (379th Bomb Group), whose landing gear collapsed on landing at Kimbolton on May 3, 1945.*

# New to the Combat Zone

**When war came and young men were volunteering "right and left" Ben Smith found himself doing this "incredible thing—the last thing he wanted to do:"**

"I became a radio operator-aerial gunner on a B-17 crew. Flying, especially military flying, did not appeal to me at first. In training we flew worn-out aircraft and had many hairy experiences in those old B-17s. I used to lie awake in bed dreading the time when I would have to lay it on the line or forever be lost in the infamy of disgrace (I learned later that I was not the only one.) This was so real to me. Outwardly, I was lighthearted and jovial, well liked by my friends. They thought I was a pretty cool customer, but inside I was sick, sick, sick! My bravado was sort of a rallying point though phony as a three-dollar bill. I wore a 'hot pilot's' cap, smoked big black cigars, and drank boilermakers. The only one who wasn't fooled was me."

[Smith was assigned to "Chick" Cecchini's crew. They came together at Salt Lake City, and were then ordered to Alexandria, Louisiana, for overseas training.]

"Many of the things we learned in training were useless in combat. I spent a lot of time studying radio procedures that were discarded in the War Zone. It was my considered opinion that a combat radio operator could have been checked out on everything he needed to know for combat operation in two weeks at the most. We learned hundreds of 'Q' signals and used only five or six in combat. Our instructors showed us how to repair transmitters and receivers that were malfunctioning. Apparently they did not know (as we learned later) that it was impossible to repair a radio at high altitude in sub-zero weather. We were taught to send and receive code at high speed, yet all transmissions in the combat zone were done at agonizingly slow speed. We had gunnery training but not enough, and, what there was, was of very poor quality. Shooting at a tow-target was nothing like the deflection shooting that would be encountered in combat, where the attacking aircraft had to be led like a bird or a clay pigeon. The tow plane was leery of coming too close, as it was a more likely target for the trigger-happy gunners than the sleeve it was towing. Only once were there

"They came barreling in from all directions"

simulated fighter attacks comparable to the ones we would encounter in battle. Even so, the fighters were careful not to get very close.

"The crew's bombing scores were excellent and we placed high in all categories for flying performance. The ground school was something else. We knew it was a joke and skipped as much as we could get away with. Our crew was on the carpet a lot about apparent indifference to the ground school curriculum. Chick was not much more diligent than the

rest of us here. We did perceive that he was an A-Number-One pilot and came to have great confidence in his ability and judgment. The crew was always bragging a lot about the big Paisan to the other crews.

"We had no idea what was in store for us, whether we were going to the Pacific, Africa, Italy, or England. The crews started off training all together in a provisional group, which bore the name of its temporary commanding officer—Jones Group, Smith Group, and the like. Naturally, we were curious about combat losses and made a lot of inquiries of our officers and instructors. The majority of them were combat veterans. They always gave us an answer. What we did not know was that they were the wrong answers. We were unfamiliar with the format in the combat zones and assumed that all the training crews would remain together in combat. So we would ask our instructors,

**Left:** *This Fez, bought in a Moroccan flea market, is a crew souvenir of the shuttle mission on August 17, 1943, when the Fortresses flew on to North Africa after the bombing raid on Regensburg.*

**Right and opposite page:** *The "all guns blazing" comic-book style AAF recruiting poster (right) glamorizes the role of the air gunner, while the example shown opposite extols the virtues of the teamwork that would be needed when flying as part of a Fortress crew.*

**Below:** *Servicemen inspect the damage to* Princess Pat *in the 303rd Bomb Group, which nosed over Molesworth on July 25, 1944. Nobody was seriously hurt, and the aircraft was salvaged.*

'How is the Jones Group doing?' (This was a group that had finished training before us.) They would answer, 'Most of the guys got through.' If they had answered, 'None of them survived,' that would have been more nearly the truth. But they couldn't say that. In retrospect I am not sure they handled it badly; they gave us something to hope for. It would have done no good to scare us. We were scared enough already. At that time we probably could not have handled the truth very well, and they knew it. So we were given the placebo that our B-17s were blasting the *Luftwaffe* out of the skies and pulverizing the German war machine with impunity. We did read about the Schweinfurt mission flown October 14, 1943, and the punishing losses that amounted to a third of the attacking force. We did not know what to think of this news as we had heard quite a different story up until then."

# Death in The Skies

**Technical Sergeant Dwight N. Miller, radio operator on *Lady Stardust II* (452nd Bomb Group) described a nightmarish return from a mission to Brux, then in Czechoslovakia, on May 12, 1944:**

"Our radio room had the old open hatch and I could see and hear everything plainly. The sky was full of tracers. In the smoke a tail and parts of a fuselage went past. Some ships were on fire and 846 to the right was

Above: *452nd Bomb Group target list showing the first 100 missions, which was once fixed to the wall of a hut at Deopham Green, Norfolk. The mission to Brux on May 12 described on this page was Mission No.48. The 452nd Bomb Group (H) flew 250 missions in total.*

flaming from No.3 [engine]. Focke Wulfs came right over us. Two exploded to the right, one to the left, and some were on fire. A P-47 was going down burning. Someone baled out and immediately his 'chute opened, right in the midst of everything. A Focke Wulf exploded by his side and his 'chute folded in rags. I didn't fire a shot because three B-17s were above us. I heard something banging, like a base drummer going mad. It was the landing flap on the right wing. It was hanging down waving in the wind and hitting the wing.

"Then I heard a sharp snap. The lieutenant formation officer in the tail turret of the crippled lead ship above had baled out and he had fallen right into the Plexiglas nose before bouncing off and into our right wing. Some 'stringy stuff' slid back across my window. The lieutenant's harness and lines were hanging on our wing. Our bombardier and navigator were injured and thrown onto the catwalk. I opened the door and looked toward the cockpit. The nose was gone. Blood—a lot of it—and a terrific wind blinded me. I was covered from head to foot. It went on through

Below: *A B-17F radio operator tunes in the Command transmitter. The top two sets are the transmitters and the bottom two sets are the receivers. The radio hatch gun (seen above the radio operator) was stowed when not in use, as here.*

the ship painting it red and freezing. The bomb bays were solid red and slippery. The blood came from the engineer 'Uncle Dudley' Orcutt. The right side of his head was gone. He didn't look like Dud. I had no doubt he was dead.

"I took the extra oxygen bottle and started up the catwalk. There was a hard wind coming from the front. I was holding on to the left rope when it broke. It was weakened from an exploded shell, I guess. I fell on the right rope. I dropped my oxygen bottle and it went tumbling down. I spent some time trying to get the bomb bay doors up with my knife. The crank and extension were gone so I gave the job up. I took some wire from the bomb pins and fixed the rope back.

"I got some first aid kits and hunted for some Sulfur powder. There was none. The right waist gunner grabbed a bandage and put it on his head. The expression in his eyes reminded me of a patient taking his first look at the stub of his leg after an amputation. Red was still bleeding and as he breathed, blood came out of the hole in his eye. I wiped the blood off his face. He returned the act and said, 'I thought you were a walking dead man.' [Next] The tail gunner yelled, 'Tail gunner hit.'

"From the way he said it, I knew he was in a lot of pain. I grabbed the first aid kit and ran to him. After laying him down in the waist, I began slicing my way to his wound, which was in his back. It was a terrible hole and I hurried to get a bandage on so he wouldn't lose too much blood. I gave him a shot of morphine. We were alone, flying just above the ground, like a coyote sneaking among bushes in fear of yelping hounds close behind . . .

"Then came the call over the interphone that we loved to hear. 'There is the Channel ahead.'"

# The lifesaver

**After flying his missions in the** *Memphis Belle*, **23-year-old Technical Sergeant Robert I. Hanson had this to say about being a radio operator on his return to the United States in 1943:**

"If you are in a new combat crew, you would do yourself a favor to sit down and have a good bull session with men who have been through it. Talking to them, hearing what they did and how they did it, you can pick up things it would take you a long time to learn for yourself. Also, you should get accustomed to talking over your interphone. Learn not to talk in an excited, high-pitched voice. A little noise on the interphone going over always helps, because everybody is nervous. When you are in combat, use the interphone to keep the rest of the crew informed about what you can see. In a fight, the interphone is one of the most important things on your ship. You will find that Jerry is fond of putting out false signals and false beams to confuse you. You have to be careful. There should be others on the crew besides the radio operator who can take code. There is always a chance that somebody will be hit, and it may be the radio operator. The ball-turret gunner or the tail gunner should be able to take messages by blinker code if the radio operator can't see them. Practice wearing your helmet before you go over. If it doesn't fit, get it fixed. You probably won't be able to get it fixed over there. At best, our helmets aren't satisfactory. The wind whistles in and if you pull them tight they hurt your eardrums. The British helmet is far superior to ours.

"In the Lorient [France] raid, when we got the tail shot off, Captain Morgan put the ship into a terrific dive and we dropped two or three thousand feet. It pretty nearly threw me out of the airplane.

I hit the roof. I thought we were going down and wondered if I should bale out. Then he pulled up again and I landed on my back. I had an ammunition box and a frequency meter on top of me. I didn't know what was going on.

"The radio operator is one of the most important men in the ship; one boy has had four navigators shot up but has brought the plane home himself each time. Many of the boys have received good training, but they have to go to school when they get over there because they have never been taught anything about the new signals they get over there. They are taking transmitters out of ships because they said they didn't need them. But if a plane gets into a mess on its return to England from a raid, only the radio will bring it out."

# The SCR-578 OR "Gibson Girl" portable radio

The term "Gibson Girl" is associated with this radio because of its "hour-glass" shape, which was attributed to the personification of the feminine ideal in the satirical pen-and-ink illustrated stories created by Charles Dana Gibson, during more than 15 years spanning the late 19th and early 20th centuries. The unit was developed for use in case of forced landings on water. The radio and the associated accessories were contained in a yellow, buoyant waterproof bag (far left). Originally carried on the flight deck, the "Gibson Girl" could either be released just before impacting the water using the small, tethered parachute provided, or simply thrown out by a crewmember after ditching. The pack was soon repositioned in the dinghy escape hatch and made accessible from outside the aircraft. The set automatically transmitted a coded signal.

*Top left, below, and bottom: The aerial wire was carried aloft by either a metal frame box kite (below) or a balloon (top left, smaller tin); the balloon was inflated by a hydrogen generator (tall tin). At bottom is shown the distinctive curved, yellow hand-crank generator whose shape mirrored that of a Gibson Girl's waspish waist; the generator provided power for the distress radio signal*

*Below, left and right: On July 26, 1943, an airborne lifeboat was dropped by a Royal Air Force Warwick from their base at Bircham Newton in Norfolk, England, near to the crew of a B-17 who had ditched in the North Sea, and taken to their life rafts. Steering westward, the crew were picked up by fishermen who delivered them safely to an Air-Sea Rescue (ASR) motor launch. Two or more four-man or six-man life rafts were normally carried aboard bombers.*

# The Bombardier

"Dick Elliott picked up the target immediately and called 'Skipper, target dead ahead, set up and follow PDI!' Dick opened the doors just long enough to release the bombs. We already had our strike camera running. It was on intervolometer but our bombsight was not. Dick, knowing that he had the rate killed and the course was beautiful, set the selector switch on 'Salvo.' Bombs were away at 1454 hours. All fell in the MPI. The roar on the intercom was 'PICKLE BARREL!'"

—Lieutenant Bob Hughes, pilot, *Nine Little Yanks and a Jerk*, second Schweinfurt raid, October 17, 1943

**W**hen the US entered World War II, the standard precision bombsights in use by the AAF were the Norden "M" series and the Sperry "S"-Series. The bombardier's station was directly behind the large Plexiglas bubble capping the B-17's nose, and the Norden bombsight was mounted in front of him. Either side of the bombardier's seat, levers and panels of dials and switches fed data to and from the Norden. Bottom right was the window defroster tube known as the "Elephant Pecker," which provided heat for the bombsight. Precision bombing's crowning refinement was the AFCE (Automatic Flight Control Equipment) which, during the bomb run, allowed the bombardier to take over flying the aircraft from the pilot, giving him lateral control of the aircraft through the Norden bombsight's connection to the A-5 or C-1 autopilot. The bomb run began at the IP (Initial Point). Once the bombardier had picked up the actual aiming point he would ask the pilot to confirm that the automatic pilot (AFCE) was engaged because he needed to integrate the AFCE and the bombsight to control the heading, turns, and drift, while the pilot maintained the correct airspeed

*Left: Nose area of the B-17G showing the bombardier's station with the Norden bombsight and, overhead, the Sperry optical gunsight for the chin turret. Left is the bombardier's control panel.*

and altitude. Once the cross hairs of the bombsight had been set, the bombardier would remain hunched over the aiming device making final adjustments and corrections for the bomb run until "bombs away." During those few minutes, when pilots had to fly their straight-and-level best, every Fort was literally a "sitting duck" in a shooting gallery. So, with what protection their flak suits and steel helmets afforded, pilots would concentrate on maintaining a good formation at all costs, giving the bombardier a constant altitude and airspeed—essential to good bombing.

Bombardier school was a 20-week course. There was no shortage of candidates and those who failed pilot training swelled the numbers. During 1941–45 no fewer than 45,000 bombardiers graduated from AAF schools. Because every bomber crewmember had to be an expert gunner, their training included six weeks at a flexible gunnery school where they were taught everything about the weapons they would use, as well as ballistics, turret operation, and maintenance and gun repairs. They also shot at air and ground targets from a moving base and from a turret. At the conclusion of the course, bombardier trainees were awarded silver wings, appointed flight officers or commissioned as 2nd lieutenants, and sent on to unit training.

Firing at drogue-towed targets and "shooting" at airplanes with camera guns was no substitute for the reality of flying up front in the nose of a B-17. Hunched behind the bombsight on a long, unwavering bomb run, exposed to flak or manning cheek or chin guns during head-on attacks behind a Plexiglas nose with only a flak helmet or suit for protection was the bombardier's lot. After "Bombs Away" the bombardier might also have to remove a hung-up 500-pounder while perched precariously on a narrow bomb bay four miles above the earth. In the ETO, bombardiers, among others, also found that the weather, flak, and fighters conspired against them to such a degree that "pickle-barrel" bombing accuracy was impossible. In 1943, during the spring and summer months (April to September), of the 1st Division's bombs that were dropped only 13 per cent fell within 1,000ft (304m) of the pre-assigned MPI on visual missions under conditions of good to fair visibility. Colonel Curtis E. LeMay, CO, 305th Bomb Group, worked hard to find the best method of combating fighter attacks without compromising bombing accuracy, and vice-versa. LeMay developed and employed squadron (six-ship) bombing tactics, utilizing toggliers. Toggliers were gunners who had been specifically trained to permanently replace a limited number of squadron bombardiers. When the squadron lead bombardier dropped his bombs, the toggliers flipped a bomb release toggle switch and bombed with him. Using the togglier, bombing as a group came later, when all ships would drop on the group lead bombardier.

Depending on distance to target, the B-17 usually carried a mission bomb load of between 4,000 and 6,000lb (1,814 to 2,722kg) of either General Purpose (GP) and/or High Explosive (HE) and/or incendiary bombs. Usually, bombardiers armed the bombs while the plane was still over the sea. Each bomb had an 8in (20cm) vane or propeller on the nose fuze, which was prevented from turning by a cotter pin through a hole. Each cotter pin had a bomb tag with warnings. As the pin was removed, a wire attached to the bomb bay was inserted through the cotter pin hole. When the bombs were dropped, they slid off the arming wire, which allowed the bomb's propeller to turn in the wind. After falling about 500ft

(152m) the propeller wound itself off the fuze, which was then armed and would explode the bomb upon contact. Sometimes bombs were fuzed at one-tenth of a second at the nose, and one-fortieth of a second at the tail. A one-fortieth of a second timing would allow the bomb to penetrate a roof before exploding, and the one-tenth of a second fuze would insure that the bomb would explode before deep penetration. During the bomb run, the formation was most vulnerable to enemy action, as the bomb bay doors were open for the entire trip from IP to target. This alerted the German anti-aircraft gunners that the Forts would be flying a long, straight course to the target from anything up to 30 minutes or more.

Page right, clockwise from top left: *The Eastman-Kodak K-20 Aero-Ecker camera was remotely operated by the radio operator to take 5in x 7in strike photos; when hand-held, it was used for reconnaissance purposes. Nose area of the B-17G (far right) showing the Bendix turret and bombardier's position; operating manual for the Bendix electrically operated chin turret (left, bottom); fuze pin warning tag; bomb-release mechanism with shackle.*

## The Norden bombsight

As the bombardier synchronized on the target, everyone hoped their luck would hold. It was always a relief to feel the ship lift slightly as the bombs left the racks and the bomb release light glowed on the instrument panel in the cockpit—for then they immediately turned to a pre-designated heading to get out of the flak.

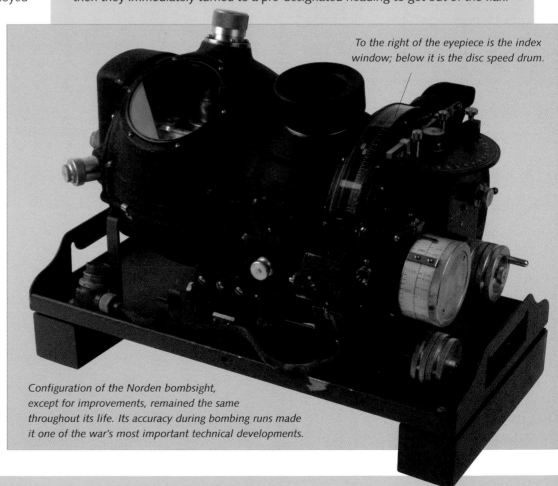

*To the right of the eyepiece is the index window; below it is the disc speed drum.*

*Configuration of the Norden bombsight, except for improvements, remained the same throughout its life. Its accuracy during bombing runs made it one of the war's most important technical developments.*

PIN NOT TO BE REMOVED
UNTIL FUZE IS ABOUT TO
BE PLACED IN BOMB.
IF FUZE IS REMOVED
FROM BOMB REPLACE
PIN AT ONCE.

OPERATION AND MAINTENANCE

*The*

# BENDIX
# CHIN TURRET

*For the Boeing B-17
Bombardment Airplane*

*Prepared by*
TRAINING DEPARTMENT
AAFGS                    LVAAF

# Some close escapes

Above: *An 8th Air Force bomb dump "somewhere in England." The site is covered by camouflage netting.*

**William A. Boutelle, a bombardier in the 303rd Bomb Group, remembers the nerves he suffered during his first combat mission:**

"I'd heard plenty about raids and, while a lot of the stories conflicted, I knew a little of what to expect. As we approached the coast of France, though, my knees felt weak and the long time in which I had to set up my bombsight seemed to be flying by: I found myself rushing so fast that I made mistakes. I kept trying to look for the first flak and fighter and work my sight figures, too. I settled down and set up my sight and looked up just in time to see the first fighters. There were two Focke Wulfs coming up at 11 o'clock low, so I reported and grabbed my gun, even though they were a mile out of range. They soon made an attack apiece from 12 o'clock with no results on either side. I did expend 15 rounds at one as he flashed by with his wings spouting 20mms like Roman Candles. About that time a formation of 10 to 15 fighters showed up and sat on our right wing, about 2,000 yards [1,829m] away. Then they came barreling in with a short burst for us, and all they had for the group below. The tail gunner said it was 'Some show.'"

Above: *Ralph Reese and other gunners on the crew of Smoky Liz outside their hut at Deopham Green in 1944.*

**As well as the expected dangers—from fighters and flak—there were always unexpected events to contend with on missions, too. Ralph Reese, a gunner who rode as radioman, recalls a series of such events on his eleventh mission on May 1, 1944 (the target was rocket installations at St. Omer, France):**

"Everything was going well until we passed the IP, when another B-17 nearly collided with us. The pilots saw the other ship in time and they dived the ship sharply for 100ft [30.5m] to avoid a collision. This sudden dive forced the twelve 500lb bombs to fall from their shackles onto the bomb bay doors. Ammunition was thrown out of the boxes and [there was] chaff all over the radio room, too. We flew back to the Channel and the bombardier put the pins back in the bombs. One bomb nose fuze was nearly off, and a wire had shorted out near it. Everyone clutched at their 'chutes, ready to jump as the fuze blew. Thank goodness

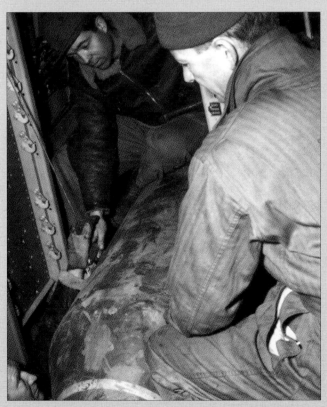

the wire remained quiet. Then the bomb bay doors would not open, electrically or manually. Finally the bombardier worked the doors open, so the bombs fell out. The pilot stated that if the doors had not opened he would have flown near the shoreline and we would have baled out."

Right: *Four 1,000lb bombs in the bomb racks of a B-17G. The maximum bomb load of a B-17G was 9,600lb but loads of around 4,000lb were usually carried on long-haul missions.*

Opposite, top: *Chemical Company personnel loading magnesium incendiary cluster bombs on to a trailer. On the left can be seen clusters still in their cases, which were used for leaflet bombs.*

Opposite: *Armorers manhandling the bombs into place in the Fortress's bomb bay. This was dangerous work, often carried out in freezing conditions in the early hours of the morning.*

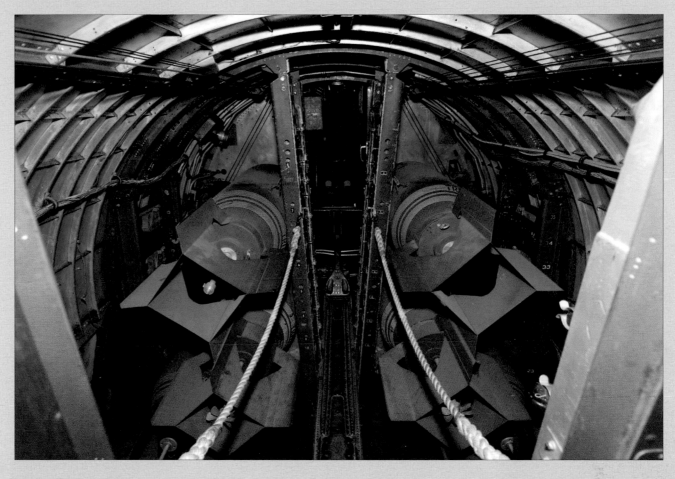

**Dick Johnson, a copilot in the 303rd Bomb Group, remembers encountering very heavy flak on a mission to Hamburg in May 1944— and a close escape for his bombardier, Ed Cooper:**

"Flak explosions [over the target] were constant and unrelenting, being so close that many could be heard to explode and throw fragments against the sides of the airplane. The angry, red center of some of the explosions meant that they were very close. To hear flak explode, it had to be within 50ft [15m] of our plane, otherwise the very loud engine noise would drown out the noise of an explosion farther away. Likewise, to feel a jolt from a flak explosion, it would have to be within 25ft [8m] or less from the plane. I saw plenty of red centers and heard several of them during our 41-mile (!) bomb run. Our ground speed against the wind was barely over two miles per minute, allowing the German defenders a good chance to track us in the straight and level flight from the Initial Point to the target. We busted the target wide open. One group ahead of us had also hit the target and smoke was visible during the entire bomb run. There were many great explosions among the oil storage tanks and on the cracking plant itself. From our vantage point at 26,500ft [8,170m] we could see clearly that the target was completely covered by bomb bursts. We hadn't bothered to carry any incendiary bombs on this trip, but it seems that they would have been redundant. Our plane suffered over 263 flak holes of various sizes and yet not a crewmember was hit, and the airplane flew as if nothing had happened to it. Our bombardier, Ed Cooper, almost lost it on this mission. Flak was so thick that it fell like rain at times from explosions above the formation. One of these pieces of shrapnel came in the nose window and struck Ed on the breastbone and drove him six feet back into the navigator's compartment. There is no doubt that the flak suit saved his life, because when we returned to base we helped him cut the piece of flak from the suit. The flak suit is composed of small plates of tantalum steel that overlap each other like scales on a fish. There were always three thicknesses of these plates. The first layer had clasped the flak fragment so that it could not be removed. The second layer was bent sharply around the first and the third layer was only slightly bent. Ed sported a large bruise on his chest for several days, but was not injured enough to take him off flying status."

# Perils of the bomb run

**Captain Tex McCrary of 8th Air Force Public Relations put theory into practice by flying a few missions himself. Here he describes watching a bombardier in action:**

"The nose of a Fort is as vulnerable as a fishbowl in a shooting gallery. Guess you know how a bombardier sits out there in front, with one eye on the bombsight as the Forts go into their bombing run . . . I watched little Bush on three runs, watched him only, for signs of nervous strain. There were none. He crouched up there in the nose, with the belts of ammunition flopped down his back; red, black, and blue noses of the shells looking like an Indian chieftain's feathered head-dress. Every time he

because if a safety pin was dropped or lost, the crew might have an armed bomb aboard on landing. This is exactly what happened when **Nick G. Plackis, a bombardier in the 390th Bomb Group, flew his 22nd mission on October 5, 1944, to Münster:**

"Just after 'Bombs Away' I had to free two jammed bombs in the bomb bay. Our load was six 1,000lb bombs, three on each side of the compartment. The three in the right bay salvoed as programed. Of the three on the left, the bottom one went down fine. But the middle shackle malfunctioned and did not release its bomb, so when the upper bomb came off its shackle, it landed with a shuddering clunk, felt throughout

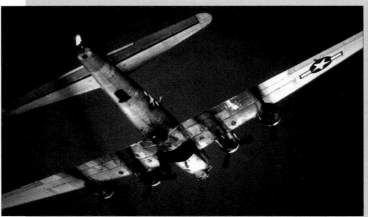

*Above, left to right: Bomb doors open, this 100th Bomb Group Fortress maintains formation over the target and waits for the signal to bomb. Center: 500lb bombs from a 388th Bomb Group B-17F in 1943 hurtle down over the MPI (Mean Point of Impact). Right: a flak-helmeted bombardier in front of his bombsight of the B-17 during the bombing run.*

yelled 'Bombs away!' into the intercom, he would whip his arm and snap his gloved fingers like a crapshooter trying to roll a seven with a million dollars in the pot. And then he would jump up and man his nose guns—because the Jerries pile in on you in the bombing run; they get cocked when they see your bomb bays open, and they throw the works at you. Bushy loved his guns better than he loved his bombsight. You could get so much more 'personal' with a gun. There was a fighter out there blazing at you and you had a gun in your fists to blaze back—it was kill or die in split seconds . . . I don't want you to get the idea that Bushy was a husky ham-fisted lunk who loved to kill—anything but. He looked like the trap drummer in a college orchestra and he played on his guns that way."

**If the target was cloud-covered, and crews returned with the bomb load when they were at a lower altitude and off oxygen, the bombardier would return to the bomb bay to insert the safety pins. This was scary,**

our Fortress, as it smashed into the center hung-up bomb, preventing the upper bomb from falling free. When the skipper sent me back to assess the situation, I realized what I was facing was not going to be a picnic. I saw that when the upper bomb released from its shackle, it also pulled out the wire retainers sometimes called 'pins' that go into the front and rear bomb fuzes. When these pins are pulled out, it frees the small propeller spinners on the fuzes to rotate a certain number of turns in the windstream, supposedly on its way down to the target. After which a spring releases the spinner, activating a plunger to pop out, arming the bomb, so if the plunger is touched—BOOM!

"I knew I had to do something fast when I saw that spinner on the front of that 1,000-pounder turning on its fuze in the windstream of the open bomb bay at 27,300ft [8,320m] altitude. The space between the front of the jammed bombs and the forward bomb bay bulkhead was too narrow for me to squeeze into while wearing my chest-pack 'chute, or carrying an oxygen walk-around bottle. So I had to squeeze down into the compartment and straddle the open bomb bay without those luxuries, while trying to release the jam. Just seconds prior to freeing the lower bomb, the spinner on the upper bomb popped off and I caught it in my hand as the plunger popped out, arming it. I had no choice now, since my only way out was to desperately release the bombs, otherwise if I tried to climb out, either my shoulder, chest or back would touch and activate the fuze plunger, making us history. So, you can be sure I was quite relieved when both bombs gently left the compartment. Lucky, too, that I was holding on when the bombs dropped out since I was not prepared for the amount of suction they created. As groggy as I was from lack of oxygen, I scrambled up to the catwalk, assisted by our radioman, who shoved his oxygen mask onto my face, saving my life. I guess this event could qualify for 'ABOVE AND BEYOND THE CALL OF NORMAL DUTY.'"

**Death from lack of oxygen was another occupational hazard, as Lieutenant Jule F. Berndt, a navigator in the 490th Bomb Group, remembers:**

"Everything seemed to be going satisfactorily until just a few minutes before the IP when the pilot made a crew check to determine who was depressing their push-to-talk button on the interphone (depressing this button caused a buzzing noise in the system). All crewmembers checked in except the bombardier, so the pilot instructed me to take a look at him. The bombardier was slumped back in his seat against the side of the ship. He was breathing heavily and his face was discolored and covered with sweat, even though our altitude was 25,000ft [7,620m] and the temperature was –31°F [-35°C]. I grabbed an extra oxygen bottle, and attached the stricken man's hose to it. After a few minutes of breathing on pure oxygen the bombardier was able to continue his duties, although hindered by the after-effects of anoxia."

Above: "Pickle Barrel!" A Fortress bombardier wearing an A-2 jacket over his flight suit, A-6A flying shoes, and no gloves poses for the camera.

Far Left: A Type A-14 Demand Oxygen mask, which was standardized for USAAF use on July 1, 1943.

Above Left: A Diluter Demand Oxygen Regulator, which automatically insured that the right mixture of air and oxygen was being supplied, and a Type A-1 Oxygen Flow Indicator.

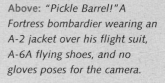

Left: Close-up of a Type A-1 Oxygen Flow Indicator. The Blinker (red ball) indicated that oxygen was flowing.

# Through skies of fire

**Clyde Crowley, a bombardier in the 95th Bomb Group who flew his 33rd combat mission as part of 2nd Lieutenant Charles H. O'Reilly's crew in *Queen Mary*, describes an eventful mission in which he freed a hung-up bomb—only to be shot down and taken prisoner:**

"It was the turn of Sergeant Bates, a togglier in my squadron, to fly but he had gotten himself grounded because of a cold. I had a bit of a stuffy head myself but my flight officer said that if I flew the mission, he would see if he could get my tour of duty ended and send me home. This sounded like a good deal. When I went to briefing and learned that the target was to be Hamburg my spirits dropped. I snapped on my 'chute before takeoff; something I rarely ever did. The day was a very cold and clear one. At the target area the flak was heavy. We started our bomb run. I opened the bomb bay doors after arming the bombs. When we reached the target I dropped the bombs. The radio operator, who could see into the bomb bay, called me on interphone and said one bomb was hung in the rack. I tried again to unload the bomb but it wouldn't go so I asked Lieutenant O'Reilly to jettison racks and all. He did this, and as soon as the radio operator announced that the bay was clear I closed the doors. With a combined sigh of relief everyone seemed to be chatting at the same time. But not for long. The radio operator saw an enemy aircraft approaching. Our gunners fired but he got through and near enough to hit us with at least one 20mm shell. The ship was on fire. The pilot gave the order to abandon. Since I already had on my chest pack I

probably was the first to get out. I kicked out the escape hatch and was gone. Four others managed to get out before the plane disintegrated. The rest of my tour overseas was spent in two Stalag Lufts."

**Lieutenant Franklin L. Betz, a navigator in the 379th Bomb Group, describes what it was like on the bomb run:**

"High above the peaceful-looking German countryside we flew, in tight formation. Our course to the IP took us far enough south of Berlin to avoid the [city's] formidable anti-aircraft defenses. A lump rose in my throat when we turned onto the IP for the 13-mile [21-km] run to the target. Five miles above the ball-bearing factory, the Germans had the sky enveloped in a murderous box barrage of flak and the air was filled with black puffs of exploding shells and unseen fragments of deadly steel . . . The formation flew in a straight and unwavering line to the target. There was no turning back, no evasive action. The lead bombardiers were busily aiming their Norden bombsights on the target and the lethal loads of bombs would drop automatically from the bomb bays when the cross-hairs in the exquisite bombsight centered on the buildings far below. At that moment, bombardiers in other planes of the group would release their bombs by flipping a toggle switch and the destructive explosives would hurtle toward the doomed factory. The plane rocked from the concussion of bursting shells as we entered the envelope of fire. 'Bomb bay doors open,' the engineer called. 'Bombs Away!' cried the bombardier. The plane lifted perceptibly when the tons of bombs dropped from her belly."

**For Harry W. Love, bombardier on Bugs Bunny (390th Bomb Group), October 18, 1944, was his "day of infamy," or date with destiny anyway. It was also his 21st birthday:**

"Five or ten miles from our rendezvous, we began to pick up massive concentrations of flak fire. One of the first bursts came within 100 yards of the front of our plane. This was followed by five or six more immediately thereafter, each one closer than the preceding one. It seemed that we were well tracked down below by the anti-aircraft crews. I announced to the crew that the bursts were directly in line. The pilot confirmed my communication. Two or three seconds later we received a hit in the nose of the plane, directly above the chin turret, leaving a hole 15–20 inches [38–50cm] in circumference. I immediately back-tracked away from my chin-gun position, and took up a station to the right (which was the cheek gun). The cyclonic rush of air that came through was impossible

*Above: A Stalag Luft 3 metal ID tag; if a prisoner died, one half would be sent home.*

*Above and right: Prisoner of War Post for Staff Sgt John W. Affleck, who was incarcerated in Stalag Luft I in Germany. It was sent via the International Red Cross.*

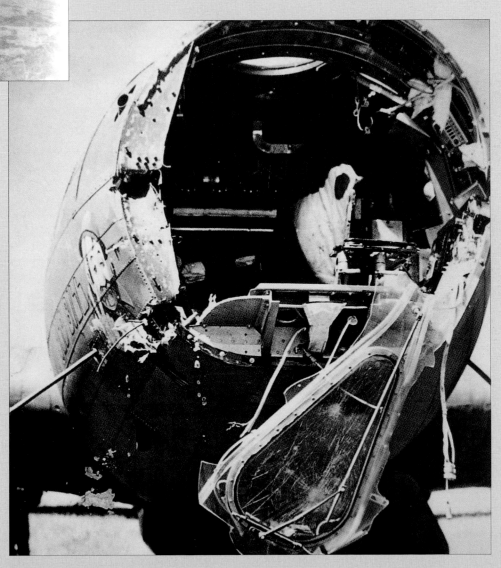

you.' Looking back at the wing again I could clearly see the oscillation increasing. It was obvious to me that the wing could not stay on much longer. At this point, firmly believing the alarm bell and intercom were no longer operating, I directed the engineer to bale out. The engineer would have to bale out first, the navigator second, and then myself. I ordered the engineer to bale out. I pushed the navigator, stating, 'We have to go; the wing is coming off.' The navigator looked doubtful and shook his head. At that instant, the wing came off!"

*Left: B-17Gs dropping magnesium incendiary clusters. In 1943 100lb and 500lb cluster bombs became widely scattered as soon as they hit the slipstream, and in 1944 the M17 cluster bomb, fuzed to explode at 5,000ft (1,500m) above the ground, proved much more effective.*

*Below: B-17F Old Bill after a May 1943 raid; 20-mm cannon fire from fighters had riddled the Fortress, shooting out the Plexiglas nose.*

to control. I recall vividly the navigator stating over the intercom, 'Nobody will know how close the bombardier came to buying it. The bursts of flak came through within inches of his right leg.' The anti-aircraft gunners on the ground weren't finished tracking our plane [though], for at that instant we received a direct hit in one engine (starboard side) with shocking impact. Massive vibrations developed and fumes and smoke filled the plane. Drugan [the pilot], without hesitation, pulled out of formation and attempted to put out the flames by sideslipping the plane. Looking at the right wing it was obvious that the damage was extensive. The entire right wing was oscillating up and down 20°–30°. I assisted the navigator in putting on his chest pack. As bombardier I always wore my backpack throughout the mission.

"I called to Drugan in the customary technique. 'Bombardier to pilot, do you have any instructions?' He replied, 'Bombardier, I hear

*Above: Prowlin' Tom in the 390th Bomb Group, which crashed at Framlingham on March 23, 1944.*

# Castles in the Air?

**Late-model B-17Fs and almost all B-17Gs were armed with twin .50 caliber guns housed in a chin turret fired by the bombardier. The bombardier manipulated the turret using controls that resembled the handlebars of a bicycle, and aimed the guns using an N-6 sight Unit. The chin turret was the only surviving innovation from the YB-40 "destroyer escort" concept, which was an attempt to alleviate bomber losses using B-17 "gunships."**

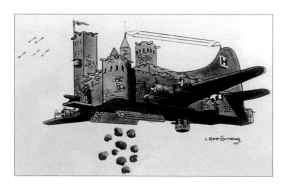

*Left: This "Castle in the air"—complete with battlements and multiplicity of guns—was one of several created by Ross Greening during the time he was incarcerated in a German Prisoner of War camp.*

The idea of "destroyer escorts" had first been proposed in August 1942—at that time, fighter escorts did not possess the range to accompany the bombers deep into Germany, and the only logical step was a heavily armed B-17. Lockheed thus converted a Boeing-built B-17F into the XB-40, fitting two additional gun turrets—a Martin turret in place of the radio compartment guns, and the Bendix chin turret—and replacing the single waist guns with twin .50s, making a total of 14 guns. Both the waist and tail guns were hydraulically boosted for improved control. Although it was still capable of carrying a bombload, the XB-40 seldom did so, because of the added weight of the guns, armor plate, and 11,275 rounds of ammunition. The XB-40 flew for the first time on November 10, 1942, and 22 YB-40s were subsequently built by Douglas (these were identified as Vega-built aircraft). Thirteen of these aircraft were flown to England in January 1943 for operation by the 327th Bomb Squadron, 92nd Bomb Group.

The first raid in which YB-40s were involved took place on May 29, 1943, when four of the planes accompanied the Fortresses on a mission to St. Nazaire. However, the YB-40, which weighed almost five tons more than the standard B-17, did not add materially to the combined firepower of a group. The *Luftwaffe* regularly attacked only stragglers and the YB-40s were unable to protect them from concentrated attacks. Sixty-nine YB-40 sorties were flown between May 29 and July 28, 1943,

*Left: Part of Lt Claude W. Campbell's crew in the 303rd Bomb Group at Molesworth pose for the camera. Among the equipment around them is the navigator's briefcase.*

*Above: On June 28, 1943, bombs hurtle down on St. Nazaire, France—home of the formidable concrete pens housing Germany's 7th and 10th U-boat flotillas.*

and losses were not made good. Three flew with the 303rd Bomb Group formation to Huls on June 22, 1943, and one failed to return, as Howard E. Hernan, top turret gunner in *The Old Squaw*, recalls: "We were flying No.5 position in the low squadron. Two YB-40s flew on the lead ship's wings and another YB-40 flew in the No.6 slot. Just before the IP the YB-40 in front of us in the No.2 position suddenly went down. I couldn't understand how come he went down when there was no flak. Fighters had not then attacked us so it wasn't a fighter. I would think he had an engine malfunction and just couldn't keep up. If they lost an engine they were in trouble. The last I saw of him was after he dropped below us and made a big sweeping left turn to the path that we were to take when we came off the target.

"He probably thought we could catch up with him after we had completed our bomb run. With all the armor plating around the tail and waist gun positions, the Martin turret over the radio room and all the extra ammunition, the YB-40 just had to be tail heavy. Of course, it weighed the same when it got off the target as it did when it got there. When we dropped our bombs we were somewhat lighter and it made a lot of difference. I believe it was a mistake to spread the YB-40s around the group. My opinion was that they should have been left to fly as a squadron, and then if they wanted to attract any fighters, to bear out a little and let them in."

*Above: The XB-40 "gun ship" converted from the second Boeing-built B-17F by Lockheed Aircraft Corporation, photographed on November 14, 1942. Lockheed Vega at Burbank, CA, also built 2,750 Fortresses during the war.*

*Below: In the ETO armorers and gunners took the lead from the early B-17s used in the Pacific where field modifications such as this introduced a whole array of frontal defensive armament to combat head-on attacks by enemy fighters.*

# From Hamm—to Spam

Ten days after Harry W. Love's eventful October 18, 1944, mission, Lieutenant Kenneth H. French, a bombardier in the 490th Bomb Group, took part in a mission to the marshaling yards at Hamm, Germany—then, one month later, flew his last mission:

"There were about 45 flak guns and six rocket guns on the target and they certainly weren't sleeping. We had a couple of bursts just underneath us that lifted the plane right up. It was too close for comfort but luckily we didn't receive any damage at all. We were carrying 20 250lb GP bombs with fuze settings of 1/10 and 1/40 and dropped them in train from 25,300ft [7,711m] at 100ft spacing. Our ground speed was about 165mph [266kmph] and the temperature recorded at our highest altitude was -44°F [-42°C]. Bombing was by PFF and the results were unobserved. No enemy planes were seen but Me 410s and Ju 88s were reported in the area. Time of mission was about five hours, 45 minutes. Though everybody got through OK in the end, the bad weather and the flak made this a most uncomfortable mission and I never want to fly another like it again."

[A month later French flew his 30th and last mission.]

"Everything went well until we approached the target area, when the lead plane informed us that its PFF equipment was faulty. (That was their excuse, though we could see they wouldn't need the 'Mickey' because it looked as though we were going to be able to bomb visually.) Our squadron took over the lead as I was flying as deputy lead bombardier today. Carrying out the changeover caused us to overshoot the IP by about five minutes. We turned over a flak area and went up through the Leipzig area, flak pecking away at us all the way from the time we turned on the IP. We were getting all the heavy stuff and it wasn't missing us a bit either. We had been briefed for over 400 guns on the target but there seemed to be three times that many. About halfway down the bomb run we got hit by flak, which cut the control cables to our rudder. All you could do was just sit there listening to the shrapnel ripping through the plane. We were carrying 20 500lb GPs and just before bombs-away a shell burst in our bomb bay, knocking two bombs, shackles and all, off the racks. It's hard to figure why they didn't explode. Just a second after that a piece of flak came through the Plexiglas in the nose and hit my right hand, which was gripping the bomb release switch, and this caused the rest of my bombs to go out. I was also cut about the eye with flying glass. The piece of flak also hit my oxygen hose and severed it from the regulator, cutting off my oxygen. When the flak hit my hand it cut away

*Left: B-17s drop food over Holland. During the winter of 1944–45, 15,000 Dutch civilians died of starvation—the Germans had withheld supplies in revenge for the help Dutch railway workers had given the Allies at Arnhem.*

most of my middle finger. I knew it was gone and it was just before I passed out that I noticed my hose was off the regulator. At that instant I went out like a light, presumably as much from lack of oxygen as from shock." [The pilot managed to land the Fortress at Brussels, in Occupied Belgium. French and the rest of the crew were taken prisoner—and what was left of the bombardier's finger was amputated.]

*Above: B-17Gs of the 100th Bomb Group dropping supplies in 1945. The first "Chowhound" food drops were made to the Dutch in May 1945.*

By 1945, bombing accuracy in Europe had risen to such an extent that 44 per cent of all bombs were falling within 1,000ft [304m] of the target. At the end of the war, the bombardiers' expertise at hitting the target was put to another use—dropping food to starving Dutch civilians as part of the so-called *Chowhound* missions. Bill Carleton, an engineering officer in the 100th Bomb Group, took part in one of them; he recalls flying over Amsterdam at rooftop height:

"I remember a little Dutch boy looking up and trying to race us on his bicycle. As we approached the target area, the Dutch had arranged stones to say 'Thank You' in large letters just as we crossed the field. There were planes ahead of us who made their drops and people were running across

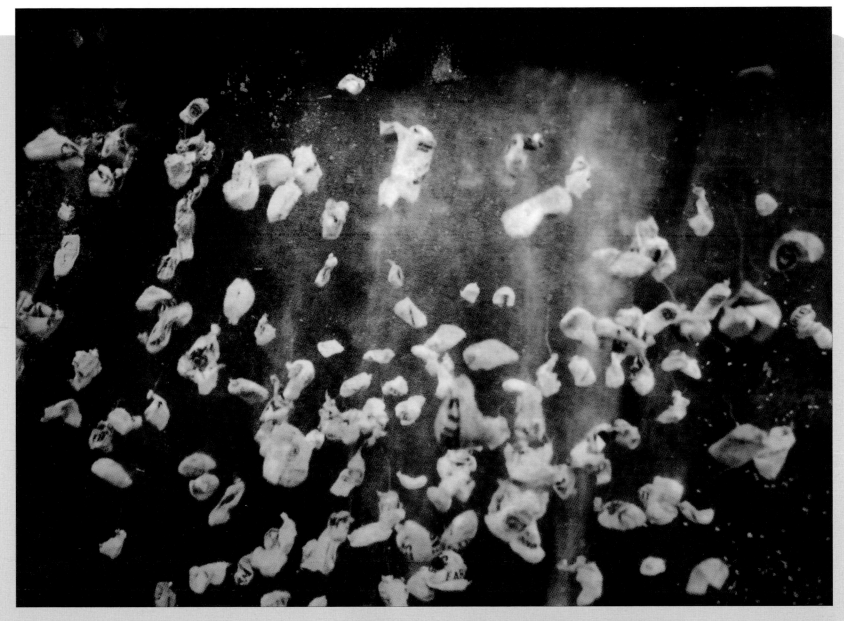

Above and right: *Six supply-drop missions were flown to Holland by the 8th Air Force; the Dutch showed their gratitude by arranging stones on the target area spelling out, "MANY THANKS."*

the target area to get the food, unmindful of the fact that they could be knocked to kingdom come with a can of spam. Planes all around us were starting to drop their food but our plane flew across the field without any salvo—the bombardier had gone to sleep! He awoke with a jerk and made the drop into the Zuider Zee. Such folly, but how typical. The best of intentions, the worst in execution.

"I hoped the forthcoming peace would be better than that!"

# The Engineer / Top Turret Gunner

*"Squinting through the ring sight of a .50 caliber gun, down the spine of a giant Flying Fortress, right smack into the teeth of every kind of Nazi fighter plane that you can find in the recognition charts—that's when you realize why the skies of Germany's industrial targets have come to be known as 'The Big League' . . . "*—Captain John R. "Tex" McCrary

**W**hen the B-17E was ordered on August 30, 1940, it incorporated a series of combat developments to overcome the limitations inherent in previous models. The RAF had discovered to its cost that the Fortress I (B-17C) was virtually defenseless against attacks from the rear, and the lesson was not lost on Japanese fighter pilots in the Pacific. Fortress gunners were also hampered by the limited amount of traverse afforded to the top and belly gun positions. Chief among the radical improvements made to the B-17E was the addition of a ventral "bathtub," a new empennage, and the extensive redesign of virtually the entire fuselage aft of the radio room to include a tail gun position and twin .50 caliber Brownings. Equally significant was the addition, directly behind the flight deck in place of the commander's sighting bubble found on earlier B-17s, of the electrically operated Sperry top turret, which added greatly to the B-17's defensive firepower, and made the aircraft a clear threat to marauding fighters. Fired by the flight engineer who stood on a steel platform inside the turret, it had a much-improved field of vision than on the previous Fortress variants, and this was further improved

*Left: The top turret of a B-17G. The unpainted natural metal finish (NMF) skin cut down production time and reduced drag to give an increase in speed of about 8mph (13kmph).*

in later models of the turret. The turret was a completely independent unit turned in azimuth and elevation by hand controls. The location was positioned well forward so that it could augment the nose guns in forward defense. The twin .50 Brownings could be rotated 360° horizontally and upward of 85°, and could be brought quickly to bear on any attacking fighters approaching from any direction. When not occupying the turret the gunner stood, or sometimes sat, in a small jump seat between the two pilots, assisting them in monitoring the numerous gauges on the instrument panel and calling out airspeeds during takeoffs and landings. Also, from his two positions, the engineer could easily observe the engines and both wings, which contained the self-sealing fuel tanks.

On the B-17F it was found that in one position the gunsight in the upper turret was covered by turret structure bracing and so the frame bar was removed at air depots. Metal side panels also obstructed the mid-upper gunner's view and the operation of the gun charging handles proved troublesome. These failings were reported to Washington in early 1943, but it was several months before the problems were rectified with a redesigned dome. Until then, enterprising staff at the field depots in England manufactured their own clear perspex panels. Early in 1943, at the engineering section of the Bovingdon

Combat Crew Replacement Center, Major Robert J. Reed, the Engineering Officer, carried out a special study of technical and operational problems. He replaced the Sperry upper turret by a 120lb lighter Martin type, which provided a sitting position for the gunner as well as improved armor protection. Meanwhile, during 1944, on the Sperry turret it was found that after considerable rotation the electrical wires and oxygen lines running up the hollow turret spigot tended to become frayed at the outlet. In several instances the fraying caused an electrical short, which in turn ignited the oxygen supply while the B-17 was airborne, causing serious fires that raged out of control. As a stop-gap solution the hollow lead-in was filled with concrete to isolate and seal the wires and lines.

All enlisted men in an aircrew were aerial gunners. At the end of the basic training period, men chosen to train as career gunners were eligible to enter the six-week gunnery school. Airplane armorer-gunner trainees took a 20-week course in the operation and maintenance of aircraft armaments. Aircraft mechanic-gunner trainees took 27 weeks training in aircraft inspection and maintenance. At the conclusion of their technical training, specialist gunner trainees were eligible to go to gunnery school. This was a six-week course in weapons, ballistics, turret operation, and maintenance; gun repairs; air, sea, and land recognition; shooting from a moving base and from a turret; firing from the air at ground objects, at towed targets, and at other aircraft with a gun camera. By 1943, 91,595 gunners had graduated from AAF schools. During 1941–45, 297,000 officers and enlisted men graduated from gunnery schools.

Page right, clockwise from top left: *Training manual for the Sperry "Upper Local turret"; cutaway diagram of the turret; groundcrew personnel lifting a replacement top turret into the top of a B-17G; when in full flying gear conditions were extremely cramped for the top turret gunner, as this Boeing-made photo of the Bendix top turret (as was used on the B-17E and B-17F) shows.*

## The Daily Status Board

In flight the engineer and assistant engineer would try to deal with mechanical and electrical problems first hand. Back at base his Squadron Engineering Officer and the line crews and their chiefs would complete the process.

DAILY STATUS 351ST BOMB SQUADRON

| DATE AIRPLANE A.C. SERIAL NO. | CREW CHIEF | TIME FLOWN TO-DAY | TOTAL PLANE TIME | TIME ENGINES 1 | 2 | 3 | 4 | SUPERCHARGER 1 | 2 | 3 | 4 | INSPECTION NEXT DUE INSP. AT | STATUS IN | OUT | DATE RE |
|---|---|---|---|---|---|---|---|---|---|---|---|---|---|---|---|
| 003 | SEIPEL | 10 | 541 | 100 | 100 | 150 | 200 | 100 | 150 | 50 | 100 | 600 | X | | CHAN |
| 530 | PARMENTIER | 11 | 346 | 100 | 100 | 100 | 100 | 50 | 50 | 100 | 150 | 400 | | | |
| 057 | CHRANE | 09 | 205 | 50 | 50 | 50 | 50 | 100 | 150 | 200 | 100 | 300 | X | | |
| 541 | STOUFFER | 10 | 705 | 75 | 75 | 75 | 75 | 100 | 50 | 50 | 100 | 150 | | | CARB |
| 857 | CHRISTOPHER | 11 | 600 | 50 | 50 | 50 | 100 | 50 | 50 | 50 | 50 | 650 | X | | SLOW TIME |
| 343 | SIERMINSKI | 12 | 750 | 25 | 200 | 200 | 200 | 75 | 75 | 75 | 75 | 400 | | | |
| 85 | NEHRNBERG | | 351 | 50 | 50 | 50 | 50 | 100 | 100 | 100 | 100 | 600 | X | | |
| 021 | WILDRICK | 10 | 550 | 75 | 75 | 75 | 75 | 50 | 75 | 50 | 75 | 300 | | | CHECK |
| 252 | HERMANN | | 200 | 200 | 200 | 200 | 200 | 100 | 100 | 50 | 50 | 1000 | X | | |
| 117 | MONTGOMERY | 11 | 470 | 100 | 100 | 100 | 100 | 150 | 150 | 100 | 100 | 450 | | | CHANGE |
| 232 | PICARD | 12 | 200 | 150 | 150 | 150 | 150 | 100 | 50 | 50 | 100 | 300 | X | | |
| | | | | 65 | 50 | 50 | 50 | 200 | 50 | 50 | 75 | 250 | ✓ | | CHANGE PL |

# RESTRICTED

# SPERRY TURRETS

## UPPER LOCAL

*For the Boeing B-17 Bombardment Airplane*

*Prepared by*
TRAINING DEPARTMENT
AAFБ3          LVAAF
4-44

OCHE
CHARGER HANDLE
K-3 SIGHT
AMMUNITION CAN
SEAT
SUPPORT COLUMN
SWIVEL JOINT
COLLECTOR RING ASSEMBLY
THRUST BEARING

GUN CRADLE ASSEMBLY
UNIT HOUSING ASSEMBLY
AZIMUTH RING GEAR
SPENT ROUND BAG
FOOTREST
PLATFORM
NOISE FILTER

## THE SPERRY UPPER

The Sperry Upper Turret is the upstairs brother of the Sperry Ball. It is mounted in the B-17, in the upper portion of the fuselage just behind the pilot's compartment. Its job is to defend the whole top area of the plane.

# A vantage point

Crewmembers who survived 25 missions and returned to the US for R&R or instruction before starting a second tour often revealed a preference for a change in position. Having slugged it out with enemy fighters from the top turret on the *Memphis Belle*, Technical Sergeant Harold P. Loch wanted to be a fighter pilot. He recalled:

"We had good teamwork on our ship. I think that is the main reason we were able to complete our 25 missions without a casualty. It doesn't pay any dividends to have trouble in the crew. All of ours were good boys, and we worked together and had confidence in each other. Before going over, bomber crews should get used to high-altitude flying. It gets cold up there and gunners should get accustomed to it. The first time most of the fellows see an electric suit is after they get over there.

"The upper turret is a good position. You can see any plane that is in position to do damage to you. Also, from there you can let the ball-turret gunner know when a plane is coming in and from what position so that he can take a crack at him. The engineer of a B-17 doesn't have much groundwork. I think he should have more, at least enough to keep his hand in. It is important that he know his engines, that he knows every gauge, switch, and fuze. Fuzes are especially important to him, because they sometimes blow out and he must know where they are. Every man on the B-17 should be able to assemble his gun blindfolded. He ought to be able to fix it quickly if it goes out while he is in the air. The biggest part of the attacks come from the nose. German fighters will come from away behind, slip up to the side just out of range and gradually get closer. If you don't watch closely, they'll nose right into you before you know it. Sometimes one plane will fly along in line with you, dipping his wings to attract attention, while a lot of other planes sneak in on you from the other side. You have got to be on the alert all the time. When you shoot at him and he peels off, don't worry about whether you got him. It doesn't pay to watch him. While you are doing that, another one might sneak up on you. Just use common sense. That's all it takes."

**Howard E. Hernan, top turret gunner in *The Old Squaw* (303rd Bomb Group) had to be alert on July 30, 1943, when the B-17s went to Kassel, a round trip of 600 miles (966km), when Bomber Command brought down the curtain on "Blitz Week:"**

"We were hit by more enemy fighters than ever before. The estimate was well in excess of 300. At one time I counted 157 flying off to our right. A fighter came down through our formation and then a whole *Gruppe* of them got ahead of us and started making pass after pass. Most of them we fought off and turned away at 700–800 yards [640–730m]. They would flip over on their backs and down they would go to get more latitude and then they would try again. Of course, the *Luftwaffe* painted their aircraft various colors and some were quite pretty. A snow-white Bf 109 dived on us. He had a beautiful Iron Cross painted on the wings and fuselage. He was coming so fast, with a strong tail wind behind him, that he came right through the formation and began making a turn to the right. So help me God he came between our wingman and us on the left, upside down, went between our wings and never touched either of us!

"On August 12 the flak was terrific and at no time had we encountered more attacks from fighters. I sweated out the whole trip. We lost No.2

Above: *A metal ID dog tag worn around the neck giving blood group and other personal details. The tag belonged to Robert E. Wolff.*

**MESS PASS**
**351st-418th Bombardment Squadrons**

Spangler, Robert E. _____ 7021014
Name _____ ASN

**JOHN B. KIDD**
**Major, Air Corps**

Above and left: *Chow line outside a mess hall in January 1945, and a mess pass (left). The base kitchens served food prepared to eliminate indigestion and sickness at high altitude.*

**Right:** *Crews emblazoned their B-17s with alluring "nose art" while the gunners often decorated the outside of their turrets with names of sweethearts. Ground crews stenciled bomb symbols to indicate the number of missions flown.*

supercharger before reaching enemy territory, and then No.1 engine began throwing gas and oil badly from the oil cooler vent. No.4 also began running roughly. My pilot had to feather the No.1 engine to prevent it from burning out. We lost oxygen on the right-hand side and had flak holes in several places. *Old Ironsides*, our hutmates' aircraft piloted by Lieutenant Arthur H. Pentz, was off our left wing. When we were this close together I could see my friend Technical Sergeant John A. Dougherty in his top turret and we would help one another. At the first opportunity we had ventured into Thrapston to buy some bicycles. I purchased a little sports model with 24-inch wheels for £5 and used it for cycling around the base, into Thrapston, and for trips to buy fresh eggs. Dougherty had purchased a 26-inch wheel bike. His had more speed but mine had more power, so we hooked them together. It was the most contrary thing to ride but we made many trips on it.

"I was basically patrolling forward before we got to the target. There was quite a bit of flak around, as there always seemed to be over the Ruhr Valley. I turned my turret around and looked over at Pentz's ship. It looked as though it was on fire from

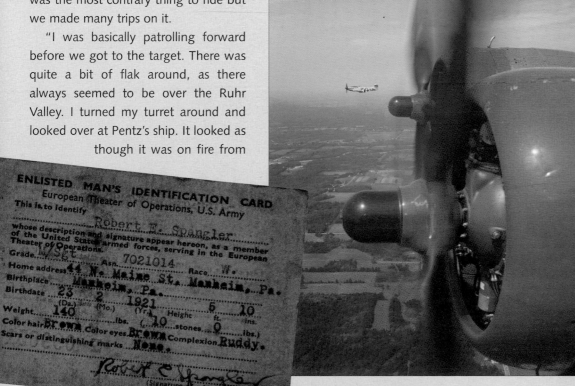

wingtip to wingtip. I just could hardly believe what I was seeing. I was actually yelling at them to bale out but they were still flying along as if nothing had happened. Pentz's ship had all colors of smoke coming out of it. Flak had got them. They flew along momentarily beside us and then dropped out of formation.

"It was certainly an empty feeling to look over the empty bunks that night. I dismantled our tandem and vowed there and then that whatever crew replaced Pentz's I was not going to make friends. I would be sociable and as pleasant as I could, but it was too hard when you lost them. Even to this day I cannot remember who moved into the hut or even what they looked like."

**Left:** *In flight the engineer watched for engine and supercharger failures, freed stuck bombs, and monitored fuel consumption and fuel tank issues.*
**Far left:** *Enlisted Man's Identification Card belonging to Master Sgt Bob Spangler.*

# Bomb-bay problems

**One of the worst chores of being an engineer/top turret gunner was having manually to crank the massive bomb bay doors shut when the electrical system, which powered the motor that normally closed them, was out. Lieutenant Franklin L. Betz, the navigator in Captain Douglas H. Buskey's crew in the 379th Bomb Group, recounts such an incident:** "As we pulled away from the target area, the plane perforated by flak but the fliers unscathed, my pilot said, 'We've got to get the bomb bay doors closed quickly. There's too much drag and with two and a half engines, I may not be able to keep up the formation.' It was no easy job. In a cramped space 25,000ft [7,620m] above Germany it was an interminable task. The temperature was way below freezing. Sergeant George Thomas was wearing a weighty fleece-lined flight suit, gloves, flak vest and helmet,

and an oxygen mask with the hose dangling like an elephant's trunk, which hooked him into the life-support system. There were wires from his throat mike and earphones to contend with, plus a parachute strapped on his back. The pilot ordered, 'Someone help the engineer close the doors.' The right waist gunner volunteered. This meant that he, too, had to disconnect from the oxygen system and hook on to a walk-around bottle that provided about eight minutes of the life-giving element, a routine any time a crewman left his position to go elsewhere in the plane. The walk-

*Below left: B-15A flight jacket with triangular leather patches sewn to the upper chest area to provide a place to clip the demand-type oxygen hose.*

*Below right: A-2 jacket worn by a crewmember of Fever Beaver in the B 351st Bomb Squadron, 100th Bomb Group.*

*Mouton collar and alpaca lining.*

*Originally, the A-2 was to be made of seal-brown horsehide but many of these most sought-after jackets were made of cowhide, and some of goatskin.*

around bottle was an aluminum cylinder six or eight inches [15 to 20cm] in diameter and about 30 inches [76cm] long. The waist gunner in his bulky flight gear had to shuffle through the radio operator's compartment, then into the bomb bay, balancing precariously on a narrow catwalk, squeeze between V-shaped bomb racks, the bomb bay doors below him only partly closed, until he reached the engineer's station behind the cockpit. Buskey continued to do a magnificent job of flying the disabled aircraft and managed somehow to stay in formation. Thomas slowly and laboriously cranked the bomb bay doors closed. Those of us on the guns were warily watching the enemy fighters in the distance, who fortunately didn't attack. Thomas said, 'Engineer to pilot. I see the waist gunner on the catwalk. He's stuck between the bomb racks. He can't move.' The radio operator, closest to the helpless waist gunner, attempted to extricate him but his oxygen bottle fell through the partly opened doors and he had to go back to his position and hook into the plane's oxygen system. The left waist gunner, on his twelfth mission, the only experienced combat crewman aboard, came forward and tried unsuccessfully to rescue his buddy who had fainted from lack of oxygen. Somehow he had freed himself but, unfortunately, he had toppled off the catwalk and dropped part of the way through the bomb bay doors that were nearly closed. The radio operator came back again and tried once more to save his pal but to no avail. He had to go back to his position for much needed oxygen. 'Radio operator to pilot. We can't get the waist gunner out of the bomb bay. He's unconscious. You'll have to hit the deck if he's to live.'

"'Pilot to crew,' Buskey called, his voice faltering. 'If I leave the formation and try to go it alone at 10,000ft [3,000m] or lower, where we don't need oxygen, we may not make it back to England. German fighters will jump us. It means losing one with the hope that the rest of us will get back.'

"The waning winter sun of late afternoon shone warmly through the transparent nose of the battle-scarred B-17 as we approached our airbase. The red flare fired from the plane by the engineer alerted the ground personnel that we had a casualty aboard and the tower gave the pilot priority to land. The plane dropped smoothly to the concrete runway and the tires screeching on touchdown sounded like a whining protest against the terrible ordeal the plane and its crew had endured. Buskey taxied the splendid Fortress to its dispersal area. The medics removed the dead body of the right waist gunner and took him away. I dropped to the ground from the plane's nose hatch, somber and weary after more than eight hours in the plane. I realized the hardening of a naive airman to combat in the crucible of war had begun."

[The loss of any member in a tightly knit crew was always tragic. The worst situation was usually when they were lost needlessly, in an accident or through carelessness on the ground, especially when the war was almost won. At Podington in late February 1945 the diarist recorded that, "on the return from the mission to a rail station at Leipzig, Lieutenant Walter A. Wesley landed his Fortress on the runway and taxied away to dispersal. While removing guns, the top turret turned and caught the engineer between the turret and the side of the aircraft, crushing his head and neck and causing death by asphyxiation."]

*Top: Bombs fall from the bomb bay of B-17G Forbidden Fruit over Schwerte, Germany, on May 31, 1944. Forbidden Fruit crash-landed on February 17, 1945, and was salvaged.*

*Above: A Fortress lands at Chelveston. The USAAF did not usually fly night missions, but special units were formed for Night Leaflet operations over Occupied Europe.*

# Fire and frozen blood

**Lieutenant Richard H. Perry, copilot of *The Eightball* in the 390th Bomb Group, was another who remembered the impact that the top turret guns could make:**

"It looked like the whole *Luftwaffe* was waiting for us at the German coast [on the way to the target, the city of Emden]. I started calling them and our boys went to work at the guns. A fighter dove in at 12 o'clock and the whole bomber shuddered with the recoil as Lloyd J. Wamble opened fire from his top turret. Wamble hit the fighter in the fuel tanks and it exploded, showering the sky with debris and smoke. For the next 20 minutes *The Eightball* came in for repeated enemy attacks and two more fighters were shot down. Finally, *The Eightball* entered cloud cover and Cabral [the pilot] asked the crew over the intercom if everyone was all right. The bombardier replied that he was but thought he had better mention that No.4 engine was on fire! Orange flames covered the wing and threatened to ignite the fuel tanks. By now *The Eightball* was over Holland and Cabral asked the crew if they wanted to bale out or keep going. All wanted to keep going. *The Eightball* made it back and as the aircraft hit the runway, the propeller of No.4 engine spun off and rolled some distance down the runway."

**Sometimes the fighters came in so close that the top turret gunner could see every detail, as they did on one particular mission that Sergeant Joe Hoffman, engineer/top turret gunner in 2nd Lieutenant Leon A. Risk's crew in the 306th Bomb Group, flew:**

"When the last wave of FW 190s and Me 109s came in we returned fire and all made a peel off and went down OK but one FW 190 cut its speed and came in on us. He fired at us from 1,000 yards [914m] and he was the one who caused most damage. But when he got in close he stopped firing and flew a close formation with us. He was so close we could not fire. We all waited for the right time. At one split second we dropped and he rose up. At this point I fired into the side of the FW 190 and got a direct hit on the pilot. His head went back against his headrest and blood was coming out of his oxygen mask. The airplane rolled off on its left wing and went down. He exploded at about 1,000 yards [914m] below. The ball-turret gunner saw the plane go down."

**When crewmen in the nose and cockpit were hit, the flight engineer/top turret gunner would help with first aid, as Leslie G. Thibodeau, flight-engineer/top turret gunner in *Pegasus Too* in the 388th Bomb Group, did on one occasion:**

"Our navigator was hit pretty badly under the armpit as he was getting in some navigational reading. The bombardier and I had to remove our winter flying clothes to keep him warm. We gave him a shot of morphine and put a cigarette in his mouth once in a while. The flak must have hit an artery, as the blood was about an inch thick all over his maps; of course, the blood was frozen."

**Crews were instructed that badly wounded airmen were to be baled out over enemy territory if their wounds were such that they were likely to die before returning to base. Loss of blood was a determining factor, and crewmen were told that Germans had given good medical care to many airmen in such straits. This was what happened to the top turret gunner of *Ruthie II* (92nd Bomb Group) on July 26, 1943. The B-17, which was piloted by 1st Lieutenant Robert L. Campbell and copilot Flight Officer John C. Morgan, a tall, red-haired Texan, was attacked by FW 190 fighters, as the navigator, Keith J. Koske, recalled:**

"On their first pass I felt sure they had got us for there was a terrific explosion overhead and the ship rocked badly. A second later the top turret gunner, Staff Sergeant Tyre C. Weaver, fell through the hatch and

slumped to the floor at the rear of my nose compartment. When I got to him I saw his left arm had been blown off at the shoulder and he was a mass of blood. I first tried to inject some morphine but the needle was bent and I could not get it in.

*Above, and opposite page top right: 306th Bomb Group B-17Gs in flight; Lassie Come Home is nearest the camera. B-17Fs escorted by P-47s en route to Emden on September 27, 1943 (opposite, top right).*

Above: Paratroopers' First Aid kit with ties (reproduction); B-17 crews tied them to their parachute harness.

As things turned out it was best I didn't give him any morphine. My first thought was to try and stop his loss of blood. I tried to apply a tourniquet but it was impossible as the arm was off too close to the shoulder. I knew he had to have the right kind of medical treatment as soon as possible and we had almost four hours flying time ahead of us, so there was no alternative. I opened the escape hatch, adjusted his 'chute for him and placed the ripcord ring firmly in his right hand. He must have become excited and pulled the cord, opening the pilot 'chute in the up-draft. I managed to gather it together and tuck it under his right arm, got him into a crouched position with legs through the hatch, made certain again that his good arm was holding the 'chute folds together and toppled him out into space. I learned somewhat later from our ball-turret gunner that the 'chute opened OK. We were at 24,500ft [7,470m] and 25 miles [40km] due west of Hanover and our only hope was that he was found and given medical attention immediately."

[Morgan meanwhile got the ailing Fortress home with Lieutenant Campbell slumped down in his seat, a mass of blood and with the back of his head blown off. Morgan flew the plane with one hand, holding the pilot off with the other; he later received the Medal of Honor for his outstanding achievement.]

Far left: A top turret gunner in the 305th Bomb Group at Chelveston poses for the camera.
Left: A badly wounded crewmember in the 379th Bomb Group receives immediate treatment after landing back at Kimbolton.

# Prepare to Ditch!

*Section Eight* (728th Bomb Squadron, 452nd Bomb Group) was hit by flak during a raid on Berlin on April 29, 1944. 2nd Lieutenant George A. Haskenson coaxed the plane back to the Dutch coast, but was then forced to ditch in the sea. All ten crew were taken prisoner. Richard Walsh, top turret gunner, describes the events:

Above: *"Goldfish Club" card issued to Robert E. Wolff for surviving a ditching on September 16, 1943.*

Below: *B-17Gs over the North Sea that claimed so many lives. Even close to home, death was never far away.*

"As we hit our IP we could see, up ahead, this great big wall of flak. I looked down on this country where so much trouble came from. From five miles up it looked like any other place in the world but you can't mistake the winding Rhine River that passes through the heart of Germany. To the right I could see the big park that we were briefed about [as a reference point] to help locate the target.

"'Bomb bay doors coming open,' the bombardier said.

I checked the doors and relay. 'Doors open and all clear below.'

'Roger' says he.

Then it happened.

"We weren't getting any flak until then, that is, direct flak, but now they were on us and we were hit, or should I say, blasted out of position and the No.1 and 3 engines were out. No.1 feathered OK but 3 did not. None of the crew was hit but the ship was a sieve. We had a hole big enough to drive a jeep through in the left wing. The fuel transfer pump worked overtime 'till the last. By now we had lost 8,000ft [2,440m] and were completely alone. Our speed was approximately 120mph [193 kmph]; dangerously close to stalling speed, if the ship was not flown perfectly. Several things happened that required fast action and skill and through all this, not one of us was panicky, but we were scared. All guns and ammo' were thrown overboard, also all of the armor we could loosen. The ball turret was dropped. That in itself was a great help because of its weight and wind resistance.

"Well, up to now things weren't too bad. We were alive anyhow. We then had a new worry: gas! The gunners and bombardier stripped the ship expertly because of some past experience. Now it was just a matter of time. The radioman was in contact with Air Sea Rescue and we were 'fixed.' With a few parting bursts of flak we left the Dutch coast and started across the Channel. Altitude about 5,000ft [1,520m]. We passed B-26 Marauders of the 9th Air Force going in and two P-47 Thunderbolts saluted us and hung around for a while. We were in constant touch with the horizon when I looked at the gas gauge, which read '30 gallons' for each

engine. Then I remembered what the books said a long way back, 'Don't use all the gas, then crash-land. Do it while the engines are turning.'

"This was it. We had to prepare to ditch. The pilots pulled their safety belts on and the rest of the crew took their places for the ditching procedure. We started down to the smooth green water (it looked like it

anyhow). At about 500ft [150m] the two remaining engines 'conked out' so we had to deadstick on the water. *Section Eight* skipped twice before mushing in completely underwater and then she bobbed to the surface like a cork. We scrambled out and counted heads. All present with no casualties. Both dinghies inflated OK and we got in and pushed away."

**Below:** *General Electric's Emergency Signaling Mirror Type ESM/2, as used in emergency kits.*

**Left:** *B-4 "Mae West," one of two of the most common US-made life-preserver vests, with mouth inflator valve. The B-3 had a rubber bladder with a separate cotton outer shell; the B-4 was made of rubberized fabric.*

ONE
EMERGENCY SIGNALLING
MIRROR TYPE ESM/2

**Left:** *A B-17 ball turret is jettisoned to save weight to help keep the Fortress airborne or prepare for belly landings. Below: A RAF Air-Sea Rescue launch pulls a stranded B-17 crew out of the "drink."*

2631

# Fighters and Flak

**"Arny" Arneson, bombardier in the B-17 piloted by Jay D. McIntosh (94th Bomb Group), recalls the work of the top turret gunner on a mission in late 1944:**

"Deep into German territory our group got out of formation and we were the prime target of this error. We were involved with FW 190s and 109s plus some Me 163s for 45 minutes. Right on their tail were P-47s and P-51s, flying through our own bullets in the attempt to knock them out. It was really a mess. Several airplanes went down in spins. The aircraft that flew group lead was a cherry red all over the fuselage. I saw one man jump without a 'chute.

"After the fighter attack our airplane seemed to be alone. There had been a gas fire on the right wing from one of the hits. The engineer/top turret gunner, Richard Eiseman, had seen this but did not have time to even comment during the attack as he was busy shooting at one of the attacking fighters. The next time he got around to surveying the damage, the fire was out. After the fighter attack was over and we had left the target area the rest of the mission was quite uneventful except that we were one sad bunch of people."

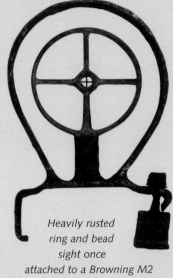

*Heavily rusted ring and bead sight once attached to a Browning M2 .50 caliber machine gun.*

out that the Germans were really guarding their oil with walls of flak. The bursts were getting closer and closer. The thin aluminum skin was really taking a beating. In fact it was beginning to look like a sieve. There were huge holes in the wings where the flak pierced the self-sealing gas tanks. Some of the engines were taking hits and beginning to falter. Nilan 'Mac' Mack, the bombardier, called me on intercom so I'd be ready to fire the flare gun (other planes were to drop their bombs when they saw the flare). I found I'd have to get out of my top turret to reach it. Here we were at 28,000ft [8,534m], 50° below, flak popping all over and I had to get out of the turret. Cussing to myself, I unbuckled my turret straps, unhooked my electrical heating suit cord, unhooked the oxygen line, and stepped out to hook up a walk-around oxygen bottle. While I was waiting for Mac to zero in with his bombsight and to call me on the intercom (right after I stepped out), I heard a big 'zing' and saw that about half of my top turret bubble was knocked out where my head would have been. I then got Mac's call and fired the flare."

**There were many facets to an engineer/top turret gunner's job, as Wayne E. Cose, engineer/top turret gunner on David "Moon" Mullen's crew in the 486th Bomb Group, recalls:**

"Our crew only had two missions under our belts and didn't realize what was ahead of us. The first one to Bremen only involved a relatively few puffs of flak, which didn't seem to be close enough to register. Little did I realize the punch behind those puffs at the time. On the second mission, however, to Mainz, I took back my thought, 'Is this all there is to it?' when a B-17 disappeared in front of us with a single direct hit burst of flak. Wow, nine men and a plane gone in one puff—those Germans are out to get us! On the Merseburg mission we soon found

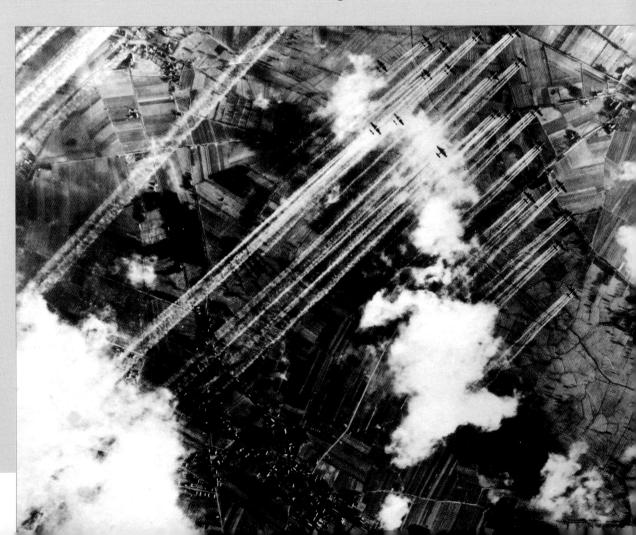

Above: *Browning M2 .50 caliber machine gun with ammunition belt. The 57-inch (145-cm) long gun first appeared in 1921 and it was produced in greater numbers than any other US machine gun in World War II.*

**On "Black Thursday," October 14, 1943, James R. "Woody" Wood, who had been a trooper in the Seventh Cavalry before transferring to the Air Corps, was flying as a replacement top turret gunner for a 91st Bomb Group crew whose regular engineer was recovering from wounds:**

"We had been working on a simplified method of target gunnery. We would set our target dimension dial at 33ft [10m], the approximate wingspan of a Me 109 or FW 190 German fighter. We set our range at 1,000 yards [914m], since fighter gunnery, as well as our own gunnery, is usually ineffective beyond this range. We held the horizontal line on his wings for elevation and range, and fired as he filled the area between the reticules. The cone of fire did the rest. The first wave of fighters was six abreast and three high, with one wave behind another at 1,000-yard [914-m] intervals. As we spotted the fighters, Colonel Milton called for the Group to close up and we tucked in beautifully. It seemed that the Germans sent the top six after the High Group, the center after the Lead Group, and the low after the Low Group. The Wing was being led by the 91st, the Low Group was the 381st, and the high was a composite group. We were as ready as possible. As the fighters closed in to range, 1,000 yards [914m], our fire began to take effect. Six of the first wave were set afire or blown up, with a couple more going down smoking. The rest split and passed on both sides of us to go after the Wing behind us. The following Wing took a beating, while we were relatively free of attack. The flak on the way in was a little rough, but the Wing behind had the worst of the fighter attacks after we convinced them that it wasn't nice to fool around with us. At the target the bombing was excellent. Our Group had no more fighter attacks after we reached France. The 8th Air Force lost 60 B-17s, but we were lucky. There were a lot of hairy situations in later years but I look back at Mission 115 as the high-water mark. I believe it was the cohesion, resulting from belonging to a close-knit group that sustained us. Most of those who cracked up were loners."

Opposite: *Contrails and cloud separate Fortress squadrons on their way to bomb a target. At this point—with no flak or fighters in sight—the formation is still being held good and tight.*

Right, above and below: *B-17G Chopstick G-George, on fire on the Berlin mission of March 6, 1944; the wrecked top turret of Sunny II after the Bremen raid of October 8, 1943.*

# The Waist Gunners

"The waist looked like a jagged screen . . . I climbed in with the medico, and, getting through the door I put my hand in a gob of blood and brains that had splattered back that way. I took one look at the body and climbed out again, careful this time where I put my hands . . . I felt no nausea, just a sense of shock, just a certain deadness inside."

—Bert Stiles, *Serenade To The Big Bird*

**W**aist gunners could see what was going on just about anywhere. On the early B-17s it was a cold place to be, but when in flak there was no time to think about being cold. There was no time to think about being scared, either. Lessons learned about high-altitude daylight bombing operations by RAF Fortress crews in 1941 led to improvements in the overall Fortress design. The bitter cold at altitude was made far worse by the Fortress having to fly with the gun-fairing blister windows removed, but the blisters soon gave way to flush teardrop-shaped windows through which the guns were fired. The top gun blister was also replaced by a stepped Plexiglas fairing that slid back to uncover the upper gun. The under-fuselage blister was replaced by a lower gun tub with the gun firing down and to the rear.

All of this proved totally inadequate in combat and the limitations were only rectified on the B-17E, when large rectangular windows with sliding hatches replaced the teardrop-shaped waist windows. These were later glazed over, with the guns being fired through mountings set in the glass. The early Forts had "prehistoric" armament, with free-mounted .50s in the waist and one .30 caliber in

*Left: The waist gunners' K-5 post-mounted .50 caliber machine guns were replaced later by K-6 gun mounts, which allowed them to swivel the machine gun inside and outside rectangular window openings, which improved visibility and increased the field of fire.*

the nose. Heavy 50lb (22kg) containers, each containing 100 rounds, had to be lifted onto the mountings at 30,000-plus feet [9,144m] and, unsurprisingly, the gunners found this "a hell of struggle." The guns jumped around all over the place and hosepiped on the free mountings—and often they failed to fire at all. They also iced up at altitude, and the gunners were forced to wash them in petrol to render them operable. The windscreens iced up, too, and eventually had to be double-glazed. Changes were made to the oxygen supply, flying clothing, and lubricants, while armor plating, self-sealing tanks and better armament were incorporated in the B-17D, which followed the "C" off the production lines.

The waist gunners' K-5 post-mounted .50 caliber machine guns were replaced later by K-6 gun mounts, which allowed the gunners to swivel the machine guns inside and outside rectangular window openings, which improved visibility and increased the field of fire. The cumbersome metal ammunition boxes were replaced by belt feeds, and plywood ammunition boxes containing 600 rounds of .50 caliber shells were mounted on the inside of the plane. Later, all .50s were power-operated, armor plate was installed and, beginning with the Boeing B-17G-50-BO, the waist-gun positions (which had been directly opposite each other) were staggered to allow the gunners more freedom of movement in combat.

Nineteen-year-old Staff Sergeant Casimer A. Nastal, who flew a first tour as a waist gunner on the *Memphis Belle*, was the baby of the crew. (Before joining the Army in late December 1941, Nastal had had a job repairing washing machines in Detroit, MI.) He said this about the gunners' role: "My first advice to gunners is [that they] take good care of their guns. This is important. They shouldn't depend on anybody else to do it for them. Every gunner should see that his oil buffer is set right. He should check his electrical equipment before taking off, because it gets cold up there and if his equipment isn't right he'll suffer. If you have escort you're likely to be less alert than when you don't have them. But if you keep alert you'll be okay. Always watch the other gunners if you can. If you are a waist gunner, watch the other waist gunner. If he needs help, give it to him. He may have attacks coming in and be short of ammunition. If he is, give him some of yours. Combat crews should never go into combat with the idea that they are not coming back. Those who have that in their minds are the least likely to get through. It's always a great thrill to get a fighter in your sights and let him have it. I don't know how many I have hit, but I have two confirmed. I'll never forget the day one came in shooting from 5 o'clock. I let him have it and I saw my tracers go into his gas tank. He went down. I didn't see the pilot get out. The Germans are a wild bunch sometimes. On our Bremen raid, the fighters came in bunches of 20 or 30. At the target, the flak started. It was bursting outside the waist windows. I could have reached out and grabbed it. I kept thinking, 'Let's get the hell out of here.' I saw two or three fighters hit by their own flak. It was so thick you could hardly see the ground. I want to go back as a pilot. I put in for fighter pilot, but if they give me a B-17 I'll take it. I guess it just gets in your blood."

## Get that Fighter

*This is Your Gun*, a basic introduction to the .50 caliber machine gun, and *Get That Fighter*, which contained advice and hints for better aerial gunnery, were two USAAF pamphlets produced specifically for the aerial gunner. The Browning M2 weighed 65lb (29kg), and had a muzzle velocity of 2,900ft (884m) per second; it was generally accepted that a flexible .50 caliber was inaccurate beyond 1,000 yards (914m).

THE CALIBER .50
BROWNING
MACHINE GUN M2
AIRCRAFT, BASIC

GET THAT FIGHTER

RESTRICTED

Page right, clockwise from top: The .50 caliber machine guns on the B-17 were fitted with either Sperry N-6A or Sperry N-8 optical gunsights; these photos show the front and back of the N-8 gunsight. The N-8 was also used in the hand-held "Cheyenne" turret of B-17s; an exterior view of one of the two .50 caliber waist guns. Beginning with the Boeing B-17G-50-BO, the previous configuration of directly opposite waist-gun positions was staggered so as to allow the gunners more freedom of movement in combat.

# Purple Hearts—for some

**When both waist gunners were wounded on his plane during the second Schweinfurt raid on October 14, 1943, all copilot Henry C. Cordery could do was pump them full of morphine—and hope for the best:**

"We were under constant attack. I don't know how long the first attacks lasted but there was a lull. I left my position to get more ammo from the radio room. Passing through the waist I found the right waist gunner severely wounded. His leg was off. The left waist gunner was also wounded. I called the bombardier. He came back and we both administered first aid. I took the protective covering off the needle of the morphine only to discover it was frozen. I must have had at least five uncovered and I put them all in my mouth to thaw them. I had considerable difficulty getting them out, as my hands were numb from the cold. Then I returned to my position and just about in time, as the attacks started again."

**In the air, combat crewmen could do nothing if one of their fellows was mortally wounded. Richard E. Perry, a pilot in the 390th Bomb Group, recalls the death of one of his waist gunners:**

"A .30 caliber armor-piercing shell entered the waist-gun area and went right through the steel helmet of Sergeant Leonard A. Baumgartner and struck him in the head. I went to the back of the airplane to administer to him. Baumgartner took his last breath in my arms."

**Bert Stiles, a B-17 pilot in the 91st Bomb Group, remembers the time a ship came in with dead onboard:**

"One flak shell had burst just outside the waist window. The waist gunner wore a flak suit and a flak helmet, but that didn't help much. One chunk hit low on his forehead and clipped the top of his head off. Part of his brains sprayed as far forward as the door into

*Left: The Purple Heart was originally inaugurated by General George Washington in 1782. It was re-established in 1932; the decoration was, and continues to be, awarded to those wounded in action while serving in the US Armed Forces.*

the radio room. The rest of them spilled out when the body crumpled up, quite dead. The flak suit protected his heart and lungs all right, but both legs were blown off and hung with the body, because the flying-suit was tucked into electric shoes . . . "

**When flak hit the nose of his aircraft on his 16th mission, Technical Sergeant Jack Kings, a waist gunner in the 388th Bomb Group, attempted to profit from the situation:**

"The bombardier, who was trying to watch his bombs leaving the aircraft, got some fragments of glass just over one eye. Turned out it wasn't very serious but it was enemy inflicted and drew blood so he'd get a 'Purple Heart.' One pretty good-sized piece hit next to me. I picked it up and tried to scratch a bloody place on one cheek just above my oxygen mask, but the weather was so damn cold and my face so cold and tight I couldn't make a scratch!"

**Sometimes, the pressures of combat became too heavy to bear. Phillip R. Taylor, who flew a tour of 25 missions as a left waist gunner in the 91st Bomb Group, recalls:**

"I do not know what raid it was but the flak was particularly severe. I could not take it any longer and kneeled down and hid my face in the junction of the armor plate in the waist. Then I thought, 'What does Bill Hoots think of me hiding like a coward here?' I raised my head and saw Billy hiding like I was. I guessed it was no crime to be scared."

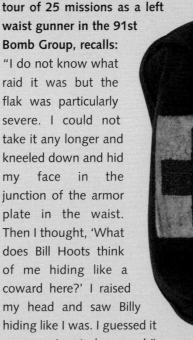

*Left: Infantry issue First Aid packet, Carlisle model, manufactured by Bauer & Black of Chicago; it contained field dressings. Many crewmembers attached them to their belts.*

Left: *A Me 210 turns away on the starboard side of a Flying Fortress after making an attack on the bomber formation. The Luftwaffe employed many fighter types against the 8th Air Force, including the Bf 109 and FW 190, and twin-engined aircraft such as the Bf 110, Me 210, and Me 410.*

a few holes in our tail, but no one was hurt. Our waist gunner fell back away from his gun for a second when he saw this plane so close and when he did start shooting again he shot through our tail and through the B-17 flying next to us."

**For Jim Collins, however, being a waist gunner did have one advantage over just about every other position on the Fortress:**

"Flak was very heavy [on one mission] and we took about 20 hits in the tail-wheel area. On approaching the base for landing, the undercarriage had to be manually cranked down by the engineer. We did not know, however, that the tail wheel was broken and when we touched down the aircraft veered off the runway, plowing a deep furrow in the adjacent field. Smelling what we all thought was smoke, every man made a scramble for the exits when the plane came to rest, listing down on one side. Our waist gunner, Mike Lasprogato, dropped to the field from the waist exit, and despite the fact that he weighed about 200lb [91kg] and was normally much slower than I was, sprinted well ahead of me, shouting, 'Run, Rip, run!' Fortunately the plane did not catch fire and no one was hurt."

**In the heat of battle, meanwhile, it was not uncommon for a gunner to fire a few rounds into the tail of his own aircraft by mistake, especially during continual fighter attacks, as Joe Wroblewski, of the 351st Bomb Group, describes:**

"One yellow-nosed Me 109 came in between our wingman and us with his guns blazing. He must have put

Left: *Death from wounds and shock could be rapid, so prompt attention was essential. Yet hands were numb from cold—a man trying to take the covering off the needle of morphine could find it frozen.*

Right: *B-17G 43-37514* My Son Bob *in the 381st Bomb Group at Ridgewell was twice forced to land on the Continent early in 1945, but was repaired each time, leaving for the ZOI in June 1945.*

# A Milk Run turns sour

Hal Kowel, pilot of *Carolee* (94th Bomb Group) remembers the second Schweinfurt raid as being **"like the inside of a bee's nest"**—and the waist gunners struggling not to slip on the sea of empty shell casings littering the floor:

"It seemed like the 94th had the 'honor' of seeing all of the German fighters on October 14. It felt like the inside of a bee's nest. Enemy fighters swarming from all directions. The crew of *Carolee* expended all of its ammunition. I don't know how many times the waist gunners landed on their fannys trying to shoot on a bed of spent casings on the floor. After the ammunition was exhausted they were throwing empty shells through the waist window at German planes. Digbey was part American Indian, and Painter a typical American teenager going into his 20s. From the call outs of the gunners, I skidded or slipped within the limits of the formation in order not to be in a German's gunsight at the closing range of the gunfire. Good flying gave way to any conceived maneuver to prevent a sitting-duck position for the attackers to shoot at."

On April 28, 1944, the 100th Bomb Group were directed to attack a NoBall (the Allied code name for V1 and V2 launch sites) site at Sottevast, near Cherbourg, France—a supposedly easy mission compared with a raid on a target such as Schweinfurt. John A. Miller, a right waist gunner, was one of many at Thorpe Abbotts who could not believe his luck:

"A milk-run! The briefing officer described our mission and our route and it really sounded sweet. We would start our run over the water and only be over land a few minutes. 'There are only about eight guns there that will be able to reach you,' he said. Wow! This was really great!

Left: *Usually, long underwear went on first, then a white silk scarf and F-1 heated "Blue Bunnies" of flannel, glove inserts, electric gloves, shoes, helmet, goggles, oxygen mask, jacket, trousers, and Mae West life preserver.*

We wondered how the 'Bloody Hundredth' happened to get such a soft mission. Colonel Robert H. Kelly, fresh from the States, had just joined our group as CO. In that short time we had learned to dislike him. Kelly had come to the group with the idea of straightening it out. At the last moment Kelly said he would fly as command pilot. At the morning's briefing Kelly stood up and told us, 'There'll be no evasive action when we're on the bomb run.' As we left the briefing room you could hear comments that 'Kelly sure picked a sweet milk-run for his first mission.'

"It was a beautiful day. We took off and soon we were starting on the bomb run. The flak was way below us as we made our run and there wasn't much of it. Then on the intercom I heard Townsend say that Kelly had called off the bomb drop and that we would have to go around again. We must have made the

Above: *The bulky metal ammunition boxes in early B-17s were replaced by .50 caliber ammunition belt feeds and plywood ammunition boxes containing 600 rounds.*

Above: *A round of .50 caliber ammunition was 5.47in long and weighed 1.71oz, with copper-colored metal jackets.*

longest 360 in recorded history. Kelly took us far out over the water and it took forever. We came back in on the bomb run at the same speed, same altitude and the same course, flying in rigid formation as Kelly ordered. The Kraut flak guns got us good! The lead B-17 received two direct hits, one between the No.2 engine and the cockpit, and the second back toward the tail position. The plane disintegrated and fell to earth. Colonel Kelly was killed.

"A second Fortress had its No.1 engine knocked from its mounting. The engine landed back on the left wing, setting it on fire. When it was directly in front of me at 3 o'clock there was a puff of smoke. I reported 'It's detonating.' As fast as I said that, it went puff, puff, and blew to hell. As he dove out of formation the left wing snapped off and it cracked in

Above: *Sgt Robert Taylor, a B-17 left waist gunner at his K-5 post-mounted, belt-fed gun, surrounded by spent .50 caliber cartridge cases. Note the plywood ammunition box containing 600 rounds of .50 caliber shells. Taylor is wearing a flak vest, combat clothing, and leather A-11 winter helmet with B-8 Polaroid goggle and sunglasses.*

# Oxygen—and frostbite

At altitude, waist gunners had to withstand the freezing temperatures and other operational problems such as oxygen deficiency, which could soon lead to anoxia and then death. If one waist gunner lost his oxygen supply, in all probability the other waist gunner could come to his aid, unless he was fending off fighter attacks at the time, and was unable to help despite their close proximity to each other. A few minutes of breathing on pure oxygen from an oxygen bottle was usually enough to revive a man, but the after-effects of anoxia could last for the remainder of the mission. The oxygen supply going out could simultaneously affect several crewmembers at once. If at the same time a regulator froze up and the oxygen mask froze, too, it placed an additional burden on the already over-stretched crew. Each ship was furnished with an emergency kit that contained an oxygen mask, so the spare mask would be passed to the gunner and the frozen one taken to the radio room to be thawed out. At Molesworth one day, Ben Smith saw two waist gunners who looked like lepers: "They were in a frightful condition, their faces swollen and shapeless. I found out that they were suffering from frostbite. Because there was no way to keep warm back there in the sub-zero weather we flew in, frostbite was a common occurrence."

two like an egg at the waist. The plane tumbled, a ball of fire, into the clouds below. A 'chute popped open in that fire. It burned immediately. The way that B-17 went down, the gyrations, how could a bombardier, of all people, get out and live to tell about it? But he did. John Jones, wherever you are, you're a walking miracle! (Six of the crew shared our hut with us in the 349th Squadron and all were KIA.)

"At interrogation we told our story about the milk-run Colonel Kelly had chosen for his first mission with us. The intelligence interrogators were awed and amazed. One was heard to say, 'Colonel Kelly hadn't even unpacked yet.'"

Above: *The Type A-14 Demand Oxygen mask with microphone— more efficient than the previous continuous-flow oxygen system.*

# A day's work done

**George Rubin, a waist gunner in the 486th Bomb Group, gave this remarkable account of a full mission—from beginning to end:**

'In the clouds now I feel as if I'm on a roller coaster as the plane rises and suddenly falls. I hold on and chew away on my juicy fruit gum, scared that we may hit another aircraft or crash land. We are caught in the prop wash of the planes in front of us. I hold on tight and as suddenly as it started it stops and now smoothly we continue to climb to 'Nightdress,' the first radio marker. We come out of the clouds into bright sunlight and begin to assemble on the lead aircraft of our squadron. We continue to climb, circling to the next radio marker and group assembly. Above the clouds now the group slowly forms high squadron and lead, middle, low and the tail end squadron. We are at 10,000ft [304m] and the pilot tells us to go on oxygen. Check oxygen mask and watch the little lips on the flow indicator move up and down as I breathe in the oxygen. Check the plug connection to my electric suit and turn up the rheostat to 'high' as the cold in the plane becomes more intense. Over the Channel the pilot checks in on the intercom and tells all positions to check guns and test-fire. Twice I charge the .50 caliber gun and fire out into space watching the tracer bullet (every 5th shell) light up the blue sky. It's good to fire the guns. It's something I know a lot about and it gives me a sense of control. I lock them in place and check the heating plate over the top of the gun, a new device that helps prevent jamming in cold temperature.

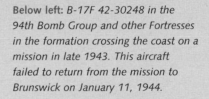

*Below left: B-17F 42-30248 in the 94th Bomb Group and other Fortresses in the formation crossing the coast on a mission in late 1943. This aircraft failed to return from the mission to Brunswick on January 11, 1944.*

*Above: B-8 Polaroid Goggle, which came complete with various colors of replacement lenses, and were standard issue for aerial gunners; some USAAF gunners, fighter pilots especially, favored the British-made Mk VIII tinted goggle.*

"The French coast appears below. It's time for Splude to enter the ball turret. I help him open the ball hatch and watch as he climbs in, plugs in his oxygen and heated suit. I close and lock the hatch. The whine of the ball motor starts up as he checks all the different positions of his turret and then he test-fires his guns. I check in with him on the intercom. I will do this now on for the rest of the mission.

" . . . On the bomb run the bomb doors open and as the bombs release Brown in the radio shack announces that all the bombs are 'away.' I have set up the K-12 camera to take pictures of the bomb strikes. It is too overcast to get very good shots but I snap away. Having something to do eases the tension.

"The plane takes a leap upward as the bombs let go. The bomb-bay doors close and we make a sharp left turn and gain altitude as we start our trip home. The lead group reports, 'Bandits at 3 o'clock!' I get my guns ready. The ball turret and the upper turret also search the sky. I put my Polaroid glasses on to check out each of the waist windows. Flak begins again. We are bouncing all over the sky. There is too much going on to be scared. I would love to shoot the .50 caliber waist guns and feel that I was doing something—anything. There is so much fear and loneliness of being a sitting duck to flak and fighters.

cleaning for the next mission, and then it's off to the debriefing hut. Intelligence officers ask me a set series of questions. After a half-hour of this it's outside again. The Red Cross gals offer me a shot of whiskey and peanut butter sandwiches. Try it some time, whiskey and peanut butter on an empty stomach. Back to the lockers. I turn in my parachute and hang up my flying clothes. Then it's back to our Quonset hut to fall into bed too tired to think or eat or anything. Later I will get up and check the bulletin board to see if our crew is alerted for a flight tomorrow. I wonder when will this end."

*This page, clockwise: The strain of the mission visible in their faces (above), combat crews make their way to interrogation for debriefing, food, a shot of whiskey, then off to their huts to "hit the sack." Gunners had to clean and adjust their weapons after each mission and armament technicians checked the barrels for wear (right). A bus converted into a Red Cross Clubmobile dispenses coffee, sandwiches, and donuts (bottom).*

"Soon the alert for enemy fighters is called off and the flak gradually stops. Back over Belgium and down to 10,000ft [304m]. I take my oxygen mask off and use the relief tube for the first time. (At altitude the urine stream freezes into ice particles.) I sit down for the first time in the last four hours. The intercom is busy with talk and how each position is doing. I help Splude out of the ball and go forward to stand behind Wiley and Demarath. Wiley has his headset over one ear. The other is red from hours of wearing it. It is a time to relax. I take out my chewing gum and press it into the armor plate around my waist gun. It sits there lined up with all the others from each bombing mission. Cookies are passed around. Maurides and Stiftinger leave the nose, stretch out in the waist and chat with Brown in the radio room. The intercom is turned to music from home. Over the Channel—then Great Waldingfield. We peel off and slowly circle with wheels down. Some of those ahead of us in the landing pattern with wounded aboard send out red flares. Jessen goes back to lock the tail wheel. We touch down, brakes squeal, and slowly we taxi back to our hardstand. I open the waist hatch and pile out with all my equipment. You feel a little wobbly; maybe from the hours confined in the plane or all that oxygen.

"The armament ground crew arrives with their truck and we dismantle all the machine guns, the bomb bay is opened and we check all the releases. The guns go back to the shop for

# Yanks at the Court of King Arthur

**Ben Smith in the Hells' Angels' Group at Molesworth recalls the particular effort crewmembers put into protecting their "family jewels:"** "There was one part of the anatomy much beloved by the flight crews. This was shown by the extreme lengths they went to protect it—the groin. All who had sitting jobs in the aircraft sat on a piece of armor, as most shrapnel traveled upward. All sorts of ingenious methods were devised to protect the 'family jewels.' The fact that this fragile piece of equipment would avail them little if their head were blown off seemed not to matter; they surrounded it with armor plate. The married men were particularly solicitous in this regard, although I am afraid that we all overdid this piece of business. I think that all these elaborate safeguards were more symbolic than protective. It was just one of the many things we did to foster the myth of our continuity."

In March 1943 new, armored flak vests, developed by Colonel Malcolm C. Grow, chief surgeon of the 8th Air Force, were worn in combat for the first time. The vest consisted of heavy canvas covered with overlapping two-inch square plates of 20-gauge manganese steel, and it protected the chest and back from low-velocity shrapnel and ricocheting missiles. In all, 300 suits were ordered from the Wilkinson Sword Company of Great Britain. In September 1943 the *New York Times* was quick to report that "A London firm, specializing since 1772 in the manufacture of swords, is now

*Above: M-3 flak helmet fashioned from a GI M-1 infantry steel helmet, with hinged ear protectors to permit the use of earphones.*

*Right: B-17 pilots wearing GI M-1 infantry steel helmets and body armor with M-3 Tapered Sporrans attached to the front of their flak vests. The Tapered Sporran was usually worn by crewmen in a sitting position, where the lower part of the body was unprotected.*

The whole Full Sporran, which had a quick-release mechanism and weighed 20 to 35lb [9 to 16kg], was cumbersome to wear and, after two or three long missions, the shoulders would become very sore. Such discomfort was a small price to pay, however, for the protection provided. On June 20, 1944, when flak was so thick that, "it fell like rain at times from explosions above the formation," Ed Cooper, a bombardier in the 303rd Bomb Group, was struck on the breastbone by one of these pieces of shrapnel. Although (as reported elsewhere) he was driven 6ft [1.8m] back into the navigator's compartment by the force of the blow, the flak suit undoubtedly saved Cooper's life: he suffered severe bruising on his chest, but remained available for active duty.

**Above:** *91st Bomb Group air-crew at Bassingbourn, in front of Oklahoma Okie, wearing GI steel helmets and Full Sporrans, usually worn by the gunners.*

**Right:** *Two of Oklahoma Okie's crew wearing the Full Sporran and the Tapered Sporran attached to the front of other armor.*

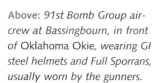

beating its products into something much more useful at the moment. It is making suits of mail for American airmen. Thus the cycle rolls around again and the American fighters, like the Yankee at King Arthur's Court, find themselves back in medieval armor."

Five main types of various weights were developed for use by different crew positions. The M-1 had armored front and back panels, while the M-2 was armored in the front only. The Tapered Sporran was designed to protect the lower part of the body; it could be attached to the front of other armor, and was intended for use by crewmen who had to sit throughout missions. The Full Sporran, which protected the entire front area of the body, was usually worn by gunners. The Thigh Sporran, meanwhile, gave protection to the lower front torso, thighs, and crotch area. By January 1, 1944, approximately 13,500 suits had been produced.

# In the enemy's hands

**For Lieutenant William C. Wiley's crew, the end came on February 25, 1945, on their 18th mission, as George Rubin continued:**
"Clarence Baugh was added to our crew as a 'toggelier-gunner.' He replaced our regular bombardier George Stiftinger, who was removed before the mission because we now dropped our bombs on a flare signal from the lead plane in each element rather than having a bombardier in each plane. We were flying in a spare plane, a new B-17G, as our *Oh Miss Agnes* was out for engine overhaul. Our primary target was Memmingen, the second Munich. There was an abort before takeoff and

*Above top: A high-flying B-17 leaving contrails in the sky; these were sometimes so dense and persistent that crews could hardly see each other on exit from the target.*
*Above: B-17F 42-29717 Mr Five By Five in the 94th Bomb Group, in a French wheat field after being shot up on the Paris–Le Bourget mission of July 14, 1943.*

we moved up and were the low squadron lead. It was a cold day and the flak was intense and heavy over the target. Overcast at the primary [target] made us shift to the second target and a run over Munich. We were badly hit by intense flak. Oxygen and C-1 (Automatic Pilot) shot out, three of the 1,000lb bombs failed to salvo and had to be dropped manually. Four of the crewmembers were wounded. Our navigator's eyes were filled with Plexiglas. Our copilot was hit in the right leg. Our radio operator was hit by glass over the eyes. Two engines and our control system were badly damaged. Flak also hit the tail section, luckily missing our tail gunner. We lost altitude and our formation. We flew south trying to find Switzerland. We were too low in the Alps to fly on and control of the ship was getting more precarious. We tried to get rid of all extra weight. I toggled the bombs out of the plane manually and we even tried getting rid of the ball turret.

"Wiley made a beautiful wheels-up landing in a field outside the town of Sonthofen. We were all okay and tried to destroy any papers and sensitive material on board. A German Youth group captured us and for a time it looked as if they would execute our officers. This was stopped by a German Alpine troop, which took over our capture and marched us back into Sonthofen. We were beaten by the townspeople as we were marched through the town to the local jail. We found out much later that the hostility was due to a bombing of the town by the Royal Air Force the night before. Our wounds were treated at the jail and officers were separated from enlisted men. We were fed bread and water and some potatoes and meat and we slept on the cell floor all night. Late the next afternoon we were moved by truck to Kaufburen. I think the move was partly out of fear that the townspeople would attack the jail. We were put in solitary confinement and individually questioned for the first time. We were fed bread and soup. We met another crew here and on the second day we were taken from our cells and given enough rations for three days—one loaf of bread, butter, and some meat for two men. With a German sergeant and seven other guards, our two crews started a trip by train to Oberusel, our interrogation center near Frankfurt-Am-Main."

**Ralph E. Tetu, a waist gunner in Lieutenant Kasimer A. Traynelis' crew in the 452nd Bomb Group, vividly remembers having to bale out during a raid on Merseburg on December 31, 1944:**
"We took a beating from the intense flak barrage. It seemed like we were singled out. The flak was very thick and I watched others go down. I had seen a lot of flak in 18 missions and Merseburg is the most vivid. I believe that was the most flak that I had seen in a single target. We lost two engines and I believe a third was acting up. We were forced to salvo our bombs and leave the formation. Shortly after leaving the group we

were attacked by a group of enemy fighters. We were heading for Sweden when the fighters hit us. They knocked out the control cables for the tail section. The cables were hanging in the waist, an oxygen tank was blown up, and the radioman got hit as he came out to man the waist gun. Traynelis gave the order to get our 'chutes on and get out. I went over to the radioman and snapped on his 'chute. Got the first aid kit, kicked out the escape door. I tried to call the pilot to see if he could hold it a little longer

*Above: Aircrews shot down on bombing missions over Occupied Europe often relied on Resistance groups to help them avoid capture. Men were issued with silk escape maps printed on both sides, phrase books and booklets on what to do if captured, and currency and compasses. Aircrew were photographed in*

*civilian clothes for snapshots intended for use by Resistance groups, who needed them for fake identity cards. The Resistance, however, largely ignored the photos as the crewmen who posed for them were all given the same shirts and ties to wear and they would fool no one, least of all the Wehrmacht!*

but he had gone. The radioman didn't want to jump as he was hit in the right shoulder. Luckily, the bomber flipped over on its right side and he and the ball-turret gunner were both thrown out. I got thrown against the waist and went down with the plane, pinned down by the centrifugal force. I closed my eyes and prayed so that I wouldn't see the ground when I hit. Through a miracle the plane got out of the spin and I managed to bail out. I went down quite a ways before I got my 'chute open. Seconds later the bomber exploded above me. The tail section went by me as I was going down. As I got nearer the ground I could see engines and debris all over the snow. I don't know to this day how the radioman got his 'chute open."

# The Ball-Turret Gunner

"He was barely 19 years old, the youngest in the crew. I do not know how he withstood that torture . . . the rest of us had the illusion of motion, of elbow room to give us security. There was nothing that Leary could do about his fate. He was as powerless as a rivet in his ball turret."—Elmer Bendiner, *Fall of the Fortresses*

Lonely and isolated beneath the ship's belly, the 43-inch (109-cm) diameter steel ball could never be called comfortable, but for some it was the best crew position of all, even if the ball-turret gunner couldn't always take his parachute with him. Various attempts were made to eliminate the defensive blind spot below the belly of the Fortress by fitting cumbersome-looking contraptions to house a pair of .50 calibers. When the combat-worthy B-17E appeared late in 1941, a Bendix twin .50 caliber machine-gun turret just aft of the bomb bay replaced the tub-like belly machine-gun position. The gun was aimed and fired by a gunner sighting through a bubble just aft of the turret, but in combat sighting proved difficult and accuracy was haphazard at best. Midway through the B-17E production run the belly machine gun and sighting bubble was replaced by the Briggs/Sperry retractable ball turret. Hydraulically suspended inside the aft fuselage, the Sperry could be raised and lowered externally while the plane was in flight. The ball turret could only be entered from inside the Fortress once the plane was airborne by rotating the guns straight down, a maneuver that rendered the entry door accessible from inside the aircraft.

Each gun had an ammunition box, with a chute for feeding the guns and leading away the links and fired shells. The top box (maximum capacity 505 rounds) fed the left gun; the lower box (maximum capacity 425 rounds) fed the right gun. Controlled power drives gave tracing rates from 0° to 45° per second in azimuth and 0° to 30° per second in elevation. The gunner's hand controls and elevation limit stop were in a unit which regulated the amount of turret movement in azimuth or elevation. When the handgrips were released they returned to their center position. The gunner sighted his twin .50s through a Sperry gunsight located between his knees. Gun-firing switches in parallel were located at the end of each handgrip; either switch fired the guns. The gunner operated the range control using his foot. Foot pressure in the support increased the range up to 1,000 yards [914m]. Often a ball turret would be removed, and sometimes the opening would be used to house a H2X radome instead. In truth, the ball turret was not even a ball. The Perspex side panels, which completed the spherical appearance of the ball turret on the E and F models, were deleted on the G model.

Being a tail gunner was a lonely job, but at least a tail gunner could swing round so he was able to see the two waist gunners. Though some ball turrets were equipped with a very small, 3-inch [8cm] window, located above the gunner's head, and through which it was possible to see the inside of the ship, many were not.

Elmer Bendiner wrote that "while the tail usually saw more action than the belly," the only spot that was worse

Left: *Despite the privations, there was one upside to being the ball-turret gunner—if the B-17 caught fire he would know it first and get out quickly, because he could see all four engines.*

was the ball turret, "where the gunner is wrapped around his gun like an anchovy, or a fetus in a womb too small." Legend has it that the ball was the most vulnerable position of all, and that only someone small could man it. Neither was strictly true. Wilbur Richardson, a ball-turret gunner in the 94th Bomb Group (Richardson also flew tail during his combat tour) was 5ft 11in [1.8m] tall. "Most ball gunners" he recalls, "were shorter than that." Richardson commented, "To get out before landing you reversed the getting-in procedure soon after takeoff. Imagine doing this in a real hurry: point the guns straight down (putting the door inside the plane). Unlatch the door, unsnap the safety belt across your back, pull yourself up, step out, reach for your 'chute, snap it on your harness before you reached the open door (the waist gunners would be long gone). That's a bunch to do. The relief tube [which enabled the crew to urinate during missions] was in the bomb bay. If anyone used it my turret would get very neatly iced up, and I wouldn't be able to see so I kept the plane supplied with some bomb fuze cans to be used and tossed out over the target, frozen of course. I went to the boneyard and cut a relief tube with about 3ft [0.9m] of hose.

When I needed it I pushed the tube out of the clip chute with the guns straight down. Much later a relief tube was installed at the factory. I wonder if my idea was copied?"

Despite the privations, Staff Sergeant Cecil H. Scott, ball-turret gunner of the *Memphis Belle*, considered that the ball turret was "the best position on the airplane." He added, "You see a lot of action in that position, you know what's going on and you are always busy. If the plane catches on fire you know it first because you can see all four engines, and you can get out as quickly as anybody else. It isn't too uncomfortable. Of course, a big man shouldn't have the ball turret. I'm small and I get along all right. I was in it seven hours one time and didn't get very tired."

*Page right: The Briggs/Sperry ball turret, which was hydraulically suspended from inside the aft fuselage and could be raised and lowered externally in flight. It could only be entered from inside the Fortress after becoming airborne by rotating the guns straight down, which brought the entry door inside the aircraft. The Perspex side panels, which completed its spherical appearance on the E and F models, were deleted on the G model.*

## Dropping a ball turret in flight

When a B-17 was hit and had to be ditched, all guns, ammunition, and armor would be thrown overboard—and, if there was time, the ball turret would also be dropped. This was a great help on account of the weight it saved, and because it reduced the plane's wind resistance. Instructions detailing how to carry out the procedure were pasted near the ball-turret hatch in the fuselage.

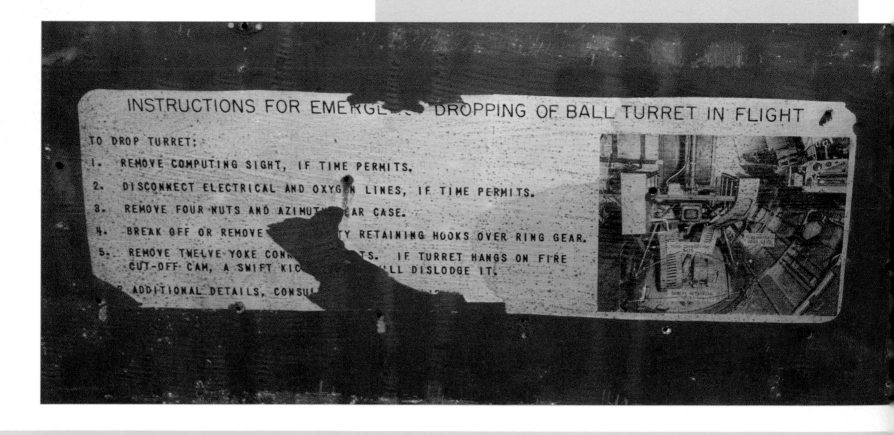

INSTRUCTIONS FOR EMERGE... DROPPING OF BALL TURRET IN FLIGHT

TO DROP TURRET:

1. REMOVE COMPUTING SIGHT, IF TIME PERMITS.
2. DISCONNECT ELECTRICAL AND OXYGEN LINES, IF TIME PERMITS.
3. REMOVE FOUR NUTS AND AZIMUT... GEAR CASE.
4. BREAK OFF OR REMOVE ... TY RETAINING HOOKS OVER RING GEAR.
5. REMOVE TWELVE YOKE CONN... TS. IF TURRET HANGS ON FIRE CUT-OFF CAM, A SWIFT KIC... LL DISLODGE IT.
... ADDITIONAL DETAILS, CONSU...

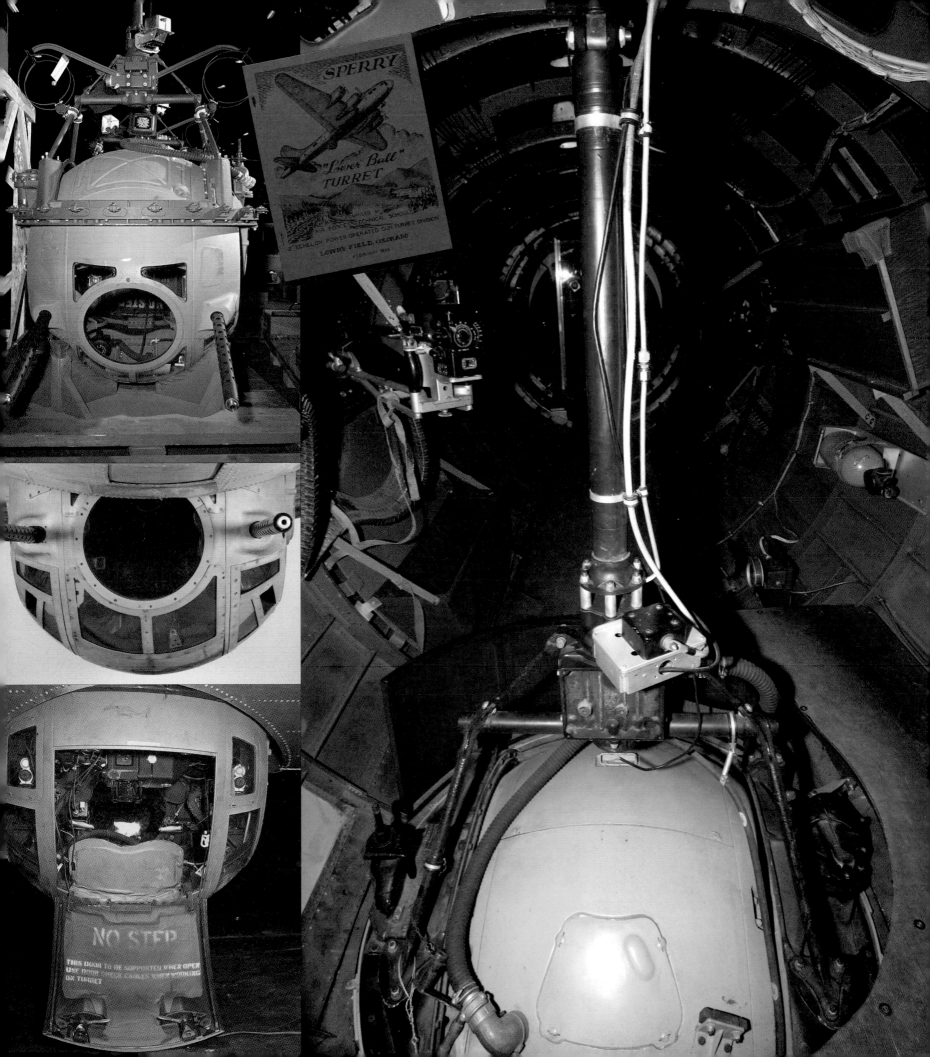

SPERRY

"Lower Ball" TURRET

2ⁿᵈ ECHELON POWER OPERATED GUN TURRET DIVISION
LOWRY FIELD, COLORADO
FEBRUARY 1943

NO STEP

THIS DOOR TO BE SUPPORTED WHEN OPEN
USE DOOR LIFTER CABLES WHEN WORKING
ON TURRET

# Flying in the "ball"

**Staff Sergeant Lee "Shorty" Gordon, an aerial gunner in the 305th Bomb Group, who flew missions in late 1942, suffered from the extremes of cold in the ball turret. On one mission his feet started to hurt "pretty bad" when they got down to 10,000ft [3,050m] because they began thawing out. Gordon remembers having to:**

" . . . take off my helmet and tear at my hair to keep from feeling the pain. My electric shoes hadn't been working. That was the fifth time I froze my feet. [Gordon was nicknamed "Shorty" because of his 5ft 2in [1.57m] frame, but what he lacked in height he made up for in guts. On December 20, 1942, Gordon filled in as ball-turret gunner on *Cunningham's Coffin* for the raid on Romilly-sur-Seine, southeast of Paris. The B-17s were met at the coastline by yellow-nosed and black-nosed FW 190s.]

*Left: It is a widespread belief that the ball was the most vulnerable position of all, and that only someone short could man it, but neither was strictly true.*
*Below right: A Sgt Flakbaite cartoon from* Short Bursts.

"THAT'S THE ONLY WAY HE CAN SHOOT—HE'S A BALL - TURRET GUN"

they were on fire because all his guns were going at once. I thought I was a gonner but I got in a quick burst and he flipped over as he went past. I tried to swing after him and get in another burst, but he was going too fast. I was damn scared at the time."

"I heard someone on the interphone yell, 'I'm hit!' and then another say, 'I'm hit!' Everyone seemed to be shot up badly so I waited for the order to bale out. This was one mission I was wearing my 'chute. I was still searching forward when I saw the No.1 engine on fire. I stepped on the interphone button but it was dead. I wondered if I shouldn't get up into the ship and tell Cunningham. It was burning on the underside and he couldn't see it. I decided to stick in the turret because there might be more fighters coming. Finally, Cunningham saw the fire through a flak hole in the wing and pulled the fire extinguisher on the engine. That stopped the fire but the prop' was windmilling out of control, and I was afraid it would tear off the engine.

"We were over the water on the way back when I suddenly remembered that I didn't have my Mae West but then I heard someone say that enemy fighters were approaching from 11 o'clock. I ran my guns to that position nearly straight ahead and waited. I could hear bullets hit our ship but I couldn't see the fighters. That was one of the worst things that could happen, hearing the other gunners fighting but not being able to help them.

*Above: The chin turret was adopted on B-17G models and on some Douglas-built F models from 70-DL on; many Fs acquired them at US and ETO modification centers. B-17F-75-DL* Gremlin's Delite *in the 381st Bomb Group was one such late model.*

"The bombardier spotted two FW 190s coming in head-on and called out the direction of the attack. I turned my turret to the front and raised my guns. Cunningham pulled up the nose so I could get at them and there was a Focke Wulf about 100ft [30m] away. His wings looked like

"I heard the bombardier calling out, 'Two enemy aircraft coming in low from 3 o'clock!' I turned and saw them and gave the first one a long burst at 800 yards [730m]. They were FW 190s. I hit the first one. Both of them saw my tracers and started to break off. Then I gave the first one another good burst at about 600 yards [549m] and saw my tracers going into his engine. He caught fire and went into a dive. I followed him for about 5,000ft [1,520m] then started searching for the other fighter.

One of the waist gunners saw the first FW 190 splash into the water. It was easy to see because we were only at 15,000ft [4,570m]. The other apparently turned back."

**"Shorty" Gordon's last mission was to Bremerhaven on February 26, 1943, in *Sad Sack*, which was piloted by Lieutenant George E. Stallman. Ralph S. Cohen, Gordon's armament and gunnery officer, was flying top turret gunner in the *Martini* crew:**

"Stallman's plane was to the right and below our plane. Going into Bremerhaven we met frontal attacks by the German fighters. During a breather I saw one fighter come in below us and to the right. He was in a firing position on Stallman's aircraft. However, he was coming in too high for 'Shorty' to fire on him. I didn't think at the time he had hit anything but on looking a few seconds later I saw Stallman's plane going down and saw a parachute break out of the ball turret. I knew then it was Stallman's plane as 'Shorty' was the only gunner I knew who could and did wear a 'chute in the ball turret. Most had to come up into the plane and snap on their 'chute and exit through the gun port window or door. I saw 'Shorty's' 'chute open but we turned north to go out some distance before turning back for England."

**Gordon had in fact rolled out of the turret, and had opened his backpack 'chute at about 24,000ft [7,300m]. He remembered:**

"The silk streamed out and I felt a terrific jerk. I had not bothered to adjust the straps. If I had not had some luck I might have slipped through my harness. The opening jolt jerked my boots right off my feet and I came down in my stockinged feet." [On landing, Gordon was taken prisoner, but escaped from PoW camp no fewer than three times. He was caught the first two times but his third attempt was a success, and in February 1944 he reached England. Gordon became the first American airman to receive the Silver Star for escaping.]

*Above: A B-17 hit in the fuel tanks by an attacking FW 190 fighter; in minutes fire will engulf the tanks and bombs, causing an explosion. With little chance of escape, survival was down to luck.*
*Left: Aircraft Mechanic's Type B-1 trousers made of lightweight seal-brown quarter inch sheep shearling and trimmed with fleece. Each leg has a horsehide tool pocket.*

# Greenhorn gunners

**Technical Sergeant Jack Kings, a waist gunner in the 388th Bomb Group, talks about the greenhorn assigned to fly the ball turret on the crew's 12th mission:**
"These men were hard to find because they had to be so small to get into the turret. Operations people were always on the lookout for replacements. (I had tried flying the ball one mission and had to take off everything but my heated underwear to get in the damn thing, and had to abandon that idea because of the cold.) Ground-type personnel who thought flying was a big deal had a chance to try their

into the oxygen outlet. This turret was operated electrically from inside. However, I could override the system from outside. If I did not hear or see the turret move every now and then I would contact him on radio.

"One of these times I got no answer so I overrode the system and cranked the turret to where I could open the hatch. The first thing I saw was the end of his oxygen hose on his mask dangling loose. At this altitude you don't last long without oxygen. I got him by the back of his jacket collar

Below left and below: *2nd Lt Francis L. Shaw's crew was shot down on April 11, 1944, flying* Battlin' Betty. *Inset (below) is a photo of ball-turret gunner John L. Hurd, made after his capture.*

Below: *The ball gunner sighted his twin fifties through a Sperry gunsight between his knees. Gun firing switches in parallel were at the end of each handgrip; either switch fired the guns.*

luck. They were given a brief flight physical, sent over to the bay, where a machine gun had been mounted on a pedestal, so they could fire out over the water at nothing just to get the feel of the gun going off. They were issued flying clothing and used as fill-in crewmembers. That is how we got this guy. He got real sick so we just put him down in the turret, and told him to hook his oxygen mask

and had him almost out of the turret when 'Goldie' Goldstein, the radio operator, got to us. To get this guy out and lay him on the deck I had to drop my oxygen hose loose, plug his hose into an outlet, then grab a walk-around bottle that would last about three minutes. His fingernails and lips had turned blue. Scared hell out of us for a second or two. 'B.J.' came on back to see how things were. We put the guy on the deck in the radio room, hooked him into oxygen and told him not to move until we got our fight over and back to base. I knew the enemy was reluctant to come at the ball turret as long as it was moving, so I lowered the guns about 30°, unlocked the gear train, and for the rest of the mission just gave it a short spin now and then. Needless to say, that 'gunner' never flew again. He had enough that day."

**Claude Campbell, a pilot in the 303rd Bomb Group, recalls a similar story:**
"This day we had a new ball-turret gunner, Peter P. Catozza, a 17-year-old boy who had been working in the armament shop. We trained him as best we could because he hadn't been through gunnery school. Over Le Mans [in France] we shot our July 4 fireworks off at the swarm of Focke Wulf 190s. Catozza fired off all his ammunition before we got to the target in his excitement. After that he naturally wanted to get out of the turret. But we made him ride it out in the ball turret the whole way because any German pilot who noticed that a turret was no longer turning would be invited to try and attack. That broke him of the habit of wasting ammunition."

down and lost altitude. I was asked to leave the ball turret and have the radio operator look at my injury. He was unable to do anything as I had too many clothes on. About this time the pilot gave the order to bale out. I hooked on my chest-type parachute and placed my GI shoes inside my 'chute harness. We were over flat country and somewhere east of Hanover. I looked out of the bomb bay and then decided to jump out of the waist door. We were somewhere between 15,000 and 18,000ft [4,570m and 5,490m]. The two waist gunners and I were waiting to jump when I heard a loud crash. The ship started to rock to the left and knocked us against the left side. I thought to myself, 'It's now or never,' so I gave a big push and all three of us went out the door. It was very noisy as I left the ship and shortly after I pulled the ripcord. The 'chute opened and then the world was quiet." [Hurd landed, injuring his ankle, and was captured. He finished the war at *Stalag Luft XVII*, Krems, Austria.]

**The ball-turret gunner could see when his ship was in trouble, and could initiate bale-out action quickly. This is what John L. Hurd, ball-turret gunner in Lieutenant Francis L. Shaw's *Battlin' Betty* (401st Bomb Group), did on April 11, 1944, when he flew his 11th mission:**
"My squadron was hit hard by flak and we lost four B-17s in this action. There were many flak bursts around our ship. From my position in the ball turret I was able to watch under the wings for fires. Immediately the No.3 and 4 engines started smoking and shortly afterward my ball turret was hit and I was injured in the right butt! Our bombs were salvoed to guard against explosion just as one of our B-17s blew up. *Battlin' Betty* finally came clear of the flak and we slowed

*Right: Page from a gunnery manual showing the specific parts and functions of the Sperry Ball turret mounted in the belly section of the B-17 Flying Fortress.*

**THE SPERRY BALL**

The Sperry Lower Ball, mounted in the belly of the B-17, is a deadly and efficient defender of the bomber's once soft underside. Its guns sweep in a full circle and offer protection from any fighter who dips below the bomber's level; its sight, the Sperry K-4, computes deflections automatically even when the gunner, swinging around below the plane, is unable to tell exactly which way he is facing.

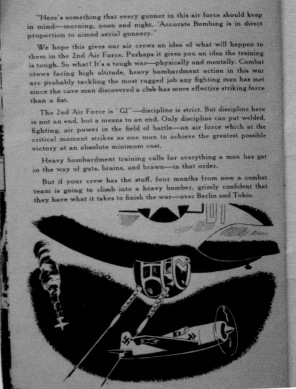

"Here's something that every gunner in this air force should keep in mind—morning, noon and night. 'Accurate Bombing is in direct proportion to aimed aerial gunnery.'

We hope this gives our air crews an idea of what will happen to them in the 2nd Air Force. Perhaps it gives you an idea the training is tough. So what! It's a tough war—physically and mentally. Combat crews facing high altitude, heavy bombardment action in this war are probably tackling the most rugged job any fighting man has met since the cave man discovered a club has more effective striking force than a fist.

The 2nd Air Force is 'GI'—discipline is strict. But discipline here is not an end, but a means to an end. Only discipline can put welded, fighting, air power in the field of battle—an air force which at the critical moment strikes as one man to achieve the greatest possible victory at an absolute minimum cost.

Heavy bombardment training calls for everything a man has got in the way of guts, brains, and brawn—in that order.

But if your crew has the stuff, four months from now a combat team is going to climb into a heavy bomber, grimly confident that they have what it takes to finish the war—over Berlin and Tokio.

# Flak So Thick You Could Walk On It

Above: *William C. Stewart (left), a ball-turret gunner in the 92nd Bomb Group.*

*Flieger Abwehr Kannonen—flak—was the crews' major problem on missions—much more so than any fighters were. In 1944, flak destroyed 3,501 US planes—600 more than met their doom by fighter opposition. Crews referred sardonically to flak so thick you could "smell it," "walk on it," and "land on it." When they became "flak happy," combat crewmen were sent on "flak leave" to the "flak house" or the "flak shack." They named their B-17s Flak Magnet, Flak Queen, Flak Eater, and Flak Dodger, to name but a few.*

For William C. Stewart, a ball-turret gunner in the 92nd Bomb Group, the flak was an unpleasantly memorable feature of his first mission, to Dresden on February 14, 1945—but on his second mission, to Berlin, on March 18, he really found out what intense flak was like:

"I turned the turret, keeping watch for enemy fighters all the way to Dresden. When we neared the IP I turned the turret facing forward and saw the black bursts of flak directly in front of us at our level. We flew to that place in the sky where the flak was heaviest and I heard the bombardier shout, 'Bombs Away!' The plane rose in the air and settled back. We had dropped our bombs on Dresden . . . We finally reached our home base and were given one shot of whiskey before eating and I felt a little light-headed afterward. The debriefing officer asked his questions and it was then that I learned, when the other crewmembers answered, that the flak was 'meager.' I thought it was worse than that but this was only my first mission. The plane didn't get hit so this may have had something to do with it. I was to learn later on what 'intense' flak really was.

"On March 18 [the date of the mission to Berlin] the day was bright and crisp; more like a Technicolor movie than real life. There were a few small wisps of white cotton clouds interspersed through the picture, but mostly it was clear. The sun glittered back from reflections of the shiny aluminum skin of the other ships in the formation. Before we reached the IP, I could see the stretch of this great city. The streets were like a checkerboard beneath us

and, once in a while, an ant-like motor vehicle appeared. The movement of the scene below was unbearably slow, and it seemed as though we were motionless. The black bursts of flak were also hanging ahead and right; at our altitude the sky was completely peppered with the stuff. As I looked ahead I said to myself, 'And we're going to have to fly through that?'

"I turned the ball turret to the right, at about 3 o'clock position and I could see the lumbering hulk of a Fortress about 4,000ft [1,220m] below us going in the opposite direction. Its nose was pointed downward with its right wing toward my left. Its right outboard engine was engulfed in red-orange flames streaking back about 10ft [3m]. I watched transfixed and uttered 'Get out, Get out!' One, two, three, and then four small white blossoms appeared. Small black puffs

Above: *German flak gunners had to lead the target by one to two miles (over two kilometers)—the interval of travel by the target until the explosive shell arrived. A slow turn by the target aircraft usually was enough to cause the flak to miss.*

*Left: B-17s flying through a box barrage. In such heavy flak bursts, flak vests provided some protection. By January 1, 1944, some 13,500 suits had been produced.*

what must have been a 105mm anti-aircraft shell through the wing. It left a hole that a man could put his head through near the inboard Tokyo gas tank. There were hundreds of smaller holes throughout the main body, wings, and tail sections but no one was hit. I had learned what accurate and intense flak was."

*The flak jacket protected the chest and back from low-velocity shrapnel and ricocheting missiles.*

appeared around one of the small white parachutes as the airman slowly floated down. The Germans were shooting at him with anti-aircraft fire. They could have used the 88mm ammunition better by going after the rest of us still flying.

"Over Berlin the ship lurched and twisted from impacts, but we kept going and finally unloaded our bombs onto a railroad station in the heart of the city. I turned my turret to about 2 o'clock and could see strips of aluminum skin peeled back from the right wing. When we landed we found we had taken

*Above: A flak vest. It consisted of over-lapping plates of 20-gauge manganese steel covered by canvas.*
*Above left: A flare is released just prior to the bomb run, and the flak onset.*

# Some mid-air battles

When on May 12, 1944, the Fortresses flew an eleven-hour round trip to Brux in Czechoslovakia, groups were under constant fighter attack for four-and-a-half hours, and ball-turret gunners like Wilbur Richardson had a ring-side seat:

"Attacks were made from 12 o'clock, [then the fighters] circled and charged from 6 o'clock level so neither ball or top turret might get a line on them. As the upper and lower turrets could fire in all directions Bruton and I were kept busy twisting and turning constantly. The navigator or the bombardier called out 'Bandits 10 o'clock low' or 'Straight in at 12 o'clock.' If I weren't shooting to the rear, assisting the tail gunner or some other direction, I'd swing forward ready to follow through coming from the nose. It was a busy time returning the fire of those fast-moving targets with winking flashes on the wings coming our way.

Above: 94th Bomb Group ball-turret gunner Wilbur Richardson, whose account of the horrific, 11-hour mission to Brux, Czechoslovakia, is given here.

"We were hit in the No.1 engine. It lost a lot of oil and we had to feather it just prior to the target. It was a struggle to keep up with the group with bombs still aboard. The flak over the target was moderate, which I almost welcomed because we had a brief respite from the fighters. We received some flak damage including the loss of some oxygen in my ball turret as well as some on the left side.

"Soon after bombs away we endured the second half of the German fighter attacks. Twin-engined fighters joined the 109s and 190s. They sat out behind the bomber boxes in groups of 10 to 20 to fire rockets and cannon just out of effective range of our .50s. With the loss of oxygen we could not remain long in our group formation, and we had to lose altitude relatively fast to make it with the oxygen we had left. Stragglers always attracted attention and on our way down 109s and 190s came at us and we received many hits. Bruton claimed one fighter and the tail and I claimed two apiece.

[By the time they got back to England, they'd been in the air for well over 11 hours]. "Because we were late and the crews at debriefing had reported seeing us go down in trouble we were listed as MIA. We returned to our barracks just in time to stop our belongings from being picked up. 061 never flew again. It became a hangar queen to keep others in the air."

Staff Sergeant Sam N. Fain, ball-turret gunner in *Lady Stardust II* (452nd Bomb Group), flown by 2nd Lieutenant Milan "Mike" Maracek, describes another mid-air pitched battle:

"I saw the FW 190s and Me 109s clearly; mean fighters to tangle with. They made frontal attacks and came in 15 at a time in a staircase formation. I picked up one in my sights and fired a five-second burst. They were firing cannon shells at us. I felt them hitting our ship and I began to sweat. I picked a FW 190 up in my sight track for one second

and opened fire. I followed him. He was going by off our left waist . . . I got him. He exploded in a ball of fire. I swung my turret to 6 o'clock and could see five of our Forts going down on fire and exploding, throwing flames around the sky. I saw seven men bale out of a Fortress. An enemy plane circled them once and came in firing at the 'chutes. They all caught fire and I could see the men falling to earth. I fired at the enemy ship for eight seconds. I saw smoke trailing from his engine and hoped that I got the rat. I looked down at the ground and saw many fires, small and and large, burning. They were enemy fighters and our Forts. Another man baled out of a Fort in front of us. His 'chute hit our propeller blades. They cut the top

out of his 'chute. I saw him falling, looking back at his flapping shroud lines. I tried to shoot him. He fell to the ground, still alive. We limped over the target. Our bombs went out. We made it . . . "

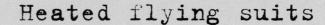

*Below: 100th Bomb Group lost a dozen B-17s on December 31, 1944; this battle-damaged Fortress also crashed, catching fire, at Thorpe Abbotts.*

*Bottom: William F. Cely, pilot, and Jabez I. Churchill inspect* Frenesi, *their badly damaged B-17G.*

# Heated flying suits

**Ellis M. Woodward, a pilot in the 493rd Bomb Group, talks about the physical endurance, as well as the courage, that his ball-turret gunner displayed:**

"Staff Sergeant Blair Archer was our ball-turret gunner, and he constantly amazed me at the way he mastered his job. The thing that was the most amazing about the ball turret was the fact that when the ball-turret gunner entered the turret, he was going to be required to spend anywhere from five to seven hours in it. The temperature inside the turret usually ranged from -40 to -60° Fahrenheit [-40 to -51°C] and during the time the gunner was in the turret, he was unable to move his legs. We almost always had to lift Sergeant Archer out of the turret, because he was unable to get out by himself. In effect, he was semi-frozen, but he always had a positive outlook."

**Wilbur Richardson also talked about the physical discomfort suffered by ball-turret gunners. He soon learned to shave close:**

"High-altitude flying necessitated an oxygen mask and facial hairs could cause a good deal of irritation. Also, it could get awfully cold. The temperature varied from -10° to -70°F [-23° to -56°C]. Because of this there was little or no food or water. Our Blue Bunny heated suits did not always work efficiently."

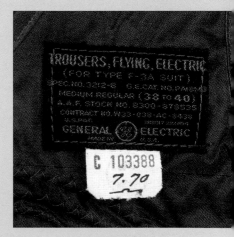

*Above: Label showing the F-3A's manufacturer's details.*
*Far left: Electrically heated one-piece flying suits developed by the General Electric Co. were standardized in 1941. The two-piece F-3A suit appeared in October 1944 and was designed to be worn over long underwear and underneath the A-15/B-11 suit. The F-3 would protect in temperatures as low as -60°F (-51°C).*

# Hit over the target

***Lucky Lady***, **piloted by Dick Noble, was one of 14 losses from the 452nd Bomb Group on a May 1944 raid to Brux, then in Czechoslovakia. Ralph J. Munn, the ball-turret gunner, recalls:**

"There was the usual amount of flak but no fighters until we were quite deep into Germany. As usual, the enemy was reluctant to attack until our P-47 and P-38 escorts [had] made the turn for home base. Until just short of target we had considerable action, mostly high-level attacks down through the squadron. When we reached the IP the flak was a solid carpet. Up to this point we had not had a casualty outside of small to fist-size holes. I had always made it a practice to turn my turret to 12 o'clock when the bomb bay doors opened. Bruce dropped a salvo, and at the same time Dick turned into the down-wind leg. We were hardly off the target when we took a direct hit in the bomb-bay area. In the meantime I had turned around to 6 o'clock to see what was happening. A fraction of a second later, there was another very bad jolt. This one knocked out my source of power, my electrical suit, boots, and gloves. I was hit in the back and the turret took considerable damage. My guns and the intercom

*Below, left to right: Bombs dropped from a 94th Bomb Group B-17G over Berlin on May 19, 1944, knocked off the left horizontal stabilizer of Lt Marion Ulysses Reid's B-17G* Miss Donna Mae *below, which went into a fatal, uncontrollable spin.*

were out. It was slippery in the turret. I was then aware that I was isolated and had no control over what was to happen next. The second hit took out the left inboard engine and the ball turret. The engine out was an invitation for the remaining fighters to attack. But I think that with the bomb-bay doors down, they assumed we were so badly damaged that they could work on a more active victim. I did not see another fighter until we reached the mountain foothills in eastern Belgium.

"By this time, Moody and Brush had manually cranked me out of my turret. I was bleeding but did not feel pain. About right here two fighters pulled up on our right wing, very close. Dick called everyone to hold their fire and prepare to jump. I later learned we were out of fuel and too damaged to make it back to the Channel. One of the men in the waist pulled the emergency lever for the exit. The door was supposed to break away with the slipstream. Two men at a time took turns and had to beat it off with ammunition boxes. The frame never did give. We managed to beat the skin off enough to get through the opening with 'chutes on. I had made a fast trip up to the bomb bay to see if we could jump from there. No way. The keel girder was torn completely in two in several spots. I could not see a hole large enough to get through without being hung up. When I arrived back at the waist Moody came over and said,

'Dick just called and to get ready to bale out.' Within a matter of minutes we all evacuated the "Not so *Lucky Lady*." Surprisingly, it was a very orderly departure, no hesitations either. All of us had had enough for that day."

**Seven days later, on May 19, 1944, Wilbur Richardson and the rest of the *Kismet*'s (94th Bomb Group) crew made their first trip to Berlin:**
"What made the trip memorable was that on the bomb run the ship above us missed us with his bomb load. One of the 1,000-pounders fell behind No.3 engine (I saw this one go by my ball turret). I quickly followed it down only to see it hit the left stabilizer of *Miss Donna Mae*, which was out of position below us. Apparently, it jammed the elevator in a down position. It lost altitude rapidly and began a steep dive. I watched in vain for 'chutes. None appeared. Others indicated that the Fort started to break up although I didn't see it."

**The July 13 mission to Munich, meanwhile, was the 30th and final mission of their tour for both Richardson and some of the rest of the crew:**
"No.30 would be remembered for just that, no matter what. [But] mine was just a bit different: I was seriously wounded over the target by 155mm flak. There was one very small hole in the wing and a very large one in my turret, and me. Just the two. *Kismet*-fate. I stayed in the turret to count the bombs away. I thought I could stick it out longer but I was losing too much blood. I reported to the pilot and he said to get out and the waist gunner could take my place as bandits were reported in the area. The radio operator and the right waist stripped off my flight clothes and new pants and shirt I had just purchased. I was treated and placed in a survival electric blanket bag. A short time later we were hit by fighters. I jumped up at the sound of shooting and grabbed the radio gun. I didn't have any intercom so I wasn't sure what the action was. I saw only one that I could shoot at from that position. After a bit I realized I had nothing but a T-shirt and shorts on and I was getting awfully cold so I hit the blanket to get warm. It was three and-a-half hours back to the base and I was still losing precious blood. We left the formation to get back to base as soon as possible. Another ship joined us as a waist gunner had an arm wound. Upon landing I was strapped on a stretcher, placed in an ambulance for a ride to an Army hospital. I didn't get back to the base for over five weeks. A nurse tossed away the large piece of flak that hit me."

**Above and top:** *S/Sgt Maynard "Snuffy" Smith MoH, a ball-turret gunner in the 306th Bomb Group, became the first EM to receive the Medal of Honor in May 1943 for his actions on May 1, his first mission. The comic strip in the Washington Sunday Star of July 25, 1943, captured his heroism.*

# The Tail Gunner

"I slipped the burning Fortress out of formation and released the bombs over Cologne before advising the crew to bale out. Eight took my advice before I dived to just 4,000ft. The flames were extinguished in the dive and I was able to land in Belgium . . . As I crawled out I noticed the tail gunner still at his post. 'Some trip wasn't it?' The tail gunner did not answer. He was dead."

—Douglas L. Johnson, pilot, 390th Bomb Group, Cologne raid, October 1944

The aesthetically pleasing but toothless "Shark-finned" Forts had no "sting in the tail"—but the lessons were learned when the "Big Ass Birds" went from "Bush League" to the "Big League." For, as RAF Fortress aircrew and US B-17 gunners early in the Pacific war found to their cost, the absence of a tail-gun position was an open invitation to enemy fighters. (As mentioned earlier, the powers-that-be were aware of the problem more or less from the beginning, but not much had happened.) Stories of US gunners cutting the tail cones off their 17s and putting in broom sticks are straight out of Hollywood, but certainly guns were added wherever and however they could be. When the B-17E was introduced, one of the innovations in the overall Fortress redesign was a crude tail-gun installation with the gunner kneeling or sitting on a bicycle seat in a glass enclosure under the rudder. As the tail gunner aboard *Tondelayo* in *Fall of the Fortresses* says, "It's a good spot for praying. You're on your knees all the time." The two .50s were fired using a ring-and-bead sight outside the window for

Left: *This remarkable view of the inside of the tail turret enclosure shows better than any words can describe just how lonely and forbidding this position must have been for the tail gunner who, apart from his intercom connection, was cut off from the other Flying Fortress crewmembers.*

sighting purposes. A larger vertical tail with a long dorsal fin was also added, and the span of the horizontal stabilizer was increased by just over nine feet (2.7m).

The B-17F and G retained the conventional tail-gun installation, but when the United Air Lines Modification Center at Cheyenne, Wyoming, completely redesigned the tail gunners' enclosure, a modified tail-gun arrangement gave the twin .50s greatly increased elevation and azimuth range. The "Cheyenne" or "Pumpkin" installation (as it was named) also improved all-round visibility by using larger windows and the ring-and-bead sight was replaced with a new reflector sight. Large wooden trays to hold 500 rounds per gun were situated on each side of the gunner. The new turret was installed during various stages of production at all three B-17G plants.

The tail gunner was an important member of the B-17 team: as well as protecting the plane from rearward attacks, he kept the pilot posted on the formation behind, and reported back on what he could see generally. In 1943, Staff Sergeant John P. Quinlan, the tail gunner on *Memphis Belle*, talked about what it was like to fight in this position: "I like being a tail gunner. It's my own private little office back there. I sit down all the time and when I get a chance I relax. I get a lot of good shots, too. The tail

## What a Life

This specially posed image of a Fortress rear gunner sighting through the ring-and-bead sight on the April 6, 1942, cover of *Life* magazine, shows the "conventional" tail-gun installation as used in the B-17F series and early B-17G series. When daylight attacks by the USAAF began in August 1942 *Luftwaffe* fighter pilots, who attacked mostly from above and behind, found that Fortress firepower was extremely effective.

gunner is in a good spot to help the pilot by telling him over the interphone what's coming up from behind. But he should be careful to call out only the ones [that is, fighters] that are attacking. If he calls everything he sees—one at 5 o'clock, one at 7 o'clock, one at 6 o'clock—he'll get the pilot so confused he won't know what's going on. He should call out only the ones that are after him. Don't be afraid to use your ammunition, but don't waste it. That is the best advice I can give. You've got to be alert all the time. You never can tell what will happen. The time they shot my guns out and hit my leg, I hadn't expected any trouble at all. I thought that mission would be a cinch. It was a short raid and we were going to dip in and pop out again. Just after bombs away, I thought I saw flak. It wasn't, it was fighters. A fighter will climb until he thinks he can give it to you, then he'll dive on you. That's what this one did. I looked up just in time to see his belly. It always gives you a funny sensation to see the big black crosses on the wings. I could hardly miss him. I got him. He burst into flames. I guess I was gloating over the one I got. Then I saw the other one. It looked like he had four blowtorches in his wings. All of a sudden, it sounded like somebody hit the tail with a sledgehammer. It got my guns and me. But the one I got the biggest bang out of was the Lorient [France] raid. The plane went up, then down. I lost equilibrium. I didn't know whether to jump or stay there, I didn't know what was going on. That was the time the horizontal stabilizer got on fire. I guess it was the wind that put it out."

*Page right, clockwise from top left: Rear view of the "conventional" tail gun enclosure, as used in the B-17F series and early B-17G series; the pre-War ring-and-bead gunsight used only on hand-held guns was replaced with a new reflector sight (top, center), which projected a sight reticule image on a transparent reflector plate, which, at infinity, moved with the gunner's eye. So, although the gunner's head might be in continual movement in turbulent conditions, the sight line and target remained together; views from the rear (top right) and side (bottom) of the "Cheyenne" (or "Pumpkin," as it was also named) installation. The Cheyenne improved all-round visibility by using larger windows. It was installed in the B-17G-90-BO (Boeing), B-17G-50-DL (Douglas), B-17G-55-VE (Lockheed Vega) and subsequent batches of the Flying Fortress.*

# Two tail-gun tales

**On April 29, 1944, Sergeant Louis J. Torretta, a tail gunner in the 447th Bomb Group, flew his 28th mission—to Berlin, in bad weather:**
"The target was the Freidrichstrasse Bahnhof, the center of the mainline and underground railway system in Berlin. The navigator that was leading us screwed up and we were 25 miles [40km] off course and separated from the rest of the formations. We thought we were just going to have flak to watch out for. We had an escort at the coast but being as we were off course the group that was supposed to relieve them could not find us, and the ones that were with us had to leave as they were getting low on gas. About five minutes later the copilot called over the interphone and said it looked like a formation of Forts up ahead. Lieutenant Irwin, our bombardier, said, 'Hell, those aren't Forts; they're 109s and 190s.' And then they came in.

"The first attack, by about 80 fighters, came from 1 o'clock high. Their first pass at us they got Donahue. He was flying No.5 in our squadron. No.2 engine caught on fire and he went down in a steep dive. No 'chutes were seen. Then they made another pass and this one came from 10 and 11 o'clock high and low. This time they knocked Hughes out of the formation and he fell behind. And about ten of them jumped him and three were seen to bale out. He dove for the clouds. He was under control and that is the last we saw or heard of them. The third attack came from 12 o'clock and 6 o'clock low and 9 and 3 o'clock level. This time they got Dowler. Then a 20mm cannon shell hit and blew up in the tail about 16 inches [40cm] behind me. I was wearing my flak suit and that is the only reason I am here to write this today. The force of the explosion and where it hit pushed me up against the armor plate with such force that it almost knocked me out. I heard the waist gunner call the pilot and say they knocked Torretta out of the tail. Then I could hear the pilot cussing. I was getting my senses back and I tried to call the pilot and tell him I was still with them and all right but my interphone had been hit and I could hear them but I couldn't answer. Finally the smoke cleared out of the tail, and I motioned to the waist gunner that I was all right and that my interphone and oxygen was shot out. I switched over to my emergency supply. The waist gunner asked if I was hit. By this time I could feel the warm blood running down my back so I motioned to him that I was hit but I did not think it was serious. A few small fragments of the exploding shell had

Left: *The crew of B-17F* Skunkface *in the 91st Bomb Group at Bassingbourn inspect the damage after their return from a raid on Bremen in late 1943.*

stuck in my back a little below where the flak suit ended. In all this we got one big hole about a yard in diameter in the tail. Also, a portion of our left wing was blown off and there were a number of small holes. I claimed one fighter destroyed as he blew up almost on top of me. (I am pretty sure he was the one that hit me.) Our crew claimed four destroyed."

**Apart from being an excellent gun position the tail gunner's station provided a convenient location for a copilot to check on formation. On June 19, 1944, it became the turn of 2nd Lieutenant Dick Johnson of the 303rd Bomb Group to man the tail turret when the Group went to the Pas de Calais [France] to bomb V-1 rocket installations:**
"Although it was considered a milk run, it was anything but that, as far as I was concerned. The lead plane in our group and others always carried a copilot in the tail-gun position to check on formation. This was because

Below: *On September 11, 1944, B-17G* Heaven Can Wait *in the 100th Bomb Group got back to Thorpe Abbotts with its tail compartment shot up and splashed with blood after S/Sgt Charles Emerson was fatally wounded in an attack by a Bf 109.*

I took off my flak helmet to use for that purpose, but managed to contain myself. It got to the point that I wouldn't have cared if I were shot down. I even contemplated taking off my oxygen mask for a while to see if that would ease the air sickness, but decided against it, since I knew that oxygen starvation was insidious, with no warning of any sort. We had periodic oxygen checks during all altitude flights and when someone didn't answer, the nearest crewmember took a walk-around oxygen bottle to check him out. For a brief moment I was resentful for having been assigned this position. It gave me new respect for our tail gunner, Carroll H. Brackey."

*Below: The "Cheyenne" or "Pumpkin" tail-gun position with the oxygen regulator, which ensured the right mix of air and oxygen. The wooden tray, left, was one of two holding 500 rounds per gun.*

*Above: Damage to a tail-gun position of a B-17F in the 305th Bomb Group at Chelveston, caused by fighter attacks.*
*Right: A "Walk-Round" oxygen bottle. It had about 15 minutes' supply, but could be recharged from the main oxygen cylinders.*

a cockpit officer could name any ship by position to tell the lead pilot who might be out of formation. Today was my turn in the barrel. When I got into the tail-gun position with electrically heated suit and gloves I was out of my element. I made out OK during formation and departure. But when I was about settled down after advising the pilot that everything seemed good about the formation, I noticed that the AFCE (Automatic Flight Control Equipment, or Autopilot), which we called 'George,' was causing a good bit of movement at my new position. The swaying and yawing soon made me airsick. Not only that, I couldn't figure out how to fire the tail guns. I tried several times, finally giving up, as I figured that no enemy plane would attack from the rear, since all I could see behind me was hundreds of B-17s as far as the eye could see. I soon developed the dry heaves. It soon got so bad that I thought that I would barf my cookies with nothing to barf in. At that point

# Cut in half

**Lieutenant George B. Reeves, a pilot in the 490th Bomb Group, remembers how, on a mission to Mainz, Germany, on September 27, 1944, it all went wrong after the bomb run had been completed. The plane survived—as did all the crew, save the tail gunner, John Volin:**

"On this particular mission everything had gone smoothly until we had just finished the bomb run. Immediately after releasing our bombs there was a very close flak burst just to the right and behind us. The plane, *Rugged But Right*, lurched from the concussion and my first indications of the seriousness of the blow was the elevator control going limp and the plane starting on a gradual decline. About the same time the tail gunner, John Volin, yelled over the intercom, 'Help! I'm hit.' I ordered the engineer, Doc Cagle, to take a walk-round bottle and go to his aid. A check with the navigator and the original flight plan indicated that in order to avoid flak we should continue to fly in an easterly direction for a short period before making a right turn to the south for a short distance, and then head westward for home. The engineer had completed his check on the tail gunner and reported that he was unconscious and showed no sign of a pulse. We made the right turn and continued on the southerly track for the appropriate time, all the while

flying through the heaviest flak I ever experienced. Finally we turned westward and eventually came out of the flak. I realized later that instead of avoiding the flak area, which was shaped like a triangle, by getting east of it, we had actually gone down the upright leg and then turned west to come back along the bottom leg. However, God was with us and we did not suffer more damage. [Back at base] John Volin was removed from the plane and it was determined that a piece of flak had severed a main artery below the heart and that he had died almost instantly. That piece of flak, the size of the end of your thumb, had gone through armor plate, a rack of .50 caliber ammunition, and lodged in John's chest. The plane had about 30 holes in it so *Rugged But Right* was truly rugged."

**Tail gunner Sergeant Byron Schlag, of the 447th Bomb Group, suffered a horrific experience on April 8, 1944, when flying his ninth mission in *Ol' Scrapiron*—after the plane was hit by flak, he found himself plummeting to earth in the severed tail:**

"We were off to bomb the marshaling yards at Holzwickede, northeast of Koblenz [Germany]. It was supposed to be a 'milk run' with meager flak

and no enemy fighter action anticipated. We had to make a second bomb run because the lead bombardier had sighted on the wrong target at the IP. After we had circled, we dropped our load from 23,000ft [7,010m] and turned to begin the trip home. It had been a quiet mission, and I hadn't noticed anything unusual until the navigator reported that we were nearing Koblenz and the Rhine River. Suddenly, out of the corner of my eye, I saw pieces of aluminum flying by, including a large panel of engine cowling. Just as I pressed the intercom button to notify the pilot, I heard our engineer say, 'Pilot, look out . . . !'

"At that instant I experienced a horrifying crash as we were hit. Just before losing consciousness I cried out, 'Lord, help me!' Then total oblivion set in. Some time and several thousand feet later, I awoke. Although quite disoriented and dazed, I knew I was alive and that I was falling, right side

*Left: USAAF field ambulances stand ready as B-17Gs of the 96th Bomb Group prepare to take off from Snetterton Heath in late 1944.*

*Below: On August 24, 1943, Kayo returned from a mission to Villacoublay; fighters had wounded the tail gunner, Sgt James Frazier, seen here being taken away on a stretcher under the flight surgeon's gaze.*

**Above:** *AN6513-1A Quick Attachable Chest (QAC)-type parachute with barrel pack. It had D-rings for attaching the pack—like the AN6513-1 with square pack—with harness snap fasteners.*
**Right:** *Parachute types included the back pack, chest type, and seat type assemblies.*

up in the tail of the bomber. I pulled off my helmet and flak suit, untangled myself from my ammo belt, and started for the escape hatch in the tail. It appeared jammed and wouldn't open. I turned toward the waist door and saw only a circle of sky! The rest of the plane was gone! I was floating down alone in the severed tail. (Another B-17 had lost a wing from a direct hit by flak and it had collided with our plane, cutting it in two just behind me.) I always kept my parachute buckled on one side and I quickly attached the loose ring to my harness, then crawled back to the edge of the opening and hung my legs over the side. Below I saw what was left of our plane going

down in a flat spin ahead of me. It soon crashed into a wooded area where the large trees stripped the wings as it impacted. I was sure my entire crew had perished, including my best friend, Eddie Shibble, who had enlisted with me. I had reservations about my 'chute's opening so I pulled the ripcord. If it popped open, it would pull me free of the fuselage. If it malfunctioned, I'd take my chances and ride the tail down. When I yanked the ripcord, the 'chute did open and pulled me out, but I was already so low that I swung up and back . . . just once . . . and quickly hit the ground."

[Schlag was captured, and sent to a PoW camp. PoWs, and crewmen who had completed their tour, at least had time to reflect upon their combat careers. Abe Dolim, who completed his second tour on March 8, 1945, and who became a member of "The Lucky Bastard Club" after flying 51 missions, is more succinct. He had lost 15lb since starting combat flying and he'd become "tense, irritable, and unfit to fly or live with . . . As for the B-17, I am not ashamed to say that in 1944–45 I regarded her as a slow, flammable old lady who was really out of sorts among fast young friends and who became my potential enemy every time I flew a combat mission. Had it not been for the long-range escort fighter, the *Luftwaffe* would have driven us from the skies over Germany."]

**Below:** *A parachute descent entitled the user to become a fully paid-up member of the Irvin Air Chute Co. of Buffalo, NY, "Caterpillar Club."*

# Down in flames

**On only his fourth (and what would turn out to be his last) mission, waist gunner Ralph J. Tomek saw a sight which horrified him:**

"Sixty fighters ripped through our formation and made decisive hits on one Fortress flying in the rear element. The tail broke off and there was only one survivor. Salvador Dalteris, the tail gunner, was fortunate enough to be in the part that broke off and managed to bale out. Later, he told me that his pilot had told everyone that day to wear their parachutes on the mission. If he hadn't he would never have made it. Our ship was the next to be picked off."

**When Lieutenant Joe Wroblewski of the 351st Bomb Group flew his second mission, to Bremen, he had several problems to contend with—not least keeping up with the rest of the formation:**

"We had a hard time keeping up in formation, being 'tail-end Charlie!' 'Tail-end Charlies' had much greater fuel consumption, and they got all the prop-wash. Only the great pilots could hold a Fortress in the 'tail-end Charlie' position all the way to the target and back . . . The chin turret on *Shady Lady II* helped to multiply our problem of trying to hang in formation in a clumsy sluggish way. As a result we used up a considerable amount of fuel changing power settings continuously. At 27,600ft [8,410m] the engines kept sputtering and gave us some trouble. Just about the time we reached enemy territory, the tail gunner's oxygen mask froze and he was without oxygen until another was brought back to him. The waist gunner froze around his eyes and the ball-turret gunner froze his fingers. We were at 27,600ft [8,410m] for three to four hours with a temperature of -67°F [-55°C]. After dropping our bomb load our gas gauges showed only a little over 100 gallons [380 liters] in each tank. We all began to sweat. But as we started our descent with low power settings, our perspiration disappeared. We had fuel to burn. Physically I was bushed.

"On another mission I watched a B-17 off to our right by itself. A Me 110 got on its tail and really poured tracers into the bomber. It caught fire and, as the flames licked around the tail, I could see the tail gunner still firing back at the Jerry. Finally, the bomber climbed straight up and fell off into a spin, burning and breaking up. At about this time many thoughts began to go through my mind. My parachute was just behind my seat and the temptation to snap it on and get the hell out of it was very strong. Right then I would have settled for being just a potato peeler, mess cook, or whatever, washing kettles for the duration. But then I thought about the other crewmembers. I don't doubt that they were just as scared as I was but at least they could shoot back. Then Saxon said, 'Lead him Henkel, lead him a little more!' The tail gunner came in with, 'I got him! I got a Me 210! The pilot's baling out!'"

**Andy J. Caroles, a bombardier in the 94th Bomb Group, had a similar experience:**

"I saw one of the 447th [Bomb Group] ships go down. It was an all-silver B-17. The entire tail of this ship from the waist back was blazing fiercely and one Me 110 was sitting on his tail not more than 200 yards [183m] out, slugging it out with the tail gunner. The tail gunner finally hit the Me 110 and it peeled off and started down smoking heavily. I watched the flames eat their way forward on the ship as it flew on in formation for one or two minutes. Then, it suddenly nosed up, fell off on its back and went straight down. No 'chutes came out of it. It was a fascinating sight, and one I'll never forget."

**Staff Sergeant Adolph J. Smetana, a tail gunner in the 351st Bomb Group, recalls an October 7, 1944, mission to the Politz oil refineries that were near Stettin:**

"Nearing the target I saw this 'boiling mass' of flak. We started to make a 360° turn and I thought, 'Thank God we don't have to fly through it.' However, I was soon to discover that another group had cut us off and we were only waiting our turn. God, it was awful. I could see planes falling from all over the sky. When the first flak burst was at our altitude I knew we had just 'bought the farm.' It was a hell of a ride through that stuff. Our group just simply dissolved. We finally got through after what

*Above: Fortresses flying through flak to their target. A tail gunner was just like his fellow gunners, who could return fire against attacking enemy fighters, but when it came to flak he had to tough it out as best he could. More than one tail gunner recalled the "boiling mass" of flak nearing the target, and of ships in their formation being hit and blazing fiercely.*

*Far left: It was not uncommon for crewmembers who survived a particularly tough trip, or who were completing their last mission of their tour, to kiss the ground in thanks on their return.*

*Above right: B-17G Blue Streak in the 834th Bomb Squadron, 486th Bomb Group, which was shot down over Merseburg on November 2, 1944. All nine crewmembers were killed. Oil targets such as Merseburg were particularly well defended, and old and new crews alike feared these missions.*

*Right: A Fortress could absorb a great deal of punishment—graphically illustrated in this picture of B-17G Dottie Jane in the 447th Bomb Group, which made it back to Rattlesden on March 6, 1944, following a direct flak hit under the floor of the radio room during a raid on Berlin. The aircraft was salvaged the following day.*

seemed an eternity. We found ourselves flying in formation with only one other plane and that was all in flames. If it had exploded we would have gone up with it. I was so scared I couldn't even tell the pilot to get the hell out of here. (We were breaking in a new officer crew that day, flying their first mission.) Finally 'Pops,' the top turret gunner, screamed over the interphone to 'get his bloody arse out of it or we would never see Polebrook [their base in England] again.' He shouted many other choice words over the interphone, but our pilot did what 'Pops' said and broke off. Out of the corner of my eye I saw cripples heading for Sweden, but mostly my eyes were focused on the flying coffin in front of us. It finally went out of control and started down. Tears welled up in my eyes and I prayed that nine spots would come out of that plane. One who didn't was our usual waist gunner, who had been with us since we had been grouped together at Ardmore AFB, Oklahoma. It was his very first mission in action."

# "Tail-end Charlie"

New crews were given the most vulnerable places in the formation, and had a way of disappearing after a few missions. "Tail-end Charlie" (or "Ass-end Charlie"), the last ship in the Group, was reckoned to be the most dangerous position after "Purple Heart Corner," the lowest and furthest-out plane of the combat formation. Ben Smith, Jr. recalls:

"We heartily resented this callous treatment; but, after winning our spurs, we were as bad as the rest, [happy to get out of that position]. Our first mission was the Heinkel plant at Oranienburg in the suburbs of Berlin. We were told that we could expect heavy fighter opposition, with flak at the target described as 'intense.' In other words, the target was heavily defended. We could see from the diagram that we were flying Tail-end Charlie in the high squadron."

New crews were not spared any of the gruesome details of combat or of their chances of survival by the "veteran crews" (those who had flown at least one mission). Neither were older members of crews spared

Left: 18th Bomb Squadron, 34th Bomb Group insignia, which once adorned a wall of a hut at Mendlesham airfield. Artwork like this featured on aircraft, the back of A-2 jackets, and on hut walls.

from practical jokes by their crewmates. Phillip R. Taylor tells how he and his partner Bill Hoots conspired to bedevil their tail gunner, Johnny Walin, who they thought "lacked a sense of humor."

"Billy and I spent an entire day making a sign and nailing it high over the door at the barracks entrance at Bassingbourn. The sign read *S/Sgt John E. Walling Jr., Esq—Fart Sack Specialist—Fart Sacks Approved and Tested Here* and it had a *Good Housekeeping* seal of approval in the lower right-hand corner. The sign was the laughing stock of the base until the group adjutant rode by, was seized with laughter, fell off his bike and tore his pinks [uniform]."

Press reports constantly feted the B-17, often singling out the effectiveness of its armament for special mention. For example, after an August 17, 1943, mission to the marshaling yards at Sotteville near Rouen, France, Sergeant Adam R. Jenkins, the tail gunner of *Bat Outa Hell*, flying "tail-end Charlie" was reported to have said, "There were eight of them in 'V' formation and the leader waggled his wings and came for us. When they were about 300 yards [275m] away I figured it

Below, left and right: *"Gunners 'Gen'"* and *"Read—For Your Safety—Heed"* information, which was painted on the wall of the 388th Bomb Group Gunners' Briefing Room at Knettishall airfield in Suffolk during the War. It survived there right up until the early 1980s.

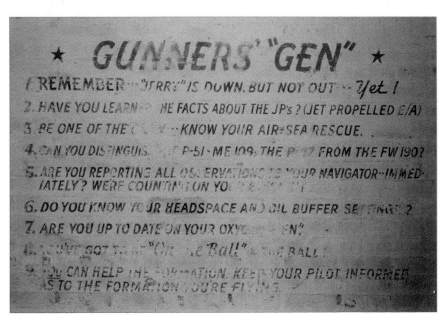

was about time for me to do something. So I pulled the trigger and it looked like the ends of his wings came off. The other seven scattered."

The reality, however, was often somewhat different from the press reports of actions. For example, Captain Howard "Pappy" Colby, a 42-year-old pilot in the 94th Bomb Group, recalled "one rough, rough mission when they were coming out of the target and doing a slow 'Purple Heart Corner.' Needless to say the fighters jumped us real bad and the top turret and the tail guns were really working overtime. After what seemed

*Left and above: Radio operator Ben Smith Jr. (left) and Chick's Crew. Standing: Lt Anthony "Chick" J. Cecchini; Lt Stan Fisher; Edward "Jasper" Veigel; Theodore McDevitt. Kneeling: Cliff "Bachy" Bachman; Clarence "Alvin" Cogdell; George Kepics; Robert J. "Chunk" O'Hearn; Ben Smith Jr.; Ward Hudson.*

about 15 minutes and a lot of damage the Germans, except for one Focke Wulf 190, left us. He wasn't giving up. He kept coming in at 6 o'clock low and then up and over. The top turret went out, and then the tail guns went out. Old 'Carrot Top'—our tail gunner—got a little excited. I called back to him and told him to get the big light we used for assembly and start blinking it when the 190 came in. Would you believe that Jerry hightailed home? Oh yes, the light had the red lens on it!"

# Lucky for some

**On March 1, 1944, 2nd Lieutenant William W. Varnedoe Jr., navigator in 2nd Lieutenant George H. Crow Jr.'s crew in the 385th Bomb Group, flew his second mission, to a railroad marshaling yard at Ulm, Germany.**

"We flew left wing off Rusecki's crew. Chuck Armbruster's crew in *Mr. Lucky* were above and to the right of us. After assembly over England, we headed out over the Channel and began to climb to our cruising altitude en route. As we approached the Belgian coast, we also reached 10,000ft [3,048m] and went on oxygen. There was a cloud deck just below the Group. It was mostly flat and smooth on top, except that there were occasional humps of cloud here and there. Just as we reached the Belgian coast, Rusecki passed into one of these humps and came up out of it in a steep climb just over us and into Armbruster's Fort. *Mr. Lucky* was contacted by Nos. 1 and 2 engines of Rusecki's B-17, which cut into *Mr. Lucky* about the rear of the radio room. Rusecki slid back, chewing up the waist section of Armbruster's plane, which was now in two separate pieces. I lost sight of Rusecki's Fort and the tail of *Mr. Lucky*, as I focused on the front half which was sliding to the left and dropping and was now mighty close to us on our level. I could clearly see Armbruster, looking back over his left shoulder, trying to see what was happening. As he continued to slide toward us, Crow pulled us left, out of formation, or there would have been three planes in the collision. Armbruster's front half went into a flat spin and disappeared into the clouds, so near below. We then edged back into the lead slot, where Rusecki had been moments before. It was very eerie seeing all that metal ripping apart only yards away, but without making a sound as if in a silent movie. The constant, deafening roar of our own engines drowned out everything. Another lasting image was the sight of the radio operator falling out of Armbruster's plane—without his parachute. The whole thing was over in less than 15 seconds.

"Crewmembers generally wore a parachute harness, but not the 'chute itself. These chest packs had clips which could be quickly attached to our harness. However, after this incident, and seeing that tumbling crewman, several of us wore our parachutes all the time while in the air, cumbersome or not. We later learned that there were only two survivors: the waist gunner of Rusecki's crew, who baled out, and the tail gunner of Armbruster's crew. Joe Jones was on his 22nd mission as tail gunner in *Mr. Lucky* with Armbruster's crew when he knew something was terribly wrong. The intercom was dead and there was no contact with the rest of the crew, but the aircraft was making some violent maneuvers. He tried to bale out his tail hatch, but it was jammed shut; he tried to go to the waist, but twisted metal blocked the way, so he sat back down in the tail. Joe remembered a new technique some airplanes were experimenting with, namely, using a drogue parachute as a brake. So he popped his 'chute and tried to stuff it out of a broken window, but the air rushing by was too strong and this came to naught. In the end, he says he just sat down and had a smoke, waiting. Six days later he woke up in a British hospital!

"The tail of *Mr. Lucky* had landed in a cow pasture on a farm near Slijpe, Belgium. A local ferryboat steward, beached by the War, named Gilbert Deschepper, found him, cut him out of the tail with an ax and, evading German sympathizers, took him to that British hospital.

*Above and opposite: AN6513-1A QAC barrel-type parachute pack. Type QAC and Type A assemblies were attached to the harness by snap fasteners and bayonet fasteners respectively. Left: Lady Liberty of the 305th Bomb Group going down on August 18, 1943. Eight of the crew were killed.*

Crewmembers generally wore a parachute harness but not the 'chute itself. The chest packs had clips which could be quickly attached to the harness.

Above: Mr. Lucky *in the 385th Bomb Group was lost on March 1, 1944, on a mission to a railroad marshaling yard at Ulm. Over Belgium* Mr. Lucky *collided with another B-17 whose propellers sliced into the plane.* Right: *S/Sgt Joe Jones was on his 22nd mission as tail gunner in* Mr. Lucky *on March 1, 1944. He was the sole survivor.*

He fully recovered. No one knows to this day why that Fortress came up abruptly like that. It is speculated that the cloud hump may have had an updraft or perhaps Rusecki, flying formation, concentrating on the plane he was flying off of didn't see the cloud coming, then, suddenly losing visibility, got vertigo. We'll never know. Some of the debris struck the Fort in the low diamond and it dove straight down to nearly the water. But, although there were oxygen leaks, two guns out of commission and the rudder jammed, it rejoined the formation and finished the mission."

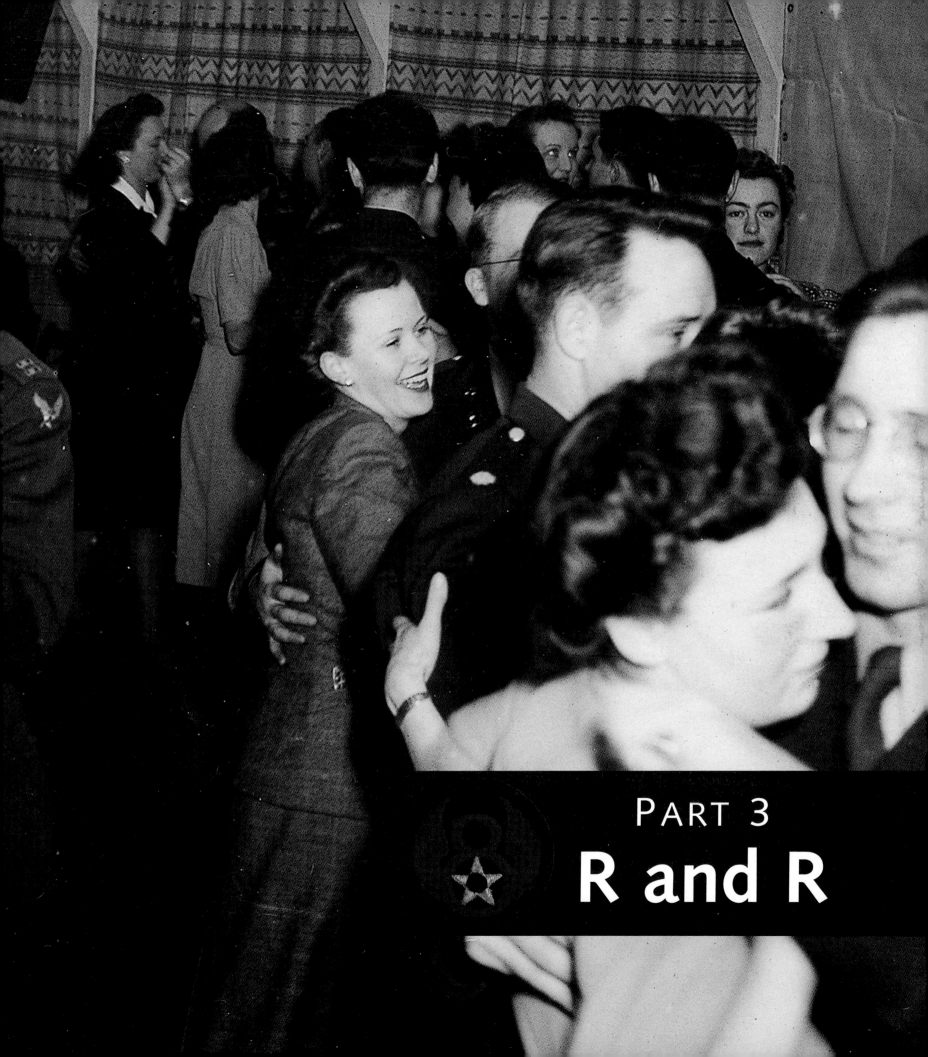

PART 3
# R and R

# Rest and Recreation

**W**hen they were not flying, combat crewmen tried to enjoy themselves on their base or in the nearby towns and villages and, if they were really lucky, they would get a three-day pass and go to London. On base there were clubs for the officers and enlisted men alike, while sergeants with the rank of staff sergeant upward had the Rocker Club, a name taken from the half circle in the sergeants' stripes, or "rocker," on their arms. Slot machines and cold beer were perennial favorites, while the library and chapel provided other forms of recreation. Many combat crewmen managed to purchase second-hand bicycles, which made for a pleasant "pubbing mission" to town, where they were always welcomed by the British people. These were happy times, when they could forget about the

other side of life—facing the enemy five miles high over Germany, often in freezing temperatures. As one combat crewman put it, "Living the good life in England, and then suddenly being in another world facing death was a paradox, to say the least."

Most found England's fog and rain very hard to get used to. Walking around in the blackout was a new experience, too—for blackouts made it difficult to navigate at night with no lights. But despite these drawbacks Paul Arbon, lead navigator of *Virgin on the Verge* in

*Above, center: "Pubbing missions" were a favorite pastime for GIs—even if the beer was "weak and warm." Left: On base there were clubs for the officers and enlisted men alike. Slot machines and cold beer were perennial favorites, while the library and chapel provided comfort of a different order.*

the 388th Bomb Group, commented that "We had money, glamor, and a devil-may-care attitude which came from knowing that every day might be our last."

Money was always a problem. The GIs were paid much more than their British counterparts but they had difficulty understanding English "funny money." Lieutenant Abe Dolim had soon learned to play darts and drink Guinness Irish beer—but learning about the "God-awful British money system" was another thing. "However did they get screwed up with pounds, shillings, and pence? We looked at a pound note the size of our dollar but it was worth four of our bucks." Staff Sergeant William Y. "Bill" Ligon Jr., a B-17 gunner in the 385th Bomb Group at Great Ashfield, Suffolk, in a letter home wrote about the "post-pay day" crap game. "Money means nothing to these guys. A pound is $4.03 but since it's a single piece of paper, it's treated the same as a dollar bill, especially in a crap game. Consequently, 'small fortunes' change hands overnight. But the boys have to relax some way. They are all, to some extent, 'flak-happy . . . '"

Romantics such as John S. Sloan at Podington looked to the England of his schoolbooks, of King Arthur, and Robin Hood, and Cromwell, and saw his time abroad as the beginning of a great adventure: "Morale was buoyed up by an excitement that neither mud nor minor discomforts could dispel." At Molesworth Ben Smith recalled, "The villagers near the air bases quickly adopted the American fliers as their own. These picturesque villages with thatch-roofed cottages were a delight to me. I was fond of the dignified, sturdy villagers, who were

**OFFICER'S PAY**

Edward K. Wilcox
  (Name)        (Serial number)
Over___0___years' service ___1st___ pa
_____, 19___.
Monthly base pay and longevity _____
Additional pay for __Flying_____
Rental allowances_____
Subsistence_____
Date __12 July /44__
Dependents (state names and address
    __Mary A. Wilcox__
  __Ascension St. Pass__
Evidence of dependency (mother) filed
_____, 19___.
Accounts of_____
Allotments, class E, $__100.00__
Insurance, class D, $_____
Pay reservations, class B $ ___18__
Other deductions, $_____
Subsequent changes in above data wit___

_____
_____
_____
Changes affecting pay will be entered be
W. D., A. G. O. Form No. 77
March 26, 1942

friendly and hospitable once I learned a few 'ice breakers' . . . The Yanks visited in their homes, shops, and churches and became a part of village life. Each day the villagers anxiously awaited the return of the mission in the afternoons, counting the planes in the formation just as we did. Our base was in a lovely section of England . . . the countryside was unbelievably green and rolling. Many stately groves of trees ringed the base and I was fond of taking long walks and bicycle rides in the countryside. Somehow, I had the feeling that I had been here in another life. I knew that my roots were here—that my people had all come from England in earlier times. Anyone with a passion for literature could not help being in love with this lovely pastoral land. Beginning with *Mother Goose*, this land had shaped my life from childhood on. I knew it intimately from my books. So I bicycled constantly over hill and down dale, rejoicing in the lush greenery of Huntingdonshire. The War seemed far away."

"How they roamed the local villages, looking for the rural pubs, which they very much enjoyed," recalled one local. "They bought anything that looked like a bicycle and learned to ride. I remember them coming from the pub riding single file, wobbling all over the road and shouting at each other, so it was quite easy to know they were coming." East Anglia was well endowed with historic old inns. GIs liked the public houses and many grew to like the seeming timelessness of everything. They tried the mild beer. It was weak, watery, and warm. "Haven't you anything stronger?" they asked. Ben Smith was quite taken with the country inns and pubs and he "never intentionally passed one by . . . These were venerable institutions, nothing like saloons. They were homey places, family-oriented. Misbehavior was not

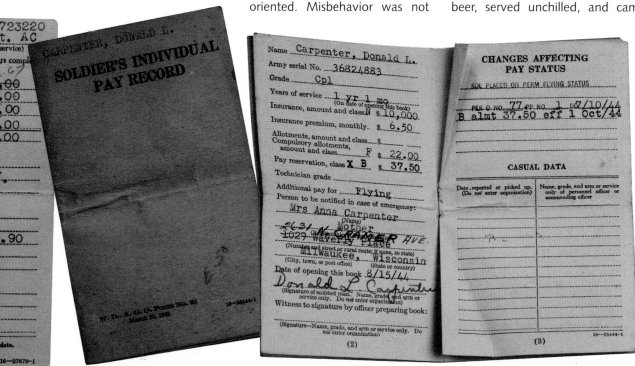

Below: *GIs were much better paid than their British counterparts but they had difficulty understanding English "funny money." A pound was worth $4.03 but was treated the same as a dollar bill.*

Above: *GIs helping with the harvest near Thurleigh, Bedfordshire, in 1943. The "Yanks," as they were universally known, did not all come from big cities: many were from rural areas.*

tolerated in them. I eventually learned to appreciate the English ale and beer, served unchilled, and came to prefer them to the American, probably because they were much more potent. Their lager was phenomenally good. All of it had much more of a malt taste than our own. There was always a plink-plank piano and the Limeys and Yanks liked to gather around it and sing the old World War I songs: *Long, Long Trail, Tipperary,* and *Pack Up Your Troubles. Roll Out the Barrel* was a standard but the most popular of all was *Roll Me Over in the Clover.* At least three or four times an evening there would be bawdy renditions of it. The Yanks were as fond of it as the British. These were the best times of all to me. I loved to sing and I loved to drink."

On train rides to London GIs could view the quaint beauty of the small towns and rural country-side of England, though many of the traveling "Yanks" thought that the deep-green hedgerows, rolling fields and slow-flowing streams of East Anglia were like scenes out of 18th-century pastoral paintings. Others, like Jim Johnson, were confused. "It was November 1943 and a very foggy night. The occasion was one of my first visits to London and we were returning on the train. The word 'Bovril' appeared at one of the stations. Nothing else was on the sign. Another GI said to me, 'It's a bad fog, really bad, he's going round in a circle. We've been through Bovril twice before!' We did not know, being foreigners, that Bovril was a drink!"

The British music-hall joke was that "Yanks" were "Over fed, Overpaid, Oversexed and Over here." Some British

that some let go, specially when "everything" seemed to be available for the buying, asking, or taking. Boasting seemed to be a popular pastime. Meanwhile the British—particularly the teenage girls and young women—believed that America really was how it was depicted in the movies and magazines. In their well-cut greens and pinks (uniforms) the airmen did indeed seem like movie stars, not least because the average GI usually had money to spend on chocolates, flowers, and stockings, or even a silk parachute, which could be used to make underwear. The airmen were kind, too, distributing ice cream, peanut butter, and chewing gum. A child's favorite question was "Any gum, chum?" The humorous response was often "Got a sister, mister?" At Christmas the airmen were particularly generous. One English teenage girl recalled, "They gave local children lovely

*Above left and right: ETO Christmas card and a program of events for a 100th mission first anniversary party. Although the beer was free, the "Programme" reminds the men to bring their own cups!*

truly believed that the "Four Overs" were justified in many cases, forgetting that many of the US airmen had entered the service straight out of school or college. They might never have had a paying job before. Suddenly, they were better fed and better paid than ever before. Freed from the constraints of family, church, and friends, it is unsurprising

Christmas parties and played Santa for them. They had things we didn't because everything was rationed. They gave us ice cream and peanut butter. I had never had peanut butter before."

English civilians met their American cousins both off-base, and at on-base parties, and many lasting relationships

*Above and left: Americans took the British children to their hearts, especially at Christmas parties on the bases (above); local people were also invited when bomber groups celebrated reaching the 100- or 200-mission mark (left).*

were formed as a result. At one base party, a GI was reputed to have met a WAAF [a member of Britain's Women's Auxiliary Air Force] one evening at 6pm, and to have proposed and had his proposal accepted by 9pm. There were many reasons for holding the base parties—each time a group completed 100 or 200 missions they were stood down for one or two days respectively to celebrate, and everyone for miles around was usually invited. Girls were brought in from town in a bus, or fleet of buses. One

American Red Cross Club girl who was sent out to recruit girls for a group's 200th mission party, was surprised by one stern WREN [Women's Royal Navy] officer's refusal to allow her charges to attend. "Didn't the girls have a good time at the 100th mission party?" she asked. "I guess they did. She said it was several days before she got them back!" After a Saturday night party more than one base put up signs on the Monday saying that all women "will positively be off the base by Thursday."

Bill Ligon wrote home about one such base party, "Well, the big party comes off tomorrow, Glenn Miller, etc. There will be 1,500 girls here from somewhere. Should be quite a spree." And a few days later, "The big party went off all OK I guess. Glenn Miller played all the good music he's ever put on records—Doolittle was here. They had a big dance that lasted till 2:00 AM . . . We had ice cream in the mess hall. The second time since I've been over here."

An English girl who lived on one of the farms on the base at Framlingham (Parham) was invited to the big party held to celebrate the 100th Mission. She described the spectacular scene: "Hangar Number 2 was beautifully decorated with bracken, with bales of straw around the side to sit on and a great many blue lights. There were thousands of

persons there from neighboring villages, British service girls, and American WACs. Glenn Miller's band played for the dance. The 200th Mission party was held on Sunday, October 8 with civilians again invited to attend. The afternoon began with a religious service, followed by a football match and then an open-air performance by a variety show from London. In the evening there were four dances to choose from—at the officers' club, the Rocker Club, the combat mess, and the Red Cross. When the 300th Mission party was held, the hangar was again lavishly decorated, this time with different-colored parachutes hanging from the roof. There were thousands of persons invited again; the entertainment consisted of variety shows and dancing and we ate with the boys in their mess halls."

Food and drink being plentiful, the parties were always well-attended by British people trying to get by on their rations. American servicemen were generally unaware of the food shortages. A B-17 pilot and his bombardier who visited Clacton-on-Sea, a resort on the east coast, saw a queue about a block long and asked what it was for. They were told that ice cream was being sold and so the airmen excitedly got in line. When they noticed that most of the people in the line were children, they reasoned that many of them had probably never tasted ice cream, so they quietly stepped aside. Ice and ice cream were popular on base and test flights were discreetly scheduled on the days of major parties to insure

*Left and below: There was always a full house when the Glenn Miller orchestra played on the bases. American officers danced the night away with their English girlfriends, and many lasting relationships were formed.*

that there were sufficient quantities of both. Ice for the Officers' Club bar and ice cream for the kids was made by taking a B-17 to 30,000ft (9km) with containers of water and ice cream sitting in the waist area. Ice formed quickly, and ice-cold drinks and ice cream could be served back at base.

*Right, below, and below center: There were no fewer than 17 Red Cross clubs around London; their main headquarters, Rainbow Corner, was just off Piccadilly Circus (below center). These hotels for the US military provided clean, safe havens from the London blackout, where free coffee and donuts were served all day and night.*

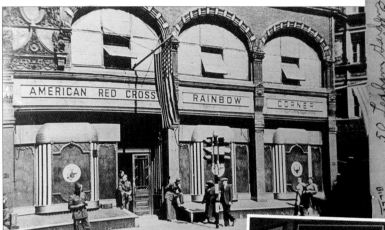

USO shows starring Hollywood movie actors and entertainers like the Bob Hope Special Services Show with Frances Langford, Jerry Colonna, and Jack Pepper (their guitarist), were very popular. But the War was never far away. One teenage girl who visited Great Ashfield to listen to Glenn Miller's band playing in the hangar met an American flier and they danced to all the big hits. The next week she did not see the young man around so she asked one his buddies where he was: "'Oh, he went off on a mission and didn't come back', he said. It was very sad." Sometimes airmen paid another price. Abe Dolim recalls the occasion when word got around that the group dances could be canceled due to "abuse of privileges by certain unprincipled individuals. For instance, a certain squadron was quarantined because of an unusually high increase in the VD rate suspiciously soon after the last group dance party. Rumor had it a small group of renegades had stashed a blonde and a redhead in one of the Nissens for nearly a week and that the girls were responsible for all the trouble. This was clearly a violation of military procedures. However, it was true that some of the girls were of questionable background and that it was difficult to arrange transportation for others who lived at great distances. Certainly, bad weather did occasion delays of a day or two—at times—and of course accommodations were scarce . . . "

All officers and men on each base were required to attend at least one lecture every year on the dangers of casual sexual behavior. The doctor would explain how to use a prophylactic to avoid VD, then the chaplain would talk about the moral dangers of "loose" behavior, stressing the men's obligations to church, country and, especially, their wives (or sweethearts) back home. Father Joe Collins, who was based at Rougham with the 94th Bomb Group, remembered these lectures as being, on occasion, surprisingly effective: "One squadron CO told me that some of his men, after attending [one of them], even canceled their London passes."

Despite the lectures, a visit to London or further afield was, for most, an eagerly anticipated occasion. It not only boosted the men's morale; it gave them another aim in life. American airmen returning to their bases in East Anglia from 48-hour passes in London normally had tales of debauchery or of sightseeing to tell. August Bolino, a navigator in the 388th Bomb Group, recalls, "Once a month we were given a two- or three-day pass to London. And this was an interesting episode, because London was blacked out and was constantly being bombed. We did get to see Piccadilly and a bunch of other sights, although I must admit I wasn't in London looking for the sightseeing. We would look for bars and good food and we would have tea at the Ritz where we could dance. It was just getting away—from the bombing and planes going down and from that kind of stuff."

Usually the talk was of "Piccadilly Commandos," that army of prostitutes that thronged Leicester Square, of Soho theaters and their burlesque shows (complete with corny gags, and good-looking girls—some of them naked). Abe Dolim recalled an occasion near Hyde Park when two aircrew officers were walking back to their hotel. "As the officers approached a building entryway, they heard a loud, unmistakably Yank voice say, 'Five pounds! Whattayagot, a diamond-studded snatch?'" Aircrew who could afford it stayed at the Strand Palace and the Savoy hotels. Others made their way to American Red Cross clubs. These hotels for the US military were clean and tidy,

and they served free coffee and donuts all day and night. There were 17 Red Cross clubs scattered around London and their main headquarters, Rainbow Corner, was just off Piccadilly Circus. The Jules Officers' Club on Jermyn Street near Piccadilly was where most of the "action" was. Lalli Coppinger, a volunteer Red Cross hostess, wrote, "The Washington Club was smaller, cosier, more intimate than Rainbow Corner. Homesick Yanks could sit on a couch in a fairly quiet lobby and write letters home, get a room for about the equivalent of two dollars, eat in the cafeteria, dance up a storm to a good band and maybe meet a nice girl who wouldn't steal their wallet. The girls were screened. I was one of them for about two years. I learned a lot about the young American male, far from home, 1940s type. They weren't the kind that we English girls had become familiar with through American movies. Sure, they were from big cities, some were sophisticated, but they were also from every small town and hamlet in the US. Their average age was 19–23. I met a few who were even younger than 19—they'd lied about their age. And there were many who had never tasted hard liquor or smoked and who had little or no adult sexual experience. At the most vulnerable time of their lives, with adrenaline pumping, raging hormones and all, they were let loose in London—at that period the largest city in the world—with just about every temptation known to man available to them. London was renowned for its wide variety of entertainments, as many an unsuspecting GI found out, not always to his advantage. But they learned fast and these were the men who frequented the Red Cross Clubs, the 'safe havens' from the blackout!"

One time Wilbur Richardson was in London by himself looking for a good place to eat. "I went into one of the major hotels. As I went by the doors there were a couple of our MPs [Military Policemen] walking up and down the street. I sat down and was about to order when a waiter comes over and says, 'There's an MP who would like you to join him.' Well the first thing I thought of was the two MPs I'd seen out there, so I said I don't want anything to do with MPs, and if they want they can come and talk to me. The waiter went away, and I had my meal and then left the hotel. I got to wondering why an MP should want me. It was only later that someone suggested that the MP was a British Member of Parliament."

Above: The officers and men were continually reminded about the importance of using prophylatics—including on matchbook covers, as here.

Right: Once a month men were given a two- or three-day pass to London where they would look for bars and good food before returning to their bases, normally with tales of debauchery or of sightseeing to tell. For many, London was their last leave—and they lived it to the full.

# "Overpaid, Over Sexed, And Over Here"

**Dan M Bloyd remembers the thrill of anticipation when a three-day leave in London came up:**

"The crew had three days off and we all traveled together to London. An Army 6x6 took us to the train station in Bury St. Edmunds, the closest station to the Base. It was a typical English train. The doors to each compartment, which could seat eight to ten, opened from the side. It had a coal-fired engine so smoke and soot were still a problem. The train ride was uneventful but there was pleasant rural scenery to watch until we approached London.

"We officers checked into a nice hotel while the enlisted men all elected to stay at the American Red Cross billet. It was located in a large building just off of Piccadilly Circus. The first order of business was to find a good restaurant that did not look like a mess hall. We did, but in a way, it was a disappointment. The shortage of food was evident by the selections on the

FOR U.S. ARMED FORCES IN U.K.

*London*

" Millions of Londoners, through us, extend to all members of the American Forces very cordial greetings.

" Many of our people have had the pleasure of meeting you personally. We want you to know that we are delighted to see you, that we have very warm feelings in our hearts for you, and are ready and anxious to do all we can to make your stay in our country enjoyable.

" We wish each and all of you the best of luck, with the sincere hope that you will take with you, wherever you go, the happiest memories of London and its people."

LORD MAYOR OF LONDON

CHAIRMAN OF THE LONDON COUNTY COUNCIL

menu. Forget the sizzling steaks but the food was well prepared and tasty and a change from the mess hall.

"London was a fascinating city to a kid off a Kansas farm. It was huge, busy, and dark. The black taxis with the driver sitting outside were everywhere. Incredibly, they had a very short turning radius and could make a U-turn almost anywhere. They, along with the double-decked buses, generally had the streets to themselves, except for the military vehicles. Few private autos were seen.

"London was much more than just historic sights. Joe was from Baltimore and he enjoyed going to see vaudeville shows. One afternoon we attended a

**Above:** *An English volunteer Red Cross girl serving coffee and all-American food in the Rainbow Corner dining area.*

**Above right:** *Booklets on all Britain's major towns and cities, giving details of sights and places to stay, were produced for US personnel.*

performance at the famous 'Windmill'. 'We never closed' was their motto, referring to their staying open all through the Blitz. While waiting in line to get in I was amazed at the sidewalk entertainers. There were Cockneys with their coats covered with buttons working the crowds and speaking a dialect that was almost impossible to understand; young girls selling flowers; mimes and street performers with their colorful costumes. War seemed a long way away. It was a different world from anything I had known. It was also my first introduction to live theater. The music was lively, the comedians were corny and we forgot why we were in England. There were three or four nude young ladies on the stage for almost

*Cards on this page: A visit to London or further afield was looked forward to. The city really came to life at night and clubs and pubs were ever-popular.*
*Below: Two English girls, plus admirers, join in the celebrations on VE Day. Piccadilly Circus was notorious for its prostitutes—or "Piccadilly Commandos."*

every number. It seemed that women could appear nude on the stage as long as they didn't move.

"The Officers' Mess at Grosvenor Square was the best place to eat but it was segregated by rank . . . Anyway, the food was good, plentiful and the price was right. After-hours clubs flourished. For the equivalent of $2.00, you could join a club for the evening. There was usually a band with a singer and, most importantly, mixed drinks could be purchased. There was a shortage of men in London, so opportunities to meet members of the opposite sex were always possible.

"Three days in London wasn't very long but it was an unforgettable experience; then it was back to the Base, and on with the War."

Above: *The Eagle Public House in Benet Street, Cambridge—a favorite watering hole of US and Allied airmen. "Smoked" on the ceiling are the names and numbers of US bomb groups and RAF squadrons.*

Above: *458th Bomb Group men relax in the crew room at Horsham St. Faith in 1944.* Right: *USAAF personnel often spent a 72-hour pass in Cambridge—it offered sightseeing and pretty girls, but didn't involve a long train ride.*

I guess the place will really come to life at night then. But it's by no means dead at night now. But there's nothing blacker than a London blackout . . . The war news continues to look good. You asked in the last letter if I was flying on missions—yes, I am. I can't say how many, but I have to fly 35 before I can come home, unless of course I get home when the European War is over—and I expect it to be before I get 35 missions."

For many, London was their last leave and they lived it to the full. Bill Ligon never got his 35 missions in. Two days after writing his last letter home the 22-year-old was killed in action on a mission to Berlin.

Now and again crews ventured to other cities. Some spent a 72-hour pass in Cambridge. Others didn't know what inspired them to go to the university town. As one of them said, "It was unlikely that they were thinking of our higher education there after the War was over. Again, more sightseeing, visiting the university, some good eating and pretty girls." August Bolino recalls, "We were in a hotel in London one time and a wing of that hotel was hit by a flying bomb. It scared the hell out of us and in fact, after that, I decided I would rather go to Cambridge. Both because it was a university town and didn't involve a long train ride, and also because I didn't see any sense in going to London and risking being bombed. We usually wound up at Dorothy's, a dance hall on the second floor of an old building in Cambridge."

Bill Ligon loved London. He would write and tell his folks all about it: "What a place! Stayed in the nicest hotel in Piccadilly. I don't know how they charge so little. In England they serve breakfast at no extra cost in all the hotels. For two days in a swell room and breakfast, $7.60, or $3.80 apiece. And if you put your shoes outside the door at night they pick them up and shine them—no charge. Of course, some things are very expensive though . . . As a nation, the United States is sometimes called a melting pot. I can tell you now that as a city London is every bit as much a melting pot as the US. And there is no racial trouble in London. I've seen more races here than anywhere in America. I could spend six months in London and find something of interest or mystery, something still new to me . . . I guess you heard about the lifting of the blackout soon.

But after a time Cambridge and even London ceased to excite most people. Aircrews tended to be more interested in finishing their tours and going home. With missions coming so hot and so fast for those who survived them, "R & R" (Rest and Recreation), or furlough, as it was known, was inextricably linked to the combat tour. Leaves were often issued upon the completion of 10–15 missions. Late in the War a policy was adopted whereby 30 days (later 45) TDY (Temporary Duty) in the US would be given to qualified personnel who agreed to return to the theater for another year or fly another combat tour.

Left: A prized "Lucky Bastard" certificate, which was "awarded" to combat crews who survived a 25-, 30- or 35-mission tour. This one belongs to Fred "Pappy" Daiger, who completed 20 combat missions in the 100th Bomb Group.

92nd Bomb Group, recalls: "We had four officer crews in one Nissen hut. The night before a mission I would go over to the barracks and write letters and get some early sleep because you never knew when you would be alerted to fly a mission the next day. One night one of the officer crews packed all their belongings. It made me wonder what insight they must have had when they knew they would not survive the next

As early as 1942 the 8th Air Force had recognized that the morale of combat crew personnel in the ETO was "not all that it should be to obtain the maximum efficiency in operational missions." Flight Surgeons discovered that the absence of a fixed, limited tour of combat missions contributed to crewmembers' anxiety or emotional breakdown. Signs of "combat fatigue" were not just obvious to trained medical minds. Fellow airmen, too, were quick to spot those who were becoming "flak happy," as it was universally known, as Captain Franklin "Pappy" Colby, a Squadron Commander in the 94th Bomb Group, recalls: "The nervous strain of continuous raids was more than some of them could take. Some of the boys were developing the equivalent of 'shell shock.' It raised the very rough command problem as to how long these lads would still be fit to fly a combat mission, especially the pilots whose nine-man crews were trusting him with their lives." John A. Holden, a navigator in the 452nd Bomb Group, recalls that "The crew that we resided with were on their 28th or 29th mission and they were all crazy. One in particular would wake up in the middle of the night and shoot his .45 off at mice. A .45 reverberates and makes quite a bit of noise and disturbs your sleep!" Larry Goldstein, a radio operator in the 388th Bomb Group, saw "many men who absolutely refused to fly another mission after seeing their buddies go down on a raid or be victims of mid-air collisions." One B-17 pilot claimed that he only got through his missions "by smoking 60 cigarettes and drinking a bottle of whiskey each day." Some men just gave up and took the first opportunity to take an easy way out, as Bill Rose, a pilot in the

mission. Sure enough, the next day they went down. We had another crew who went on a bombing mission to southern Germany. After bombing the target we turned around and came home, but this crew took off for Switzerland. When we got back I checked their clothes in the hut. Everything was there except for their Class A uniforms, which they had worn on the raid to prove their identity. They had just given up fighting . . . The squadron flight surgeon drank with us and palled around with us but kept a very watchful eye on us. He knew what shape we were in, how many combat missions we had flown and what the crew situation was. He was the one who dispensed the pills. In February–March 1944, I was on pills to put me to sleep and on the morning of a mission I was on pills to wake me up and get me going. Sleeping at night became so bad that we started taking pills from our escape kits."

Above: "Lucky Bastard Club" members' names in the 452nd Bomb Group displayed on a hut wall at Deopham Green, Norfolk, could still be seen in the 1970s, when this photograph was made.

When combat fatigue was diagnosed the flight surgeons would recommend that those crewmembers who were affected should be sent to enlisted men's and officers' "rest homes" in quiet backwaters in southern England, which had been established on the recommendation of the 8th Air Force Surgeon. Members of the combat crews were sent to the "Flak Homes" or "Flak Shacks," as they were known colloquially, free of transportation charges, for an average period of seven days' rest and recreation, with a daily allowance. At first the Air Force ran these rest homes alone. After two had been established, a large part of the responsibility was transferred to the American Red Cross, so as to make them as un-military as possible. Howard E. Hernan, an air gunner, recalls that after the Schweinfurt raid, "We got to go to a rest home run by the Red Cross, which was much needed. The officers went to Stanbridge Earls while we went to Moulsford Manor. We were treated royally and got to wear civilian clothes. There were butlers, waiters, and maids to take care of us." From August 1 to December 1944 17 Air Force "rest homes" accommodated 6,581 officers and 6,809 enlisted men. Cliff Hatcher, a pilot in the 94th Bomb Group, was sent for a "flak furlough" at Coombe House shortly after the Brunswick mission of January 11, 1944, when the group lost eight B-17s. He recalled that they were in such bad shape that their flight surgeon, "Doc" Miller, went along with them! For "He too was getting 'flak happy' riding along with his boys."

*Above: One pot-bellied stove could consume the weekly ration of 52lb of coke in one day if the hut was to be warm.*

Abe Dolim recalls that "From 23 to 30 June I spent a quiet week at Aylesfield House, Alton (the 'Flak House' to the trade), where we slept late and let ourselves be pampered by butlers and the Red Cross ladies." Richard Timberlake in the 388th Bomb Group, who was very badly injured by flak on January 28, 1945, and was later repatriated Stateside, adds, "Every evening we reverted to our dress uniforms—forest greens and pinks—and had supper served by the butler in the beautiful dining room. Of course, we talked shop to let off steam, although everyone was careful not to let off too much. Then there was after-dinner dancing and relaxation. The week was such an oasis in the desert of war that it could pass only too quickly.'

## Shades of Twelve O'Clock High

Forrest J. Eherenman, the navigator in Lieutenant Corson's crew in the 379th Bomb Group at Kimbolton, returned to England in 1966, determined to visit his old base. Arriving in the nearest town, Bedford, he finally persuaded an old man to take him there and back for £10: "After all, he explained, not many people besides himself could even find the site of the former air base. After some negotiations, we settled for [a fare of] £5 10 shillings and soon we were riding past thatch-covered farmhouses and country churches that were only vaguely familiar. It was the first time that I had ever seen them in the daytime. I don't think I recognized the turn-off to the base at all. After a jolting ride down what seemed a seldom-used lane, the driver stopped and said, 'This is it.' 'It' was barely recognizable. The macadam runways were piled in fifty heaps of rubble, outlining what had been the perimeter track like those that I had walked 'tours' on for various infractions of military regulations. I located what

*Below, left and right: Walhampton House near Lymington (left) and Furzedown House (right) near the village of King's Somborne, both in Hampshire, were two of the 17 rest homes available to 8th Air Force combat crews. Attended by butlers, waiters, and nurses, the men could forget the horrors of combat for a while.*

had been the officers' mess hall, but all that was left was a chimney and a concrete slab. I was surprised to find the concrete slab because everything else that had covered the ground, even the roads to the squadron sites, had been torn up to make way for the plow. The whole place was one big barley field. Gone were the latrines, shops, and administrative buildings. All that was left were a few of the Nissen huts that had once housed our crews. I was drawn to one of these, ESP or something and so help me, it was the one in which I spent my sack time in 1943–44. How did I know? It was the stove!

"No Englishman could afford to fire that monster. We had scrounged sheets of armor plate and conned a friendly sergeant in the shop into welding the pieces together. Six feet, by three feet, by three feet, with grates at the bottom and a stove-pipe hole in the top. It took a two-ton truck and six guys to install it in our hut. Nightly forays to the mess hall's coke bin kept it burning, but we were warm that winter. Though it used to glow cherry red and was a fire hazard, the danger, compared to flying missions, was inconsequential. We noticed that when Colonel Preston made his inspections that winter, he tarried longer in our hut. He never inquired about the source of fuel, although he did arrange for a six-foot fence to be erected around the mess hall coke bin: but not until the spring, when we didn't need to fire the furnace anymore.

"Rats troubled us that winter. They ate our dirty socks, shoes, anything. One night when I was awakened by gnawing, I could see a pair of beady eyes glowing in the semi-dark about six feet away, under the bombardier's bed. Fumbling carefully in my barracks bag, I drew my Colt .45 and calmly blew him to Kingdom Come—the rat, not the bombardier. There was massive consternation and condemnation in the hut until my explanation for firing the gun in the middle of the night satisfied the CO, the sentries, and the guys in the huts next door, all of whom came running. The next day all handguns were ordered to be turned in to the armament shop. (I didn't turn mine in.) We impaled what was left of the rat on a metal rod, which we thrust into the ground at the corner of the hut. Until the carcass dried there was a disagreeable odor, but rats or mice never annoyed us

*Far left and left: Movie star Major Clark Gable (center) visiting a USAAF base in Norfolk. The 1949 movie classic* Twelve O'Clock High *(poster, far left) owed much to the early events that were experienced by the 306th Bomb Group. The fictionalized 918th Bomb Group that features in the movie was created by writer Bernie Lay, Jr. Lay arrived at the number 918 by multiplying 306 by three.*

again. On the sidewall of that hut, an inch or so above the floor, there is a 45-caliber bullet hole, the only thing remaining in England to show I was once there.

"From a distance, the control tower looked like it always had, but I found that one wall had been torn out to shelter a farm tractor. The steps to the tower still adhered to the remaining walls. I climbed them. I got the strangest *déjà vu* sensation when I stood on top, gripping the pipe railing. It was a day like most of the English days I remembered— half rain, half fog, and downright yucky. It was not difficult to recall the other times I had climbed those steps and peered into those same skies, waiting to count the number of returning aircraft. The taxi driver took my picture. We got back in the cab and I returned to London."

**Above:** *Many rusting, corrugated Quonset and Nissen huts that once dotted the English landscape in woods and far-flung thickets of every 8th Air Force base still survive. Today they are used for storing farm machinery and other such items.*

# Glossary of terms

**ETO**  European Theater of Operations.

**H2S**  British 10-cm experimental airborne radar navigational and target location aid.

**Happy Valley**  Ruhr Valley.

**HE**  High Explosive (bomb).

**Heavies**  Bombers.

**HEI**  High Explosive Incendiary (bomb).

**Holy Joe**  Chaplain.

**Hot Crock**  Garbage, nonsense, untruth.

**IAS**  Indicated Air Speed.

**IFF**  Identification Friend or Foe.

**IO**  Intelligence Officer.

**IP**  Initial point at the start of the bomb run.

**Iron Ass**  A hard, demanding, tough officer.

**Jug**  Short for Juggernaut, P-47 Thunderbolt.

**Junior Birdman**  An inexperienced pilot.

**KIA**  Killed in Action.

**KP**  Corporal Punishment, fatigues.

**Kriegie**  From the German word *Kriegsgafanganen* (PoW).

**Latrine Rumor**  Unfounded rumor.

**Liberty run**  Night off in town.

**Light colonel**  Lieutenant colonel.

**Little friend**  Allied fighter aircraft.

**Looie**  Lieutenant.

**LORAN**  Long-Range Navigation.

**Lucky bastard**  Someone who has completed his tour of missions (and who has been given a certificate for The Lucky Bastards' Club).

**Lufbery**  A fighter maneuver.

**Milk Run**  An easy mission.

**MP**  Military Policeman.

**NCO**  Non-Commissioned Officer.

**Noball**  Flying bomb (V-1) or rocket (V-2) site.

**Non-com**  NCO.

**Over the Hill**  To be absent without leave.

**PFC**  Poor [expletive] civilian, or private first class.

**Piccadilly Commando**  A London prostitute.

**Pill roller**  Medic.

**POM**  Preparation for Overseas Movement.

**Poop**  Information.

**PoW**  Prisoner of War.

**PR**  Photographic Reconnaissance.

**Prop Wash**  Air disturbed by preceding planes.

**Pubbing mission**  A pub crawl.

**Purple Heart**  Medal awarded for wounds received in combat.

**Purple Heart Corner**  Reputed to be the most vulnerable spot in a bomber formation.

**PX**  Post Exchange: the military store.

**R/T**  Radio Telephony.

**RCM**  Radio Countermeasures.

**Red-lined**  To be canceled.

**Re-Tread**  An older officer who has been recalled to active service.

**RP**  Rocket Projectile.

**Sack**  Bed.

**Sack Time**  Bedtime, sleep.

**Sad Sack, Sack Artist**  GI who was always asleep.

**Second John**  Second Lieutenant.

**Section Eight**  Discharge given for mental breakdown, insanity, etc.

**Shack Job**  An easy woman.

**Shack Up**  To sleep with a woman.

**Shortarm**  A VD inspection.

**Shuttle**  Long bombing mission with a stop en-route.

**Sky pilot**  Chaplain.

**Snowdrop**  Military policeman, so-called because of his white helmet.

**Tour**  A series of missions.

**TS**  Tough Shit.

**UEA**  Unidentified Enemy Aircraft.

**UHF**  Ultra-High Frequency.

**USAAF**  United States Army Air Force.

**VHF**  Very High Frequency.

**V-Mail**  A letter greeting card written on a special form; they were photographed on microfilm, flown to the US, and delivered in hard-copy format.

**WAAF**  (British) Women's Auxiliary Air Force.

**WREN**  (British) Women's Royal Navy.

**Wolfpack**  A fighter outfit.

**ZOI**  Zone of the Interior (i.e., the US).

**Zoot Suit**  Flying suit.

# Bibliography

Bendiner, Elmer: *The Fall of the Fortresses* (Souvenir Press, 1980)

Bloyd, Dean M.: *Flak at 12 O'Clock: A Teenage Kansas Farm Boy's Experiences* (Writers' Club Press, 2000)

Boiten, Theo and Bowman, Martin W.: *Raiders of the Reich. Air Battle Western Europe: 1942–1945* (Airlife, 1996)

Boiten, Theo and Bowman, Martin W.: *Battles with the Luftwaffe* (Jane's, 2001)

*Bombardier's Information File, AAF: The Official Guide to the Army Air Forces* (Pocket Books, 1944)

Bowman, Martin W.: *Four Miles High* (PSL, 1992)

Bowman, Martin W.: *Great American Air Battles of WW2* (Airlife, 1994)

Bowman, Martin W.: *Castles In The Air* (PSL, 1984; Red Kite, 2001)

Bowman, Martin W.: *8th Air Force At War: Memories and Missions, England 1942–45* (PSL, 1994)

Bowman, Martin W.: *Flying To Glory* (PSL, 1992)

Bowman, Martin W.: *The USAAF Handbook: 1939–1945* (Sutton Publishing, 1997, 2003)

Bowman, Martin W.: *Boeing B-17 Flying Fortress* (The Crowood Press, 1998)

Bowman, Martin W., and Woodall, Truett L. Jr.: *Helton's Hellcats: A Pictorial History of the 493rd Bomb Group* (Turner Publishing, 1998)

Caiden, M.: *Black Thursday* (Bantam, 1960)

Department of Armament: "Fundamental Physics of Modern Bombsights: Automatic Computing Sights, Sperry Type K (.50 calibre)" (published in Operating Bulletin No 14-227A, July 1, 1942)

Dolim, Abel L.: *Yesterday's Dragons: The B-17 Flying Fortress over Europe during WWII* (Communications Concepts, 2001)

Freeman, Roger A.: *The B-17 Flying Fortress Story* (Arms & Armour, 1998)

Freeman, Roger A.: *The US Strategic Bomber* (MacDonald Illustrated War Series, 1975)

Kuhl, George C.: *Wrong Place! Wrong Time! The 305th Bomb Group and the 2nd Schweinfurt Raid, October 14, 1943* (Schiffer, 1993)

Lay, Bernie Jr.: "I Saw Regensburg Destroyed" (Extract from article originally published in the *Saturday Evening Post*, November 6, 1943)

Lay, Bernie Jr., and Bartlett, S.: *Twelve O'Clock High* (Ballantine Books, 1948)

Link, Mae Mills and Hubert Coleman: *Medical Support of the Army Air Forces in World War II* (Office of the Surgeon General, USAF, 1955)

Maguire, Jon A.: *Gear Up* (Schiffer, 1994)

Maguire, Jon A.: *Silver Wings, Pinks and Greens: Uniforms, Wings & Insignia of USAAF Airmen in World War II* (Schiffer, 1994)

McCrary, Captain John R., "Tex" and Scherman, David E.: *First of the Many* (Ballantine, 1944)

O'Hearn, Robert E.: *In My Book You're All Heroes* (Privately published, 1984)

Sloan, John S.: *The Route As Briefed* (Argus Press, 1946)

Smith, Ben Jr.: *Chick's Crew: A Tale of the Eighth Air Force* (Privately published, 1978, 1983, 2006)

Stiles, Bert (ed.): *Serenade To The Big Bird* (Norton, 1947)

Sweeting, C. G.: *Combat Flying Equipment: US Army Aviators' Equipment, 1917–1945* (Smithsonian, 1989)

*Target: Germany: The US Army Air Forces' Official Story of the VIIIth Bomber Command's First Year Over Europe* (Simon & Schuster, 1944)

Windrow, R. and Hawkins, T.: *The World War II GI: US Army Uniforms, 1941–1945* (Windrow & Greene, 1993)

Woodward, Ellis M.: *Flying School: Combat Hell* (American Literary Press, 1998)

# Picture credits and Acknowledgments

Page number and position are indicated as follows: L = Left, TL = Top left, TR = Top right; C = Center; CL = Center left; B = Bottom, BL = Bottom left, etc:

**Author's collection:**
12-13; 15: TR, C, BR; 16: CR; 17: TL, TC; 18: TL (illustration); 21: TR; 23: T, BR; 24: T, CL, CR; 25: CR, BR; 26-27; 31: CL (3rd from top); 33: TR; 34: BL; 35: TR, BL, BR; 36: TR; 37: BL, TR; 38: BL, BR; 40: TR; 41: BL, TR; 44: BR; 45: TR; 46: TL; 48: L, BR; 49: BR; 50: TC, CL, BR; 51: TL, C; 52: L, B; 53: BR; 54: BL, BR; 60: TL; 61: BR; 62: TC, BL; 63: TL, B; 64: C (illustration); 65: TL, B; 66: L, BR; 67: T, CR, BR; 69: BL, BR; 74: TL, TR, BL, BR; 76: CL, C, CR; 77: TR; 79: TL, BL, BR; 80: TC (illustration), BL, BR; 81: T, BR; 82: TC, CR; 83: T, BR; 84-85; 87: TR; 88: BR; 89: TR, BC; 91: TR, CR; 92: BR; 93: CL, TR, BC; 94: CR; 95: CL, BR; 96: BR; 97: TR, BR; 98-99; 103: TL, BR;104: BL; 105: TR; 106: BL; 107: TL. CR, BR; 110: CL, BL; 115: BL (3rd from top); 116: TC, CR (illustration), BL; 117: CR; 118: L, CR, BR; 120: TL, BR, 121: TL, C; 122: CL, CR, BR; 124: CL, C, CR; 125: TR, BR; 128: L; 130: C, BR; 131: TL; 132: C, BR; 133: C; 134: CL; 135: CL, CR, B; 136: TC, BL, BR; 137: T; B; 138: BL; 139: TR, CR; 140-141; 142: CT, BL; 143: TR; 144: BL, BR; 145: L, BR; 146: TL, C; 147: CB; 149: BL; 150: TL, BL, BR; 151: BR; 152: BL, BR; 153: TL, TR, BR.

**Boeing Images:**
14; 16: BL; 18: CR; 31: CL (second from top); 45: CL (3rd from top); 115: CL (top photo).

**Pat Bunce:**
31: R; 45: CL (second from top); 56; 112; 129: TL, TC.

**Corbis:**
148: BL.

**USAAF/Graham Simons:**
108: BR; 109: T, BL.

**Michael P. Faley/100th Bomb Group Photo Archives:**
34: TC; 60: CR; 119: TC.

All the B-17 interior and exterior photographs, and all the memorabilia photos featured in the book (except for those listed above) were made by Neil Sutherland, and are the copyright of Elephant Book Company Ltd.

**Jacket and front cover illustration:**
*Clash Over Haseleunne* by Robert Bailey
Website: www.baileyprints.com

**Author's and Editors' acknowledgments**
The author and editors wish to thank the following for their help in preparing this book: Ron and Carol Batley; Kenneth Everett; Mike Nice and everyone at the 100th Bomb Group Memorial Museum, Thorpe Abbotts, England; Larry Goldstein; Ben Smith; Wilbur Richardson; Pat Bunce; Mike P Faley (100th Bomb Group historian); Graham Simons; Natalie Finnigan, Imperial War Museum, Duxford, England; Elly Sallingboe of the B-17 Preservation Society; Mick Royall; Bill Donald; Dr Walter E Brown, President & CEO, Mighty Eighth Air Force Museum, Savannah, GA; and Major General Lewis Lyle.

**Museums**
The great majority of the items of memorabilia featured in this book were photographed at the 100th Bomb Group Memorial Museum, Thorpe Abbotts, near Diss, Norfolk, England (www.100bgmus.org.uk)

Many of the B-17 interior and exterior photographs were made at the American Air Museum, Imperial War Museum, Duxford, England (www.duxford.iwm.org.uk)